# THE
# THEMING
## OF AMERICA

# The Theming of America

## Dreams, Media Fantasies, and Themed Environments

### SECOND EDITION

### Mark Gottdiener

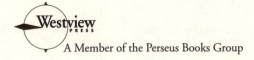

A Member of the Perseus Books Group

Copyright © 2001 by Westview Press, A Member of the Perseus Books Group

Westview Press books are available at special discounts for bulk purchases in the United States by corporations, institutions, and other organizations. For more information, please contact the Special Markets Department at The Perseus Books Group, 11 Cambridge Center, Cambridge MA 02142, or call (617) 252-5298.

Published in 2001 in the United States of America by Westview Press, 5500 Central Avenue, Boulder, Colorado 80301-2877, and in the United Kingdom by Westview Press, 12 Hid's Copse Road, Cumnor Hill, Oxford OX2 9JJ

Find us on the World Wide Web at www.westviewpress.com

A CIP catalog record for this book is available from the Library of Congress.
ISBN 0-8133-9765-0

The paper used in this publication meets the requirements of the American National Standard for Permanence of Paper for Printed Library Materials Z39.48-1984.

10    9    8    7    6    5    4    3    2    1

# Contents

# ILLUSTRATIONS

# Preface to
# the Second Edition

When I published the original version of *The Theming of America*, I meant it as a contribution for consideration by other scholars interested in the new ways in which cultural processes were affecting the built environment; I did not have classroom use principally in mind. During the years following the book's release, I was pleasantly surprised by the response of college teachers around the country who had used this book in their courses. Their often-repeated request that I rework the book to make the argument more accessible to students has inspired this second edition.

I prepared the new edition also with other concerns in mind. Not long after the first edition's release, several other books appeared that seemed to cover the same ground but that lacked analytic depth. For example, John Hannigan (1998) wrote about the very same venues covered in this book—the mall, the theme park, the Las Vegas casino—and in a similar vein, but with a narrower focus and from the perspective of urban development. I disagree fundamentally with such an approach: The increasing use of theming does involve city projects, but the phenomenon is deeply cultural and therefore more globally influential to our way of life than his approach would suggest.

Lastly, since the first edition was published the phenomenon of theming has taken on greater complexity. Our society seems to be witnessing the limits of the effectiveness of themed environments. Several notable commercial enterprises, such as Planet Hollywood, have experienced serious financial problems. Theming is no longer automatic in profit-oriented consumer services. Customers have also grown to expect more from their consumption experiences than theming alone can provide. This new edition addresses the increasingly evident *limits* to theming as well as its sustained popularity.

The relatively recent social movements that have emerged in opposition to simulated themed environments and franchising also fascinate me. Citizen resistance is worldwide. There are organized protests against McDonald's chain stores and Disney Company projects. A cultural conception has appeared among select groups of people in several countries that stands in opposition to the advance of theming and simulation. Our culture, then, is not simply rushing down the drain of one-dimensional artificiality, contrivance, franchising, and "Disneyfication." People are also beginning to define an alternative to the corporate logic of theming. This new edition takes such efforts seriously and analyzes them as part of the phenomenon.

An author is always indebted to others who have helped out at various stages. The following people helped me greatly through their nurturing support, their comments, and their often brilliant observations. I wish to thank, in particular, Robert Antonio, Douglas Kellner, George Ritzer, Joe R. Feagin, David Dickens, Lauren Langman, Jorge Arditi, Chris Mele, Talmadge Wright, Peter Marcuse, Eric Monkkonen, Chris Rojek, and Eugene Halton. Colleagues in other countries also provided me with helpful comments: Mervi Ilmonen, Arie Schachar, Noam Shoval, Anne Haila, Thomas Maloutas, Alex Deffner, Alexandros Lagopoulos, Karin Boklund, Nicos Komninos, Mike Featherstone, Bob Catterall, Leslie Budd, Martin Harris, and Janusz Baranski. Lastly, I have had the benefit of working with first-rate graduate students who have helped me refine my ideas on the emergent patterns of our society's quotidian culture: Emily Lester, Rich Mancuso, Neil Weiloch, Cindy Cooper, Chigon Kim, Andrew Pollack, and Minjoo Oh. I wish also to thank Leo Wiegman, Katharine Chandler, and Michelle Mallin of Westview for their support over the years.

This second edition is dedicated to my fantastic family—Jennifer, Felix, and Zev.

# 1

# LOOKING AT THEMED
# ENVIRONMENTS

During the summer month of July 2000, a French sheep farmer, José Bové, descended to the site of the McDonald's fast-food outlet in his hometown of Millau and, with the help of some friends, demolished the building. He was sentenced to three months in jail. According to one report (Bremner, 2000: 4):

> For ordinary people, Bové spoke for the France of petits villages, red wine, and honest *paysans* that inhabits the Gallic imagination. "We have remained a culture where the time spent at the table is not just for consuming food. It's a social and family moment. There is a frightening statistic from America that the average time a family sits at the table is six minutes. That hasn't happened here yet."

The report also mentioned that Bové's other targets are mad cow disease, genetically altered products, and the large multinational corporations that are gaining control over all aspects of business and agriculture. To Bové and many others, McDonald's is a symbol of a general threat to their traditional way of life—a threat that they believe emanates from the global forces of the world economy.

During that same year, in Florida, famous country and western star Jimmy Buffett, who previously had opened a themed restaurant named Margaritaville (after his well-known hit song), announced plans for Cheeseburger in Paradise, an "island themed restaurant" named after one of his other hits. And in Los Angeles, a limited partnership between the Hard Rock Café Corporation and several National Basketball Association

(NBA) players announced the projected opening of "NBA City"—a new, themed restaurant chain that was expected to gross $15 million a year from one million patrons (Schneider, 2000).

Later that year, in September, the Krispy Kreme national doughnut franchise opened stores for the first time in Buffalo, New York, and in Los Angeles, California, causing traffic jams in both cities. Buffalo, the home of wings and beer, and Los Angeles, best known for health food fads, witnessed the same doughnut-eating frenzy with the unveiling of the new stores.

This book focuses on the cultural trend that unites all of these events. Since the 1950s our culture has been increasingly characterized by the use of themes and signs to sell merchandise. At times, the symbolic milieus that have been created, like the Planet Hollywood chain, overshadow the quality of the products they sell. The frenzy over Krispy Kreme doughnuts in one part of the world is offset by the organized objections to franchises like McDonald's in another. As people in other countries are exposed to themed restaurants, theme parks, and themed tourist attractions, they feel the same conflicting dynamics of curiosity, celebrity, and caution that we experience. Both national cultures and local environments seem to be increasingly altered by the growing influence of franchising and theming.

People eat lunches and dinners in restaurants that compete with each other for the most attractive motifs. These include the signature logos of McDonald's, Burger King, and the like, in the franchised world of fast foods; small-scale theme restaurants that cater to particular tastes, such as Chi-Chi's for Mexican style food, the Olive Garden for Italian-style franchise cooking, and the Red Lobster for seafood; or more elaborately themed environments, such as the Hard Rock Café and Planet Hollywood. Even individually owned restaurants tout their personal themes as they struggle for business in the competitive world of dining out, by adding to the density or variety of symbolic decor.

Motifs increasingly define recreational activities both in central cities and in suburbs. Professional sports, with their aggressive merchandising and team boosterism, offer themed experiences that focus almost as much on abstract symbols worn as clothing or sold as poster images as on the spectacular players of the game. The motifs of teams and of sports figures are found on shoes, jackets, hats, and even men's suits.

Symbols also structure other experiences, such as family vacations, which increasingly involve visits to theme parks or commercialized leisure locations. Disneyland in California and Disneyworld in Florida are perhaps the most famous destinations. However, popular theme parks are scattered throughout the country. Dolly Parton, the country and western singer, has her own theme park, Dollyland, as does the dead Elvis, Graceland—both in Tennessee. Las Vegas, once a mecca for alcohol, sex, and gambling, has become the theme park capital of the United States as casinos switch over to family-oriented entertainment; but even before this change, Las Vegas was the themed environment par excellence. Nature has been similarly transformed by motifs. Government regulators and construction designers and engineers have worked over natural wonders such as Niagara Falls and the Grand Canyon, to heighten the theme of mother nature in an idealized sense.

The forms of a symbol-ridden environment pervade everyday life as well. Shopping increasingly occurs in large suburban malls or special central city districts that use defined themes purposefully to entice consumers. Architecture and decor artfully play out distinctive symbolic appeals that connect the mall shopping experience with the media world of television and popular culture. Finally, the idea of overarching, organizing themes has recently been incorporated into the construction of museums and historical monuments. The Holocaust Museum in Washington, D.C., for example, orchestrates the visitor's experience entirely around the theme of Germany's failed destruction of European Jewry during World War II. The government also recently converted its abandoned absorption center on Ellis Island, located in New York City harbor, to a popular tourist attraction using a themed milieu that documents the immigration experience. This motif is painstakingly developed and highlighted in the restored buildings of the former immigrant absorption center. Similar themed historical renovations that are specifically designed for tourists characterize new public projects across the country. Engineered to attract outsiders rather than to commemorate local sentiments, these themed environments indicate the active competition among different places around the country for tourist dollars.

In sum, the themed milieu, with its pervasive use of overarching symbolic motifs that define an entire built space, increasingly characterizes not only cities but also suburban areas, shopping places, airports, and recreational spaces such as baseball stadia, museums, restaurants, and amusement parks. Progressively, then, our daily life occurs within a material environment that is dependent on and organized around overarching motifs. This book explores the nature of this themed environment as it has developed since the 1960s, the reasons for its emergence, its connections to the economy, and its development as a new cultural form of varied thematic appeals.

## The Increasing Use of Themes in Everyday Life

Since the end of World War II, our everyday environment has been altered in profound ways. Before the 1960s there was a clear distinction between the city and the country (Williams, 1973). Cities grew as compact, dense industrial environments usually laid out along right-angled grid lines. They possessed a central sector of office towers and an adjacent area of factories tied to rail spurs and roads. Residential areas exemplified the classic contrast of the "gold coast and slum." Wealthy, privileged areas of housing were juxtaposed and in close proximity with more modest, sometimes squalid, neighborhoods of industrial workers. Lying outside the limits of the city was another contrasting space—the countryside of farm fields, wooded acres, and occasional houses separated by open space. Cultural styles of life that were either urban (urbane) or rural reflected this dichotomy of different land uses, as did depictions of city and country dwellers in novels and films (see Redfield, 1947).

Before the 1960s, fundamental class differences between capitalists and workers organized the land use of the industrial city. Neighborhoods, for example, were working class and the local community reflected ethnic, racial, and religious solidarity dedicated to the task of raising families. The center of the city, in contrast, belonged to business. During this period the symbols that provided meaning to daily life were manifested more cognitively than materially. Buildings reflected their functions with a minimum of symbolic trappings. People in neighborhoods signified their culture through the sometimes subtle markings of churches and store signs using foreign languages. Symbolic marking was muted, and inhabitants had to be perceptive to pick out denotations of place that signified particular ethnic solidarities or preferred places of business.

Since the 1960s a new trend of symbolic differentiation within the built environment has appeared that contrasts graphically with the earlier period. The use of symbols and motifs more and more frequently characterizes the space of everyday life in both the city and the suburb. Signification involves not only a proliferation of signs and themes but also a constant reworking of built facades and interior spaces to incorporate overarching motifs in such a way that we increasingly are exposed to new environmental experiences when we consume. Now these new consumer spaces with their new modes of thematic representation organize daily life in an increasing variety of ways. Social activities have moved beyond the symbolic work of designating ethnic, religious, or economic status to an expanding repertoire of meaningful motifs. Whereas symbolic elements were muted in the settlement spaces of the early twentieth century, the trend is reversed in the new consumer spaces of today.

## Understanding Themed Environments

When I refer to a *themed environment,* I explicitly mean the material product of two social processes. First, I am talking about socially constructed, built environments—about large material forms that are designed to serve as containers for commodified human interaction (for example, malls). Second, I have in mind themed material forms that are products of a cultural process aimed at investing constructed spaces with symbolic meaning and at *conveying* that meaning to inhabitants and users through symbolic motifs. These motifs may take on a range of meanings according to the interpretations of the individuals who are exposed to them. The range of responses can include everything from no response at all—that is, a failure of the symbolic content to stimulate—to a negative response, or displeasure. Themed environments do not automatically provoke desire and pleasure in their users. Such spaces also can be sources of great irritation, as can be seen in the strong negative reactions of some Europeans to McDonald's franchises in their countries.

Another important distinction concerns the way I use the concepts of "production" and "consumption." The former refers to a *social* process of creation that often involves a group of individuals brought together within an organized, institutional context, such as real estate development. Consumption involves the way individuals or groups *use* or interpret the constructed space by imputing some meaning or meanings to it. These people may be customers, inhabitants, visitors, or clients, but they are all users of the space in some fashion. Consumption of a themed environment refers to the experience of individuals within a themed milieu, including the assumption of a particular orientation to space, based on the personal or group interpretation of its symbolic content. Built forms have the power to alter human behavior through meaning, and this response is also part of what I mean by the process of consumption in space.

Visitors to a themed park consume the environment itself as well as the rides and attractions. They adjust their behavior according to the stimuli they receive from the signals embedded in built forms. Motifs and symbols developed through the medium of the park's material forms may be highly stimulating, or conversely, hardly noticed. Always, however, the physical presence of individuals within a space involves their use or "consumption" of the material environment.

In the following chapters I discuss both the production and the consumption of themed milieus. Most commentaries—for example, those about places like Disneyland—ignore the production process of the park and focus exclusively on impressionistic accounts of a visit there. I seek to correct this one-sided view by also emphasizing the process of production, and the role of that process in the larger economic organization of our society. I am especially interested in the intermixing of creation and use, as consumer experiences increasingly are packaged within themed milieus.

## Production in Consumption

Despite the dichotomization of the interrelated concepts of production and consumption, I must caution the reader against making sharp distinctions between these two social processes. To begin with, as our society progressively shifts from an economy dependent on manufacturing to one in which service industries predominate, the jobs held by the bulk of the population are increasingly associated with thematic experiences. Museum exhibits, for example, more frequently concern the elaboration of themes than in the past; service labor in restaurants or recreational areas requires employee conformity to the symbolic decor through the wearing of costumes and the like; and retailing activity increasingly locates in motifed milieus such as malls. Thus, the world of work, or production, penetrates and merges with the world of consumption.

Second, it has become harder to isolate shopping and other leisure pursuits as activities defined by consumption alone. In the past, observers of mass cultural participation often did just that by painting the users or the audience as a group of *passive* consumers, conditioned by advertising to behave in the way producers wished. More recently, analysts of culture have recognized that the gross manipulation of people by advertising is an exaggeration. We must acknowledge the relative autonomy of individuals in the act of consumption, as they blend personal history, the self-actualization of their identities, group pressures of various kinds, and the powerful compulsions of the consumer society that pressure people to make certain choices in the marketplace. As individual identities become wrapped up in modes of self-expression and the fashioning of particular lifestyles in response to the great variety of market choices, there is a blurred line between production and consumption. More and more we view the pursuit of particular styles of life and the development of contemporary subjectivities through the use of material objects as a form of production itself (de Certeau, 1984; Gergen, 1991). There is always an element of production in the act of consumption, just as there is also a corresponding aspect of use-value exploited by the production process. These intersecting, liminal activities of the economy are increasingly organized by overarching symbolic motifs within consumer milieus.

Michel de Certeau (1984), the author of an influential book on the subject, argues that consumers are always employing a creative strategy or series of strategies in their buying activities that bear a resemblance to the production process. They try to juggle desires, prices, stores, and modes of purchasing. They create uses for objects to fill specific needs. They modify commodities to suit their own lifestyle. These and other responses are common strategies of consumption deployed by average household or family groups as they cope with economic adversity (see Roberts, 1993). In short, people are not the passive, media-manipulated masses often depicted by analysts of advertising. They are very often proactive in their attitudes toward commodities and shopping. Through the daily use of strategies, they "produce" an attitude and a form of coping behavior in their social role as consumer.

Another way of viewing the links between the processes of production and consumption focuses on the development of subjectivity and the emergence of the self within a consumer-oriented society (see Langman, 1992; Gergen, 1991). To be sure, images and desires produced by the advertising industry constantly prime people to consume. When individuals enter commercial realms, such as in a visit to a mall, the themed, retailing environment actualizes their *consumer self*. This process, however, is not a passive one, with individuals acting like marionettes, pulled back and forth by powerful consumer conditioning. Instead, people *self-actualize* within the commercial milieu, seeking ways of satisfying their desires and pursuing personal fulfillment through the market that express deeply held images of themselves. Granted, mass advertising conditions much of this actualization of a consumer identity, especially aided by the group force of conformity to fashion. Equally valid is the observation that self-actualization is destined to be disappointed in the alienated world of mass marketing. However, as observers interested in the innovative (production) aspects of buying argue, the fashioning of consumer identities is much less controlled by advertising manipulation than is often supposed, and the incredibly prolific abundance of commercial products does promise the satisfaction of many of our desires, whether these are manufactured for us or not.

As an example of these aspects of production in consumption, consider the activity of dressing in contemporary society. Group norms highly regulate socially acceptable dress, and this has always been so (Gottdiener, 1995). The large fashion industry that orchestrates modes of appearance in modern society lately has targeted men as well as women both for periodic changes in style and for the production of desire. Despite the power of fashion, most individuals hold a very personalized conception of their dress patterns. They often seek self-actualization and pursue certain distinct lifestyles through the medium of appearance (see Stone, 1962; Simmel, 1957; Konig, 1973). People in our society spend a great deal of money on clothing—more than they could possibly need for purely protective purposes. They use these material objects symbolically in many ways to exploit social situations for their own advantage. Individuals may "dress for success" or to impress; they may seek approval of others—women, men, prospective in-laws, a possible employer; and they often seek identification with particular groups by dressing like them. Finally, people often mix and match objects of clothing and accessories on a daily basis in a *creative* effort to fashion a personal look or image. When considering the social process of dress as distinct from fashion dictated by the clothing industry, it becomes difficult to separate aspects of production and consumption because the two are so interrelated in the daily behavior of dressing (see Barthes, 1983).

## A Brief Note on Signs and Symbols

In the opening section of this chapter we have already begun to use concepts associated with the analysis of symbols in specific ways. This is necessary to discuss the phenomenon of the themed environment in comprehensive detail. The *sign* is defined conceptually as something that stands for something else, and, more technically, as a spoken or written word, a drawn figure, or a material object unified in the mind with a particular cultural concept. The sign is this unity of a word/object, known as a *signifier,* with a corresponding, culturally prescribed concept or meaning, known as a *signified.* Thus our minds attach the word *dog,* or the drawn figure of a dog, as a signifier, to the idea of a "dog," that is, a domesticated canine species possessing certain behavioral characteristics. If we came from a culture where dogs were not routinely encountered, we might not know what the signifier *dog* means.

When dealing with objects that are signifiers of certain concepts, cultural meanings, or ideologies, we can consider them not only as "signs" but as *sign vehicles.* Signifying objects carry meanings with them. They may purposefully be constructed to convey meaning. Thus, Disneyland, as a theme park, is a large sign vehicle of the Disney ideology. This concept, however, has two aspects that are often a source of confusion. When we use a signifier to convey simple information, usually of a functional nature, we *denote* meaning. The word *train,* for example, denotes a mode of transportation or movement. Objects that denote a particular function are called *sign functions.* Every material form within a given culture is a sign of its function and denotes its use. When we approach a building that is a bank, we understand its meaning at the denotative level in terms of its sign function as a repository and transaction space for money.

Every signifier, every meaningful object, however, in addition, conveys another meaning that exists at the *connotative* level—that is, it *connotes* some association defined by social context and social process beyond its denotative sign function. The word *train,* which denotes transportation, also connotes old-fashioned travel, perhaps the nineteenth century by association, maybe a sort of romanticism of traveling, even mystery, exoticism, and intrigue, as in the Orient Express; or in another vein, slowness, noise, pollution, crowds, and the like. The bank building, which is the sign function for the activity of "banking," also *connotes* a variety of socially ascribed associations including wealth, power, success, future prospects, college educations, and savings for vacations or Christmas. In short, every sign not only denotes some social function and conveys a social meaning at the denotative level but also connotes a variety of associations that have meanings within specific cultural contexts. Thus, sign vehicles that are material objects operate on many social levels. Understanding this fact provides an appreciation for the rich cultural life of objects. It also means that we can understand how material objects are used as signs in social interaction. Rather than considering objects as signs—that is, as existing exclusively in the mind of the interpreter—we also consider signs as objects, as material forms that are used and manipulated by social actors for personal reasons or material gain. The former is associated with the act of consuming a themed environment. The latter concerns the way producers use signs as objects for distinct purposes, such as making money. Both processes operate simultaneously, depending on the point of reference.

Because signs perform double duty in social interaction (denoting and connoting), their interpretation is fraught with ambiguity. Furthermore, individuals decoding signs use their personal frame of reference, unless taught not to, and this may lead to the interpretation of a particular sign or discourse that was unintended by its producer, who may have come from another social context. For these reasons, the meaning attached to signs is always *polysemic*, that is, there are always several equally valid ways of interpreting a sign. Due to the presence of polysemy, the understanding of meaningful interaction is always problematic. Communication between individuals is a difficult task, especially because the *interpretation* of communication invariably differs from person to person even within the same receiving context. Recognition of cases of polysemy is also an important aspect of the interpretation of signs.

Societies with a polysemic culture accomplish the task of communication by adhering to particular symbolic *codes* that may also be called *ideologies*. Codes or ideologies are belief systems that organize meanings and interpretations into a single, unified sense. Sometimes we also use *semantic field* or the *universe of meaning* to signify the concept of code or ideology. Codes are subcultural phenomena shared by others, and they vary from one social group to another. A diverse society contains various subcultures that interpret experience and commodities according to their individual ideologies. For example, some people love country and western music so much that they dress up in cowboy hats and jeans and go to bars where they line dance to it. Others hate country and western music, preferring some other genre that is consistent with the ideology of their particular subculture. A diverse society contains populations that invoke a variety of subcultural contexts in the process of communication. Simultaneously, powerful forces in society, such as advertising, economics, the media, and politics, marshal unified social organization through the deployment of specific codes that limit ambiguity and direct our understanding toward specific meanings or values. It is this operation of institutions that channel meaning—for example, Hollywood, or advertising—that makes the new themed consumer environments so appealing to a variety of subcultural groups. Where would McDonald's be, if the corporation had not spent billions of dollars on advertising over the years? The powerful forces that define the symbolic value of commodities to our society are important subjects of this book.

The themed environment is a tool exploited in business competition or place competition, rather than a symbolic milieu constructed for its own sake. We experience the themed environment, therefore, as the intersection of meaning systems and social processes—in this case, profit making, tourism, displays of affluence, business or locational competition, shopping or consumerism, and nostalgic representations of American history that comfort us with a semblance of culture.

## The Plan of the Book

The following chapters not only describe the variety of themed environments in our society and explain how they are used but also explore the reasons for their increasing presence. Chapter 2 places the concept of "themed environment" in historical context. Symbolism once literally saturated human existence, mainly through signs deriving from the codes of nature, cosmology, or religion. Ancient civilizations created themed environments celebrating state power or the grandeur of rulers who were often considered divine. The era of capitalist industrialization, which began during the latter middle ages in European society, undercut the symbolic basis of the built environment. Through the passage of centuries, cities lost their once robust symbolic milieus. Denotative sign systems that marked sign functions came to dominate the lived environment of industrial society during the early twentieth century, and connotative signifiers were only weakly present. Then, after the 1960s, things began to change. The already existing themed environments, such as movie palaces, state fairs, and department store "phantasmagorias," were joined by an increasing emphasis on fantasy and symbolic themes in other areas of commercialism. Much of the following discussion deals with this more contemporary period. Before plunging into the analysis of themed environments today in all their variety, I spend time in the early chapters laying out the historical and analytical concepts that help us understand why theming is now so important to our culture.

Chapter 2 traces changes in culture and in construction from ancient times to the present and illustrates how the creation of themed environments has resurfaced in contemporary society. Chapter 3 analyzes the role of themes in contemporary social processes, seeking to explain why motifs are more common today. An explanation is found in the dynamics of profit making and the problems encountered by our late capitalist economy in the twentieth century. This chapter makes a connection between the recent reliance on themed milieus and the problems of a mature economy that explains the growing popularity of the former. Chapter 4 more closely examines various themed environments found in everyday life, from themed restaurants and malls to gambling casinos and airports, linking the development of these milieus to the dynamics of the present economy. This discussion continues in Chapter 5, with an examination of the more spectacular examples of theme parks and "natural wonder" tourist attractions. Extensions of theming—such as its use in rock concerts, professional sports, and new housing developments, including urban renewal projects—are also considered. I then discuss other, more recent uses of themes in war memorials and museums that are less connected to the economy and more relevant to society's desire to adequately represent the "unrepresentable"—the enormity of events and historical circumstances that seem beyond our symbolic vocabulary.

Chapter 6 discusses the important topic of personal responses to theming. Earlier chapters in the book considered theming from the point of view of producers and of society. Chapter 6 introduces the "phenomenology of theming" and addresses the ways themed environments are experienced by users. Critical perspectives have called theming into question because of its negative effects on individuals as well as on society. Several negative effects are examined here, including the erosion of public space, of locally controlled business, and of traditional cultures, as well as the perceived artificiality of thematic environments and simulations.

The final chapter (7) discusses what theming is doing to the United States. A brief review of the academic field of *cultural studies* is needed in order to make observations that go beyond the level of superficial description. We may like or dislike theming, but here I have tried to supersede matters of opinion with a focus on the deeper meanings and effects of theming on our society. An analysis of the range of themes proves the limited imagination—the virtual impoverishment, if you will—of our popular culture. And an analysis of the use of theming proves just how much consumerism and profit making dominate this activity. The fact that so many people enjoy and are entertained by themed environments raises troubling questions about the formation of personal character and individual identity in our society.

## Summary of Main Ideas

1. Themes and symbols are increasingly used to sell consumer goods today.
2. Themes are linked to the appearance of new consumer spaces that are symbolic environments. These include shopping malls, themed restaurants, and theme parks.

3. There is a range of responses by individuals and groups to these themed spaces, extending from enthusiastic patronage to resistance and opposition.

4. Themed environments link two different processes—the process that produces them, and the one that results in the consumer's response. The distinction between production and consumption is often blurred in real-life activities (e.g., shopping).

5. Signs are vehicles for the expression of meaning. When a symbol is used for a particular effect, we call it a *sign vehicle*.

6. Themed objects have both a denotative and a connotative aspect: They are *sign functions* because they express (i.e., denote) an intended use; and they are connotative in that they invoke particular associations, beyond utility, in the mind of the consumer. In our culture, the latter level seems to dominate in themed environments. These connotations are often fantasies stimulated by the mass media and by our image-driven culture.

7. The meaning of spaces varies among users who belong to different social groups. This implies that signs have multiple meanings in our society.

8. *Codes* or *ideologies* organize these potentially disparate meanings into well-defined interpretations. The process of creating and maintaining these codified interpretations takes place within social institutions such as advertising, television, Hollywood cinema, politics, and the economy.

# 2

# From a Themed to an Anti-Themed Environment, and Back

## Natural Codes, Ancient Cities, and Modernism

Everyday life from the very beginning of human societies was overendowed with symbolism. We know this from the historical record and artifacts left by early image makers such as the cave artists of Lascaux. Traditional societies wrapped a symbolic context, like a blanket, around all their daily activities. From the earliest moments of human consciousness, animism evolved as a great naming exercise. Guided by the belief that every object of nature possessed its own animating specter, humans named the spirits of the trees, the rivers, the stones, the mountains, the sun, the rain, and so on. These spirits were acknowledged as presences that intervene in the affairs of people and were worshiped for their independent power to intervene. The natural world, then, was possessed by the thousand named apparitions that inhabited its many forms (Schama, 1995).

Human imputation of meaning to the natural world involved three distinct but interrelated activities. Early people *believed* in the independent life of the spirits of their environment; they developed extended *discourses* that recounted the cosmologies of their spirits; and they produced *artifacts* that

*The cave paintings at Lascaux, France, are an example of symbolic production by the earliest humans. These representations have much the same purpose as the symbols of today. Photo courtesy of Corbis/Bettmann.*

objectified their images of the spirits. The meaningful environment of the ancients was produced by the activities of belief, discourse, and materialization, articulating together in the human practice of recognizing and mollifying the power of their respective gods. Over time we have been left not only material artifacts that signify this rather extensive spirit world but in many cases also with discourses that specify legends, tales, and myths.

As several scholars of sagas point out, myths are *empowering* to those who believe in them. They enable a society to respond to the environment in positive and controlling ways. Legends, for example, encode important forms of knowledge about managing the external environment. They are the earliest examples of the close connection between knowledge and power. For instance, Mircea Eliade (1963) points to the role that myths of *origins* played in the life of ancient societies. Knowledge of beginnings was controlling knowledge. A society dependent on the cultivation of rice would be assured of a successful harvest only after the shaman of the tribe visited the newly planted rice fields and intoned the myth of rice's worldly creation (see Eliade, 1963, chapter 2). Individuals also empowered themselves by establishing a totemic connection with an animal or plant spirit.

The powers of the latter—such as leaping, running, hiding, or divination—were appropriated through the totemic practice. The wearing of material objects, such as totemic masks, feathers or fur, or tattoo markings, objectified the relation between humans and their natural spirits. Using the practice of naming, early humans reinforced this relation in discourse. People assumed the names of their totems, such as the coyote, fox, or bear—for example, "Running Fox" or "Little Bear." Belief, discourse, and material culture were melded together in the production of a meaningful or themed environment.

Scholars note the many similarities among the myths of the world's cultures (see Jung, 1964). The story of death and rebirth, for example, is common to many societies. Figures such as Osiris among the ancient Egyptians, Orpheus for the Greeks, and Christ for Christians, personify the myth of death and rebirth. Many of these same cultures also have elaborate festivals marking the winter or spring solstice—the period of decline and renewal in nature (e.g., Christmas or Easter, among Christians). Symbols such as the phoenix and the egg figure in myths of life cycles. Also common to most cultures are legends involving a hero who is godlike and omnipotent. Often the mythical hero rises from humble birth to a triumph through the slaying of some monster, but then succumbs to the failing of pride or hubris and meets a heroic death. Samson of the ancient Israelites and Achilles of the Greeks share these attributes. The former possessed strength from long hair; the latter had a critical weakness at the heel. Although seemingly godlike, both died when these flaws were discovered. These and other stories of folk heroes empowered the people who believed in them.

The conception of the natural world as a *meaningful* or *signifying* place created the earliest instances of the *themed environment*. During ancient times, everyday life consisted of fully themed spaces where every tree, stone, location, or individual had a connotative symbol attached to it. There was once little difference between the name of an object or person, and the name of the spirit that resided in that object or person. Later, the threefold process of belief, discourse, and material objectification led to the development of increasingly elaborate legends handed down by cultures. Eventually, people systematized these into cosmologies, mythologies, or religions. Following from their ancient origins in animism, the earliest religions—for example, those of the Hindus, Chinese, and Greeks—were pantheistic. A group of gods who often competed or conspired among themselves ruled the world, dominating all animal and plant spirits as well as humanity. For example, the ancient Greeks believed in the god Pan, who was lord over the woodlands and the spirits inhabiting them; the god Poseidon, lord of the sea; and Cronus or Zeus, supreme gods of the earth.

Greek mythology, a system of belief that unified the ancient Hellenic and Hellenistic civilizations, and later, Roman civilization, was more developed than the animism of primitive, traditional societies. Ancient Greeks believed that the gods not only ruled natural objects like the sun and the moon but also governed human attributes and activities. Apollo, the Greek sun god, was also the god of music, poetry, eloquence, medicine, and the fine arts; Artemis, known by the Romans as Diana, was goddess of the moon but also of the hunt and of maidenhood. Athena was one of several divinities that ruled solely over people. She was the goddess of wisdom, the industrial arts, and war.

In these examples, we can observe a transition from the spirit-naming of the natural environment by primitive societies to the more sophisticated naming of both the natural and the human/interactive environment in the sacred beliefs of ancient civilizations. This shift involved the development of cosmologies into organized religions based on the pantheon of gods, complete with specialized niches in the social division of labor for priests, priestesses, oracles, temple virgins, shamans, seers, and assorted "holy men."

As history unfolded, gods took on more human attributes and humans were more likely to be considered godlike. The Greek gods quarreled with and were jealous of each other, behaving as many humans do. Zeus was well known for his sexual trysts with young women, such as Danae and Lida. As time went on, the role of gods in human interaction increased and their reign over nature became less important. When the Romans adopted Greek mythology as their official religion, they added to the Greek pantheon several gods (e.g., Mercury) whose concern was the control of human activities. Eventually, the Roman emperors themselves were proclaimed to be gods. No similar redefinition of human ruler to divinity took place among the Greeks, even though the latter believed the gods sired earthly creatures like Hercules. After the Romans, Christians worshiped Jesus for this reason and they still believe in his divine birth. In these and other examples, the activities of the gods over time shifted from the domain of nature alone to intervention in the behavior and social affairs of people. This shift away from the natural and toward the social world occurred at an early period in recorded history.

Accompanying this development of religion from early animism to organized social systems was the same articulation of belief, the same discourse and object-making typical of early forms. Ancient civilizations, such as those of Egypt, Greece, and Rome, possessed elaborate rituals and codified texts that systematized mythology. This discourse regulated daily life. The Judeo-Christian bible, which also influenced the Koran, became the central focus for the organized religions of Judaism, Christianity, and Islam, and thus, the basis for the religious beliefs of over half the world's population. The bible, as a codified text reproduced from generation to generation, was not the only discursive component of organized religion. With Judaism, for example, discussion of the core text produced immense reams of commentaries, such as the Babylonian Talmud, as well as further elaborations that passed from oral to written culture. Around the core text—as happened for Christianity and Islam as well—arose a host of ancillary beliefs and practices, each with its own themes and material objectifications. The societies organized by institutionalized religions were thoroughly regulated by these belief systems. Every object, every action, every moment, every person possessed a symbolic connotation. Thus, societies believing in the early religions, continuing today among traditional or fundamental cultures that remain regulated by orthodoxy, were thoroughly themed environments. Individual members of such cultures existed in a medium saturated by symbolic connotations, or what T. Luckmann calls life under the "sacred canopy" (1967).

In sum, humans have always been symbol-producing beings; from the earliest times of cave paintings and artifact production, they have endowed their environment with themes and signs that held power. Over time this practice produced elaborate discourses or myths that made living itself symbolic and the world that was inhabited a realm of signs. People handed down these empowering stories through the generations, and the stories eventually formed the core of organized religious systems. Human activity is naturally a signifying activity. That is, humans crave and therefore create meaning for their actions and their environment. Symbol production was as basic to everyday life as was the search for food, clothing, and shelter. What is more, this activity of meaning-creation and -circulation remains a fundamental part of life today. In what follows, however, we shall see that the production, quality, and social context of themed environments have changed since ancient times, as has their purpose in daily life. Despite the historical shifts, both the production and enjoyment of a connotative milieu that is "themed" has always been basic to human existence and everyday life.

## Theming and Anti-Theming

The observation that social life involves the quest for meaning is commonplace, and I am not concerned with exploring it here. Instead, I have cho-

sen to focus on one aspect of this quest—namely, the extension of mean-
ing-production and -enjoyment to large-scale material environments by
social processes. In other words, I am especially interested in themed environments that are produced by codes existing *outside* the domains of religion and cosmology. A temple or mosque is a themed environment that is
an extension of the organized religious discourses discussed above. I am
more concerned with artifacts that manifest the desire for meaning objectified in other, secular material forms, such as buildings and theme parks,
or in the current modes of themed retailing, such as malls or restaurants,
because these forms increasingly dominate our culture today.

This assertion, which frames the thesis of this book, is *not*, however, a
commonplace one. Not too long ago—as late as the 1960s—much of our
material environment was decidedly devoid of significant connotations.
Our cultural artifacts did possess meaning, but only in an attenuated, highly
compartmentalized sense. In this book I have sought to explain how and
why the new modes of symbolic production that have appeared recently,
since the 1960s, increasingly characterize our culture.

Before proceeding with a discussion of contemporary themed environments, I explore some early examples of symbolic production through
themed settlement spaces, or cities. Later in this chapter I discuss the shift
experienced in Western, industrial society, from a themed to an anti-
themed environment, associated with modernism in architecture and
design. The remainder of this book discusses the revival of the desire for
themed milieus that seems to characterize our society today, and the reasons for the present shift.

## The Contrast Between Ancient and Modernist Cities

Reliance on themed milieus in the built environment began to increase in
the 1970s. Before that time, in the years immediately after the First World
War, the symbolic dimension in the type of architecture characterizing
contemporary American cities was consciously and purposely squelched,
although in every city there were still environments that pursued fantasy
themes through design. Going even further back, to the nineteenth century,
the industrial cities of capitalism had an attenuated symbolic structure
compared to the cities of the medieval period in the West and the cities of
ancient times. Thus, what seems surprising today by contrast—namely, the
increasing appearance of themed places in our quotidian environment—
was quite common, and, in fact, was normative for ancient cities. Cities

such as Athens, Rome, and Beijing during the period of empires existed as material expressions of cultural themes. All ancient cities were overendowed with built forms that were symbols. The ancient city itself was both a symbol or symbolic expression of a particular civilization and a material environment that sheltered and contained social activities within a signifying space.

## The Ancient City

All ancient civilizations constructed settlement spaces that were overendowed with meaning and material symbols. The place of daily living was itself symbolic, as the built environment encapsulated the typical resident in a richly textured, sign-filled space. Even now, many traditional societies assign great importance to signs and overarching themes in the construction of their settlement spaces.

Ancient societies most commonly built places using a cosmological ideology. Buildings were situated according to particular directions that promised luck or paid homage to the gods. The present-day Chinese practice of *feng shui* embodies these ancient cosmological practices of siting. Those who practice *feng shui* believe that good or ill fortune depends, in part, on the way living spaces are situated regarding the cosmological axis. Experts analyze buildings and houses for a preferred location and proper placement of windows and doors to protect against evil forces and to promote good luck or success. Ancient societies endowed their places with meaningful symbols to enhance fertility, to celebrate empire, to glorify rulers and gods, to achieve harmony with nature, and to promote good fortune. Perhaps the best example of the city as a symbolic construction is classical Athens, in Greece.

Classical Athens was constructed according to a combined cosmological and religious code that prescribed its situation in harmony with nature and its endowment with homages to the gods. The entire city, its environmental space and its buildings, signified through material elements the belief in the pantheon of Greek gods, so that its inhabitants lived within a sacred and meaningful space.

As suggested by its name, the ancient Greeks built Athens to honor the goddess Athena. The early Greeks conceived of the world as a circular orbit with a sacred center. Consequently, Athens was planned using the circle as its principal figure. At its center was the sacred public hearth, or the *hestia koine*. The Greeks of the sixth century B.C. considered this space the sacred center of the world, or the *omphalos,* which was also the anchoring point for the cosmological axis of the universe. Surrounding the sacred center was the *agora,* which encapsulated the public hearth and reserved the surrounding space for the central functions of the city, including its civic and political functions, and the central economic institution—the marketplace. Thus, Athenians conducted the ordinary, mundane activities of daily life, such as buying and selling, legal matters and politics, within a circular space that possessed a sacred center symbolizing the community hearth and, by extension, the center of the universe.

An elevated mesa, called the *acropolis,* dominated the entire city. On its flat top the Greeks built the finest structure of the ancient world, the Parthenon, a temple dedicated to Athena. Like all sacred buildings in Athens, the Parthenon was scaled according to the golden mean—a set of proportions dictating width, height, and length, which were believed to order the natural universe and, therefore, signified the sacred proportions of the cosmos. Because the temple of Athena dominated the acropolis and because the acropolis dominated all of Athens, the symbols of its religion, which we now know as Greek mythology, blanketed this ancient city and made it a sacred space. In their situation within the settlement space, and in their construction according to the sacred proportions of the golden mean, all buildings were endowed with cosmological and religious meanings deriving from Greek cosmology.

### Early Modernist Forms in the City: The Transition from a Signifying to an Anti-Signifying Environment

In the industrialized West, built environments underwent a transition to a settlement space with an attenuated symbolic content after the Middle Ages. Before that time, people built cities with clearly defined symbolic referents in mind. In the Middle Ages, the church dominated the city spaces of Europe. Usually, a particular church, if not a large cathedral, became the central focus for the town. By the time knowledge of the Holy Land had circulated back to Europe, people occasionally designed cities according to the crusader maps of Jerusalem. This plan consisted of one long corridor running lengthwise through the city, after the Roman *cardo* in Jerusalem, and a second thoroughfare that bisected the main street, so that the entire configuration was in the sign of the cross. At the intersection of the two main streets they located the most important church or cathedral. Thus, the entire ensemble derived a sacred significance through analogy with the city of Jerusalem. Visitors to the historically themed contemporary site of Williamsburg, Virginia, will find the same layout, with an Episcopal church standing at the town crossroads.

With the coming of capitalism at the end of the European Middle Ages (there is no definitive date), religion and local signifying practices were pushed aside in favor of the functional need of accumulating wealth. According to Roland Barthes (1970–1971), the classic city of early capitalism grew around a center that contained buildings corresponding with the most powerful forces of social organization. There was a church, a bank or brokerage house, a court or civic building, and a space for a market. Usually, the buildings surrounded a large town square that functioned as a market, just the way the agora did in ancient Athens. Apart from the church, which retained the symbolic trappings of traditional society, other buildings of the center possessed little in the way of symbolic embellishments. The structures were known best by their functions—a bank, a court, a commercial brokerage. Françoise Choay refers to this attenuation of the power of signs in the early capitalist city as "hyposignification." As she states, "*Hyposignificant* does not mean without signification, but only that the built-up system no longer refers to the totality of cultural behavior" (Choay, 1986: 170). Thus, although most societies retained richly structured symbolic systems of religion and historical tradition, they were no longer organized by some overarching, total symbolic canopy, as the settlement spaces of the European Middle Ages or the ancient cities had been. The facades of most buildings in the capitalist downtowns were relatively devoid of obvious thematic connotations, being known instead for their functions. Of course, the city as a whole did and still does symbolize domination by capital and private wealth.

By the late nineteenth century in the West, urban living had already become problematic and many social leaders were appalled at the poor living and working arrangements of people in the industrial city. The filth and congestion of factories, frequent public health crises, and the fast spread of epidemics, poverty, homelessness, and child abandonment were obvious urban plagues of nineteenth-century capitalism. In response to this social crisis of the functional city, which focused on profit making rather than the nurturing of a more humane or symbolic environment, urban reformers began to dream of alternate spatial models—models that also served as critiques of current city living. The new planning models addressed the ills of urban life through utopian planning and simultaneously infused the built environment with a richer symbolism.

Choay (1986: 242–256) mentions two seminal plans that appeared at the turn of the last century, in reaction against the ills of industrial urbanization: the *nostalgic* and the *progressivist* models. These were new codes or ideologies that directed urban development toward more desirable symbolic and social ends. The dream of nineteenth-century utopian planners oriented "itself along the two basic dimensions of time, past and future" (1986: 242). In both cases, an attempt was made to withdraw from the symbolically limited functional code of capitalism and return city building to a signifying environment based on the more expressive codes of naturalism and progressivism. Today, the two ideologies identified by Choay remain seminal influences on planners and architects who are concerned with the problems of the built environment in the capitalist city.

*The Return of Symbols: The Nostalgic/Culturalist Planning Model.* The nostalgic model, also known as the culturalist model, drew upon antiurban feelings and a yearning for the close community of past village life. Both metropolitan regional development and suburban sprawl were considered undesirable settlement patterns. Instead, it was the small town or village that fired the imagination of reformers who sought to regain the sense of human scale and community in the environment. The antiurban writings of early American thinkers are most illustrative of the nostalgic model. As described by Choay (1986: 244):

> The large city is thus criticized successively from a series of different angles; in the name of democracy and political empiricism by Jefferson; in the name of a metaphysics of nature by Emerson and mainly by Thoreau; finally, as a function of a simple analysis of human relations by the great novelists. All these writers, in unison, naively place their hopes in the restoration of a kind of *rural* state which they think is compatible, with a few reservations, with the economic development of industrial society and which alone will ensure the safeguarding of liberty, the blossoming of personality and true community.

This yearning for the more humane, naturally endowed built environment of the traditional small-town community inspired several alternate visions of city living. Two of the most influential were the "garden city" plans of Englishman Ebenezer Howard, and the naturalist model of American architect Frank Lloyd Wright. Howard believed that a complete rupture between the urban pavement and the rural countryside was mistaken: In such a design, the pristine rhythms of nature were forgotten, and the city, cut off as it was from nature, was free to grow to any size, dwarfing human scale and the ability of people to manage their own society. Howard proposed, instead, a plan for all new city building that strove for a balance between the urban and the rural. Cities would be limited in size, and surrounded completely by a circular *green belt* of vegetation; traffic would be restricted to distinct corridors; and residential structures would be airy, with easy access to gardens and green areas.

The vision developed by Wright at the turn of the century was very similar to Howard's. Society's ills at this time were widely blamed on the big, sprawling industrial city. As the poet Emerson preached, only a return to nature could cure people of the evils of capitalist industrialization. Wright envisioned a new model of building that he called "Broadacre City." As Choay (1986: 254) describes it:

> Nature here again becomes a continuous environment, in which all the urban functions are *dispersed* and isolated under the form of *limited units.* Housing is individual: not apartments, but private houses with at least four acres of property each, land which the proprietor uses for agriculture and for different leisure activities. Work is sometimes attached to housing (studios, laboratories, and individual offices), sometimes incorporated in little specialized centers: industrial or commercial units are each time reduced to the minimum viable size, destined for a minimum of persons. The same is true for hospitals and cultural establishments, the large number of which compensates for their dispersion and their generally reduced scale. All these cells (individual and social) are linked and *related* to each other by an abundant network of land and air routes: isolation has meaning only if it can be broken at any moment.

By synthesizing the urban and the rural and by returning to a nostalgic vision of small-town life, the naturalist/ culturalist model was conceived as the cure to the ills of unfettered urban growth. To the industrial functions of city buildings were added the signs of nature and of rural life. Daily living was returned to a human scale and mixed in with the routines of plant and animal life. As we shall discuss in Chapter 5, the nostalgic model, which yearns for the small-town scale of the past, remains an important inspiration for some contemporary planners, especially architects Andreas Duany and Leon Krier. Duany and his followers, who are known as the "new urbanists," vigorously advocate their town-inspired model as an antidote to suburban sprawl. According to one commentator: "Duany and Plater-Zyberk don't merely want to lay out streets and parks and buildings. They want to design a way of life. They want to bring back the neighborhood, create folksy new towns with the charm of addresses such as Annapolis,

Maryland, or Princeton, New Jersey" (Morrison, 1994). In this endeavor they pursue a nostalgic image of the small town as an ideology or code that represents a sign of antimetropolitan living.

*The Progressivist/Modernist Planning Model.* Unlike the nostalgic model, progressivist visions were oriented toward the future, and they celebrated technological progress. At its core the ideology of progressivism depends on the concept of *modernity*. Modern architects (who practiced mainly after World War I) incorporated two distinct perspectives in their designs: first, the continual technological progress of industrial expansion; and second, the innovations of avant-garde art such as cubism and abstract expressionism, which provided a departure from the ordinary visual perspective of city building. I discuss modernism more fully below, because, as a design movement, it was singularly responsible for the eradication of symbolic depth in contemporary cities until the recent period of thematic revival. Ironically, although the progressivist model celebrated the ideal of progress and the symbols of technological advancement and efficiency, such as the automobile, progressivist planning actually restricted the symbolic content of building. Progressivist architects and planners replaced the eclectic mix of old buildings inherited by the central city from the many years prior to the 1920s with an austere environment of concrete, steel, and glass, molded in minimalist geometric shapes, such as the rectangular box of the high-rise office tower.

The basis of progressivist city planning was the reduction of all urban spaces to their function, much as had been done in the cities of early capitalism. But modernist architects took functionality to an extreme in order to promote efficiency. The credo of the times was "Form follows function." Design was meant to stand in the service of efficient work and movement in the new environment. One leading architect of progressivism, Le Corbusier, conceived of the city as a "machine for living" or a tool that enabled continued progress and technological advancement. Conceived of as tools, all components of the city—buildings, roads, railways, and open spaces—were reduced to their functions in order to make them work efficiently. In the words of Choay (1986: 247): "Progressivist planners carefully separate working zones from living zones, and living zones from civic centers or areas of recreation. Each of these categories is in turn divided into subcategories equally classified and ordered. Each type of work, administrative, industrial or commercial, is assigned a label."

According to Le Corbusier, "Everything must be given form or set in order, in a condition of full efficiency" (1946: 74). In his plan for the city of

the future, or *the radiant city,* transportation routes were predicated exclusively on automobile travel and the superhighway. Le Corbusier's design
abolished the street because it was the symbol of the chaotic, poorly
planned industrial city. His radiant city reordered the space of the urban
agglomeration. Instead of the haphazard placement of housing, which was
usually low density, Le Corbusier planned large, high-rise apartment blocks
that liberated city space for use as parks and landscaped vistas. Equally
important as functional efficiency was the desire of progressive architects
to eradicate all sentimentality and traditional symbols within the city. Le
Corbusier, for example, proposed a plan for the redevelopment of Paris
that would eradicate all the picturesque old neighborhoods of the past.
Nothing should get in the way of the modernist skyline of abstract geometric shapes. As Choay describes it (1986: 248):

> The planner 'composes' his future city on the drawing board, as he would compose
> a painting. Following the principles of cubism, and still more those of purism and
> of Stijl, he eliminates every incidental detail in favor of simple forms, reduced to
> essentials, where the eye cannot stumble against any particularity; it is in a sense a
> question of constructing the a priori framework for any possible social behavior.

The progressivist vision has had even greater influence on city building than
has the naturalist. Codified in the principles of modernist design and
launched as a movement among architects around the globe, progressivism
became known as the "International School" of architecture. Virtually every
downtown center of every major city in the world surrendered to the rectangular boxes of high-rise buildings advocated by Le Corbusier. Superhighway
construction led to the demolition of old neighborhoods and picturesque
sections of cities in the obsessive promotion of "efficient" automobile traffic.
In many places, planners obliterated low-density residential housing and
replaced it with clusters of massive high-rise buildings ("projects") containing thousands of families. Decades of city building and renewal along progressivist lines by the 1960s had resulted in a city space that was truly
hyposignificant—austere, geometric, and homogeneous—a gargantuan
social space, void of human sentiment, human scale, and human variety (i.e.,
the symbols of various traditional cultures). As a built environment, the
modernist city celebrated the overarching theme of progress and technological efficiency. But as a dream of the future, it contained enough internal contradictions to prevent its code from being carried forward into the next cen-

tury. From the 1960s onward, the modernist city began to collapse under the weight of its own design failures as a human space.

Perhaps the best illustration of the limits encountered by the International School is the city of Brasilia, in Brazil (Hoston, 1989). An entirely planned city, Brasilia was built by modernist architects to house the federal government functions of the rapidly growing country. The city is situated in the relatively undeveloped plateau country, six hundred miles from the more densely inhabited coastal area. From the air its shape resembles that of a bird, signifying the flight of Brazil toward a successful future. On the ground, however, the bird motif was abandoned: Architects Lucio Costa and Oscar Niemeyer instead constructed an austere ode to Le Corbusier's principles of modernist design. The "death of the street" dictated that space be dedicated to the automobile. Indeed, Brasilia has no streets—only superhighways that link gigantic, rectangular apartment blocks with each other. The huge buildings are separated by expansive but empty plazas meant as monuments rather than as usable spaces. These plazas are ideal sites for the commission of crimes, and crime is indeed frequent. Because the traditional interaction of neighbors and passersby was eradicated by modernist design, the use of ramps, vacant parks, and concrete plazas by robbers and rapists has grown unchecked. Inhabitants also complain that it is a very uncomfortable city in which to live. It lacks human scale, the warmth and dynamism of street life that characterizes Brazilian cities elsewhere. Like similarly inspired megaprojects in the United States (such as the Pruit-Igoe housing development in St. Louis, which was demolished in the 1970s), Brasilia has failed as an urban space of habitation, while it breeds anonymity, alienation, and crime.

Despite the failures of the International School, the ideology of modernism remains a potent force in city building. Being up-to-date is particularly important in societies that have newly acquired economic wealth. For this reason, the theme of progress remains active in city building, although in actual design the structures in many cases depart from the austere internationalist style and venture into more eclectic, even postmodern conceptions.

## Thematic Exceptionalism in the Modernist City: The Persisting and Growing Influence of Fantasy and Symbols

Although building in the modernist style avoided symbols, cities prior to the 1960s had a number of places that remained thematic environments.

For this reason we cannot say that all meaning in the city was eradicated by the overarching ideology of the progressivist model. Although the following examples do not approach the scale of today's reliance on theming and fantasy environments, they do show that the impulse to indulge in fantasy and symbols has always remained a part of city building.

## Consumer Shopping Spaces and Symbolic Themes

The external facades of modernist buildings, as mandated by the International Style, avoided symbols. Inside these same structures, however, the signifiers of wealth and status structured the emerging mass market of consumerism and the new regime of corporate business. Interiors proclaimed the new and the fashionable in home furnishings. Denotation of function is a minimalist mode of signification; yet it retained a certain symbolic value through an association with modernist design (i.e., the connotation of progress or being "up-to-date"). As the middle class grew in numbers and affluence, it became the target of new marketing schemes to increase the volume of consumer purchasing through the delivery of a wide array of commodities that signified status because they were "in fashion." This emergent culture of consumption, whose origins predated modernism, relied heavily on symbols.

One particularly important aspect of this new consumer society was the invention in nineteenth-century Paris of the "department store" (see Williams, 1982; Miller, 1981; Leach, 1993). The first such store, which opened in 1869, was the Bon Marché. Every commodity in this store was identified by its function and grouped with every other associated commodity in "departments." The stores' internal structure and organization liberated consumers, who could move around at will, handling and examining the merchandise even before they reached the cashier's counter. Fantasies and themes of consumerism at this time were restricted to those of exoticism (such as the sale of imported commodities like silk) and opulence (for perfumes, home furnishings, fashions, and the like). Because Paris was the fashion capital of the world at the turn of the century, and because the department store was so successful as a generator of profit, entrepreneurs in America's bustling cities of the late 1800s, such as Marshall Field in Chicago and the Gimbels brothers in New York, copied the department store form and used its themes to sell their goods in the United States.

The success of large department stores changed the structure of labor in the cities, moving it away from dependency on manufacturing alone.

*A large urban department store that caters to the pedestrian crowds of the city. Photo courtesy of Corbis/Bettmann.*

Certain service occupations emerged that were closely connected to the promotion of consumer purchasing and the display of commodities within department stores. Window dressers, for example, developed the art of adorning mannequins in store displays for the benefit of the passerby. Stores used theatrical techniques of staging, lighting, and posing to great effect. Sales as a category of employment expanded exponentially, and with this increased activity came an increasing reliance on fantasy themes.

Advertising and pictorial promotional displays played an ever larger role in the stimulation of consumer desire and in the promotion of particular commodities. These images were so effective that today consumerism and advertising are major influences on our culture. The advertising industry developed in tandem with the great department stores, including the phenomenal mail order business initiated by Sears, Roebuck, with its catalog that could be mailed directly to every home in America. As elsewhere within the decor of department stores, visual ads exploited the themes of luxury and exoticism. Many consumer outlets now included the exoticism of technological progress, as exemplified in the so-called mechanical marvels of household "labor-saving" devices. These commodities signified the theme of progress that was the basis of the modernist code.

## Fantasy Leisure Industries and Early Themed Environments

Other interesting built environments that were symbolic and emotive also appeared during the late nineteenth century, which have influenced consumer spaces up to this day. Among these themed environments are state fairs, world expositions, arcades, and amusement parks, which were first seen around the turn of the century, in industrial cities. Along with the emergence of the cinema as a major entertainment industry in the 1920s came the construction of new leisure palaces, the exotic and spectacular movie houses that marked popular space in the twentieth-century city.

*World Expositions.* World expositions, such as the Columbian Exposition of 1893 in Chicago, were attempts by society to reaffirm the popular belief in progress at a time when large cities were sinking further into the mire of social problems associated with unbridled capitalist industrialization. The expositions of the nineteenth century were utopian dreams staged against the real nightmare of uneven development found in cities (as seen in the contrast between the great success of urban capitalism, on the one hand, and its immense social problems such as homelessness, poverty, and frequent health crises, on the other). International world's fairs, which began in the late nineteenth century in Europe, were a combination of trade fairs for the benefit of major commodity producers, and reassuring celebrations of the planner's or architect's vision for the improved urban milieu of tomorrow. They contained elaborate representations of utopian schemes for an enriched everyday life. Expositions promoted middle-class consumption as the social norm. They presented the plethora of commodities made available by the economic system in a whimsical and amusing way. Consumption itself was promoted as a form of amusement. In the best modernist style, the world expositions reendorsed a popular belief in the benefits of technological advancement and in the ability of people to plan for a promised age of capitalist cornucopia. According to David Frisby (1985: 254): "The world expositions were the high school in which the masses, dragged away from consumption, learned to empathize with exchange value: 'Look at everything, touch nothing.' Their goal as far as the masses were concerned was distraction."

The greatest fair of the nineteenth century was the World's Columbian Exposition, which opened May 1, 1893, in Chicago, on 6,000 acres of land near Lake Michigan and the University of Chicago. Over 400,000 people visited this event, including President Grover Cleveland. Among its most popular attractions was the transportation building, which was designed by Louis Sullivan in a new style of urban construction that contained a projected utopian scheme for the plan of future cities. Years later, at the New York World's Fair in 1938, the utopian representation of tomorrow contained in the transportation building was again the popular hit of the exposition. By then, the automobile had been introduced as a mass marketed product, and fantasizing about progress had shifted from dreams of an extensive public transportation network of rails to a futuristic model of an efficient highway system designed for individually owned, self-propelled cars, which would connect people almost effortlessly to homes and jobs. People were sold a belief in modernism that meant all the problems of getting to and from work could be solved through the purchase of a single commodity—namely the family car.

Another influential world's fair was the Pan-American Exposition of 1901, held in Buffalo, New York. Here too, progressivist ideology played itself out in environmental fantasy themes. One designer, Frederic Thompson, created a themed amusement ride called a "Trip to the Moon," complete with green cheese and moonshops, that proved an immensely popular attraction. The fully enclosed trip elaborated on the more common environmental experience of the "Tunnel of Love" or "Haunted House" found in amusement parks and state fairs, foreshadowing today's theme park rides.

World's fairs and international sports events such as the Olympics continue to alter our urban landscapes with ambitious public construction projects, as shown by the recent developments in Seattle and Atlanta. As a form of space they are excellent examples of themed environments because they specifically incorporate sign systems as a way of communicating to onlookers the meaning of buildings. Fairs and expositions also contain exhibits that remain useful as occasions for corporations to explore alternate themed environments that just might help them improve the marketing of their products.

The world's fair expositions of the nineteenth century also bore the seeds of postmodernism. These gigantic, pedestrian-oriented carnivals of industrialism were, in fact, the precursors of theme parks like today's Disneyland. As market fairs that enlarged and developed fantasy themes, as open-air environments oriented toward pedestrians, and as diversions offering entertaining rides and attractions, they worked out the important articulation between fantasy consumerism projecting the future as conceived by giant corporations and a built environment that was diversionary and fun. It is but a small step from the World's Fair of 1938 in Flushing Meadows, New York City, which entertained millions of visitors during the depression and the approach of World War II, to the Disneyland of Anaheim, in suburban southern California, which was erected in 1955.

*Movie Palaces.* Another example of fantasy themed environments in the modernist city also developed directly and in tandem with the emergence of the Hollywood cinema as a major industry in America. In the early part of the twentieth century, business entrepreneurs who turned moviemaking into a major industry, such as Adolph Zukor of Paramount, the Warner brothers, and Samuel Goldwyn of MGM, linked their cinema factories to chains of theaters across the country. They were joined by others, such as Marcus Loew and the Shubert brothers, who also owned franchised movie theater chains. In every city where these moguls decided to locate, a theater was built that celebrated Hollywood's excesses with imaginary and often spectacular theming. Ancient Aztec or classical Roman and Greek designs were among those commonly used as decorative motifs in the interiors of these movie palaces. Every city seemed to have its own elaborately decorated movie palace during the Depression, showing largely escapist fare, such as Hollywood musicals.

During the first three decades of the twentieth century—in other words, before the advent of television—traveling variety shows, known as vaudeville, were another popular mode of urban entertainment. Vaudeville theaters often doubled as movie houses, and they too indulged in the fantasy style of Hollywood cinema. In the 1930s, New York City's Times Square became the prototype for these multiple-block entertainment zones, which sprang up in city after city, from Boston to Los Angeles. The large urban movie palaces built in the early decades of the twentieth century in turn are the progenitors of today's spectacularly themed Las Vegas casinos (discussed more fully in Chapter 4).

### Urban Arcades and the Cultural
### Development of the Consumerist Fantasy

Another nineteenth-century adaptation to commodity capitalism, the urban arcade, also originated in the emergent consumer culture. Yet, both in spatial form and in effect, it was different from other themed milieus. On the one hand, the arcades are the forerunner of the fully enclosed shopping mall that is so common today. On the other hand, the arcades stimulated the development of a consumerist self that was in part a fantasy. The arcades I have in mind here were often labyrinthine, enclosed pedestrian thoroughfares lined with small shops of all kinds. Within the arcade, or during a walk through an arcade, the pedestrian became a consumer. The influential writer Walter Benjamin (1969) considered the arcade the preeminent modernist form. As Benjamin notes, within this milieu people are stimulated to dream of life in a "primeval landscape of consumption" and abundance. The arcade shops, with their varied kinds of merchandise, embody the increasing variety of commodity fantasies, or "phantasmagorias," that were beginning to appear in the 1920s because of the rising purchasing power and increasing size of the growing middle class.

The development of an imaginary component to shopping that departs from the basic compulsion of need is critical to the spectacular and hypertrophic development of the consumer culture characteristic of our society today. Just as the large department store made shopping easy, the arcade made fantasizing about shopping easy. The consumer arcade, through the mediation of its shops, introduced the new, the exotic, and the stylish to the urban masses. These shops were the purveyors of the modernist experience—i.e., the experience of the new, of the unique, of the stimulation of desires for novel material objects, or as Benjamin said, of "wish symbols." Now the same is true of the contemporary shopping mall, which might explain why it has enjoyed such great success.

The Parisian arcades that Benjamin studied in the 1920s were a permanent world's exposition. They were not only staging areas for consumer fantasies, and promoters of new fantasies, but also the primal ground for the development of a new kind of subjectivity—one based on "being a consumer," on the stimulation of a desiring, commodity-craving self. This consumer self was a qualitative departure from the nineteenth-century self, which had been socialized by the routine, workaday world of industrial factories. Arcade shops functioned both to create new consumer fantasies and to amplify and develop already existing themes of desire. They glorified opulence, luxury, and symbols of wealth, and they also introduced the exotic, the novel, the imported commodity, and the technological or mechanical marvel that you were invited to believe you could not live without. This development of commodity fantasy themes by the individual arcade shops fed the growing activity of the advertising industry, which circulated the new, amplified images from central city mercantile environments to the surrounding social spaces across the nation.

In this manner, the early arcades provided a key channel of desire to a society increasingly reliant on themed environments and on goods with a symbolic value greater than their use-value. They were the material link between the growing power of the advertising industry, with its promotion of consumer fantasies, and the varied products of the economy that shifted progressively more toward goods with obvious sign-value, and lately, pure images themselves, rather than heavy manufacturing.

## Suburbanization As the Expression of Theming

Beginning in the mid-1800s, as the large industrial cities of the United States were growing and prospering, wealthy residents started a movement away from the center of urban life to the country—a movement now known as suburbanization. The flight to the suburbs by rich industrialists introduced certain themes to areas around the large industrial city that remain common today as part of our consumer-oriented culture. The motifs of affluence, status, excess, and conspicuous consumption were deployed through estate living. As suburban development increased in popularity for the middle class in the early years of the twentieth century, the same themes celebrating wealth and prestige dominated housing and landscaping choices. By the 1920s there was enough demand for suburban homes that developers could switch from building on a custom basis to the construction of a modest number of mass-produced houses within a single, new community. Early suburban developments that appeared then—such as Tuxedo Park, outside of New York City; Lake Forest, near Chicago; and Shaker Heights, eight miles from downtown Cleveland—stressed the symbolic significance of their locations by extolling their exclusivity, prestige, and affluence.

Developers and real estate agents responsible for attracting home buyers to these areas advertised their ethnic and racial exclusion while celebrating these locations as symbols of status and wealth. In this early period of sub-

*A nineteenth-century urban arcade—the precursor of the mall. These*
*arcades were usually composed of small shops that were called boutiques.*
*In more recent years, the downtown section of Las Vegas was remodeled*
*in the form of an arcade. Photo courtesy of Corbis-Bettmann.*

urban development, Catholics, Jews, and African Americans were specifically excluded from purchasing homes by racist developers and real estate
agents. It was not, however, until after World War II that suburban residence became available to the masses of Americans. Today the majority of
the population lives in suburbia; however, most of these places now lack
the vigorous symbols of alternate lifestyle characteristic of suburbs at the
turn of the twentieth century.

Single-family homes built in regions on the outskirts of large cities today borrow several symbolic features from the original "nouveaux riches" mansions. They ape signs of social prestige and individual affluence. Their front lawns are miniature versions of those found on the larger suburban estates of the earlier era, and like them, are symbols of excess. Although they are devoted to the frivolous cultivation of grass rather than the growing of edible crops, the lawns of typical middle-class homes nonetheless require constant work, usually from the occupants or a contracted lawn service. In contrast, the wealthy owners of nineteenth-century country mansions kept gardeners on their staff. Suburban backyards also retain the estate function of recreation and leisure. Front doors and driveways are marked off to signify prestige. Even mailboxes are stylized for this function. Like the large country estates, middle-class suburban homes come equipped with a separate kitchen and dining room. Owners also reserve the latter for special occasions.

All of these features mimic the conspicuous consumption of the wealthy, serving as signs of socioeconomic status, but they are obviously scaled-down replicas that fit the more modest budgets of middle-class home owners. In this sense, normative plans for suburban housing—the kind of floor layout that people expect when purchasing such a home—use iconic representation to evoke the referent of nineteenth-century estate life. Without the cultural conditioning provided by the latter, we might find suburban land use patterns and housing features quite odd in their apparent dedication to excess. Indeed, since the advent of mass suburban development, untold numbers of critics have complained about the rather ordinary, banal, and boring landscape created by mile after mile of sprawling, ticky-tacky housing.

In short, the same motifs of wealth, prestige, and exclusion that were played out repeatedly, as one-note symphonies, in the development of large industrial cities were embellished over the years in residential locations outside the metropolitan areas, through suburbanization. After 1940, more people were allowed to participate in this great spectacle of symbolic excess, due to the expansion of affluence after World War II. A kind of status or prestige was marketed to the masses, symbolized by the affordable, single-family, suburban home. At the same time, mass suburban housing has not had the effect of enriching the symbolic content of our culture. For many critics of single family sprawl, in fact, just the opposite has occurred. The sameness and conformity of suburban housing and the inefficiencies of this type of development have recently become causes of concern. Yet suburbanization and mass home construction do use symbols characteristic of the consumer society. Because of these signs, the suburb, like arcades and expositions, maintained a certain level of signification, in contrast to the larger environment of the industrial city, which made little use of connotative symbols.

As discussed in Chapter 1, the large industrial city of the nineteenth and the early twentieth centuries could hardly be called a themed environment. Cities then were hyposignificant—that is, their symbolic content was attenuated and limited to signifying functionality. The bank was a sign of banking, the factory a sign of manufacturing, and the working class home a sign of shelter or neighborhood. Yet, despite this limited use of symbols, world's fairs, the phantasmagoria of commercial arcades and movie palaces, and the celebration of signs of affluence and status through the mass suburbanization of residential housing introduced certain symbolic motifs that laid the groundwork for a shift to dynamic theming as part of our culture. As time went on, the modernist stranglehold on building and planning declined. After 1960, architects and planners reacted against hyposignification. Symbols returned to the milieu of daily life. Now there is an increasing reliance on themes in all aspects of our culture. Before analyzing particular themed spaces such as restaurants and malls, I explain in the next chapter why the trend to themes has occurred and how it has been connected to the needs of a consumer-oriented, profit-making society since the 1960s.

## Summary of Main Ideas

1. Traditional and ancient cities were completely organized by symbolism. The entire settlement possessed a thematic purpose.
2. The contemporary city of capitalism limited environmental symbols to their functions. Themes were discouraged in building even though the entire city itself became a sign of industrial capitalism and progress.
3. By the late nineteenth century, a reaction to the social ills of capitalist cities led architects and planners to follow two main lines of reform, the *nostalgic* and the *progressive* models. Both of these had strongly articulated themes and reintroduced an overt symbolic dimension to the landscape.
4. The nostalgic model seeks to avoid the sprawl and massive regional growth of today's metropolis by returning to the simple, community-based model of the small town or village. The "new

urbanism" movement today retains this nineteenth-century ideology.

5. The progressivist or modernist ideology retained the early capitalist tendency to reduce buildings to their denotative functions. Thus, modernists did not revive theming in the city; but their projects taken as a whole symbolized progress and being "up-to-date," a very strong theme that was copied in cities across the globe. Modernist architecture also was inspired by abstract art, a kind of theme, in the austere use of geometric shapes.

6. Even in the modernist city of capitalism, with its limited symbols, examples existed of more vigorous theming. Fantasies of consumption and shopping themes were stimulated by the invention of the large, central city department store.

7. World's fairs and expositions created themed environments—to the great pleasure of their patrons—that foreshadowed the invention of the theme park in the 1950s.

8. Movie palaces, with their elaborate, Hollywood-inspired decors, played up the fantasy themes of the cinema and became the precursors of today's spectacular Las Vegas casinos.

9. Urban arcades stimulated both the growing consumer culture in America and the development of a consumer self by providing a fantasy-driven landscape of shopping. These arcades were the early version of our giant shopping malls or gallerias.

10. The suburbanization of single-family homes beginning in the 1800s also served to counter the limited theming of the functional, capitalist city. Early suburbs glorified the themes of affluence and of status realized through the possession of commodities—what Thorstein Veblen called "conspicuous consumption." Despite the strong presence of these same influences on consumer culture today, suburbs have also been criticized for their limited theming and their conformity.

# 3

# THE MIRROR
# OF PRODUCTION

## *The Realization Problem of Capital*

Bob Goldman and Stephen Papson (1996) wrote a book a few years ago called *Sign Wars*. Their work is an exploration of a phenomenon I described in the first edition of *The Theming of America*—namely that producers of consumer goods that are very similar or identical use signs and symbolic appeals to differentiate their products. These "sign wars" most often take place in advertising, as have the wars between Coca-Cola and Pepsi and between Nike and Adidas. A glance at contemporary media programming suggests that this list is endless. Companies fight one another for consumers' dollars, using signs as their weapons. There is an increasingly strong connection between the economic need to make a profit and the reliance on symbols in the marketing of commodities. This link is a very important clue both to the function of themed environments in our society and to their increasing use. During the period of early capitalist industrialism, in the eighteenth and nineteenth centuries, economic competition meant competition through production—that is, the need simultaneously to reduce costs and to manufacture products in quantity. During this earlier stage, conflict was often enjoined between owners of factories and their workers. Today these production criteria remain important, as do the demands of both producers and organized labor; but in addition, there is a second aspect—thematic competition, or competition through variation in symbols among products that are virtually the same. This competition is played out in the media and in all sorts of consumer environments (e.g., malls and restaurants) rather than in the workplace.

Clearly the ability to afford commodities rules the act of consumption; but presently the use of thematic appeals in marketing and the influence of fashion also regulate the social process of consuming. Thus, in addition to the relation of consumer needs to prices and budgets, which has always underlain individual behavior in a capitalist system, the consumption process involves the relation between consumer desires or fantasies and the motifs of commodity purchasing. Furthermore, the importance of the *symbolic* value of commodities, created by the social context of mass marketing, has grown considerably over the years. Presently, then, the price-consumption link that once dominated consumer choices is now joined by the symbolic value-consumption link, which involves considerations of a personal, sign-oriented nature in the purchase of consumer goods. Modernist, industrial capitalism has thus evolved from a *hypo*significant system, with attenuated or limited symbolic encoding of the environment, to a postmodern, late-capitalist, information- and service-dominated economy that produces a themed culture the material manifestation of which is a themed environment.

Due to the importance of symbols in marketing, the economy today is quite different from what it was 100 years ago. The present global relation between economic processes and the use of themes reflects significant historical changes because of fundamental shifts in the organization of capitalism. This chapter explains the current dependency of both production and consumption on symbolic appeals, while also acknowledging the importance of the more traditional consideration of production costs, profits, prices, and consumer budgets. But there is a second and equally important way in which our society differs markedly from that of the past. Consuming is not only image driven but is also dependent on new forms of space. These themed environments structure the consuming experience in ways that borrow from the state fairs, the department stores, the arcades, and the movie palaces discussed in the previous chapter. These material forms also involve the engineering of structures through franchising to sell products in the most efficient way possible. What is new and different today, then, is the increasing use of such themed environments to market goods. Symbolic and franchised consumer spaces, the general domination of themes, and the thoroughly objective orchestration of fashion characterize our society.

## The Mirror of Production

Modern economic analysis emphasizes the world of production. This was most explicit for Karl Marx, who dissected the capitalist system and exposed the conflict at its core between workers and owners of factories. In all approaches to the understanding of capitalism, however, the same basic relation applies. Capitalists invest money, or capital, in a productive enterprise, usually involving manufacturing and the employment of an industrial workforce, which then produces a commodity. The entrepreneur then sells this product in a market. When the costs of production and marketing are subtracted from the market price, the remainder is profit, or more capital. The owner of the factory (the capitalist) can then take this money and reinvest it in the factory so as to expand production, or invest it in another capital market. Pure profit is pure money under capitalism, and it can flow to any source of investment that has the potential to make even more money. Marx summarized this dynamic in his famous formula $M—>C—>M'$—that is, money, or M, is invested in commodity production, C, which, when sold, becomes more money, or M'.

This scheme seems simple, and in many ways it is. Just about anyone with some money could set up a business and become a capitalist. Many people indeed attempt it; but in reality, few succeed. Contingencies arising in the "real world" of moneymaking (the capitalist/competitive system) can be quite unforgiving. Among all of the complications that might occur when applying the $M—>C—>M'$ schema to reality, the most formidable one has been neglected for years by analysts, including Marx himself. Early analysts of capitalism focused on the first step in the equation—namely the conversion of money to commodity production within the environment of the factory. Studies of the historical rise of capitalism as a social system concentrate on the emergence of the social conditions that have produced the supply of industrial workers, on the one hand, and a class of capitalists freed from the authority of church and landed traditions, on the other. This social organization forms the basis for the accumulation of capital through commodity production.

For many years, the second step in the formula, or the conversion from commodities, C, to more money, or M', was simply assumed. We now know that this last step is far from automatic. People in business, even those with immense inventories and productive potential, have considerable difficulty unloading their products on the market in a manner that enables them to enjoy reasonable profits. Consider the domestic automobile industry in the United States as one illustration. In the 1950s the production of cars employed one out of every six workers in some capacity. The U.S. automobile industry also supported the U.S. steel industry, its tire industry, its battery, brakes, and shocks industry, and so on. By the 1970s, due to foreign competition, people were not buying American-made cars in the immense volumes of the past. Demand remained high, but alternate, competitive commodities were available as imports. Domestic automobile manufacturers found it increasingly difficult to move from the large inventories of commodities, or C, to their sale and subsequent reconversion into profit, or M'. In fact, the drop in the volume of sales produced a most critical and long-lasting crisis in American capitalism. As sales declined and American manufacturing companies readjusted to a more competitive global environment, they reduced their permanent labor forces and canceled or decreased their orders of steel, batteries, and tires, throwing those ancillary industries into a similar decline. These critical adjustments, which are called "deindustrialization" (Piore and Sable, 1984; Harvey, 1988), brought entire industries that formerly were tied to the production of cars to their knees. By the 1990s, the United States was no longer the largest manufacturer of steel or cars, and its domestic companies had to function in an environment where the conversion from commodity to profit was less and less certain. Increasing risk and increasingly uncertain profits characterize the economy today and define its parameters in a way much different from the past.

The shifting dynamic of the capitalist accumulation process, from an emphasis on manufacturing to a focus on the dynamics of profit making in a globally competitive environment, illustrates a previously neglected problem area of capitalism known as the realization of capital. The transfer of value from the commodity to its realization in sales has become increasingly riddled with risks and embattled by voracious competition. The production or manufacturing process simply "valorizes" commodities by creating value in production. In order for capitalists to "realize" that extra value, they must sell the goods they produce. Only after the sale can companies count up their profit, and only *if* they are successful in making a profit on sales can capitalists remain alive for the next cycle of accumulation. The conversion from C to M' is increasingly critical to the dynamics of capitalist accumulation as the world becomes a more competitive place. The solution of this "realization problem" has led us to a themed environment.

When Karl Marx and other nineteenth-century analysts of capitalism wrote about economic development, they neglected the realization problem, although they mentioned and were aware of it. More important for them, as we have discussed, were the dynamics of production, the problems of an industrial labor force, and the complexities of profit making in a world of competitive capitalists and landlords. In the even more highly competitive environment of the twenty-first century, the primary obstacles to the continued expansion of capital are no longer predominantly those of production—or of capital valorization in commodities at the factory—but those of consumption, or capital realization at the market.

## Baudrillard and the Political Economy of the Sign

More than any other contemporary observer of society, French postmodernist Jean Baudrillard has called attention to the new conditions under which capitalism is now developing and on which its future survival depends. For Baudrillard, the realization problem of capital, rather than the valorization problem of factory-based industrialization, currently stands at the very core of capitalism's historical dynamics.

Baudrillard unveiled his thesis in a series of books that began with a frontal attack on Karl Marx. In 1973 he published *The Mirror of Production*, which was a critique of Marx's *Capital*. Baudrillard thought that Marx was misguided and that he did not understand the true dynamic of capitalism, which was less about the world of the factory and the conversion of an agricultural labor force to the regime of industrial production, than about the world of the market and the conversion of laborers of all kinds to consumers. Without the latter social change, manufactured products would simply rot in the marketplace, and the emergent capitalist class would fall into abjection and poverty. Capitalism succeeded because it produced goods that the masses of workers could afford and that they purchased. The realization of capital, in Baudrillard's view, was the precondition for the growth of the productive powers of the capitalist system; Marx, in contrast, emphasized the historical dynamic of the production process as the precondition for capitalism.

Baudrillard considers political economists, especially those who adopt a Marxian approach, under the spell of the "mirror of production." In emphasizing production as the central process of capitalist accumulation, they show reality in reverse. In reality, the act of consumption is at the base of the survival of capitalism; and this act depends more on the transformation of individuals into desiring consumers than into industrial workers. All of the concern that Marx and other political economists have displayed for the role of the latter in the historical development of capitalism is misguided. Instead, the critical dynamics of capitalist development hinge on the ability to *realize* capital once commodities are produced.

Baudrillard claims that the record has borne him out. The industrial countries of the West have not evolved into revolutionary anticapitalist societies but into voracious consumer nations whose daily life focuses on the desire for and the consumption of commodities. Even the restraint commonly provided by the household budget does not rein in this frenzy of consuming, because many Americans are knee-deep in credit card debt (see Ritzer, 1993, 2000). Furthermore, as is well documented by studies lamenting industrial decline (see Bluestone and Harrison, 1982), heavy manufacturing has virtually disappeared from the American landscape. Production now takes place increasingly abroad, in newly developed countries. Thus, there is still an entire capitalist universe of production where the dynamics of conversion from capital, or M, to commodities, or C, reigns supreme. But, with the very important exception of the new information economy, the mass production process occurs progressively more often in areas outside the country. The population of this society remains burdened with the task of completing the realization side of the capital accumulation equation. Their way of working has changed, most commonly by shifting to information and/or service industries, but their role as happy consumers of capital's bounty remains, even if the goods that make up that cornucopia are increasingly imported.

Baudrillard maintains that the mirror image of capitalism fooled Marx and other political economists into focusing on manufacturing and the creation of an industrial workforce, which were dominant trends during the nineteenth century. The important dynamics of development in the twentieth century, especially after the Great Depression of the 1930s, instead, were a dramatic increase in mass consumption and in competition among capitalists in the market. Nowhere are these trends more evident than in the United States. This country is a net importer of goods, with a trade deficit in the billions of dollars. Other territories, such as Japan and Singapore, have developed export-led economies, the very existence of which depends on their level of exports to countries such as the United States. Although Marxian political economy might still be pertinent to analyses of export-led economies, the dynamics of consumption and not production are most relevant to the continued economic well-being of the United States.

## The Role of Symbols or Themes in the Circuit of Capital

A nation of consumers must be fed by appeals to consume even when the goods they are presented with have dubious use-values. Basic human needs are relatively simple: food, clothing, shelter, and some means of providing for these necessities. The needs pumping up a consumer society, however, extend far beyond these basics; furthermore, even the basics are elaborated by the practice of consumption, almost beyond the point of recognition. For example, shelter for most Americans is a "basic" three- or four-bedroom suburban house complete with a fully equipped kitchen and recreational room. Consumers also view the commodities that stock such a "basic" home as "necessities." They desire dishwashers, refrigerators, microwave ovens, conventional ovens, stoves, and assorted electric gadgets in the kitchen; television sets, videotape players, stereo equipment, personal computers, CD players, DVD players, Mini Disc players, MP3 players, portable phones, cellular phones, and leisure furniture in the family room; and bedroom sets in the bedrooms. Almost all of these commodities are manufactured entirely abroad or contain components manufactured abroad. Thus, the principal economic task fulfilled by Americans, as we have shifted away from industrial production, has become to desire and to acquire the goods we think we cannot do without.

For the most part, the production of this intense desire for commodities depends directly on symbolic mechanisms. Signs and themes play a central role in the proper priming of the consumer society. We may agree with Baudrillard that symbolic processes solve the realization problem of capital (this relationship is discussed in more detail later); but more than that, symbolic processes are central to the entire circuit of capital. The role of meaning systems (some call them ideologies) has been essential to capitalist development since capitalism's earliest beginnings in the competitive cauldrons of European merchant towns. The history of capital is a history of the role of signification and meaning systems in the economic life of society. This role is not confined merely to the marketing of commodities; rather, the entire process of capital accumulation is shot through with mechanisms that depend on symbolic processes for their proper functioning.

## Signs and the Constitution of a "Capitalist Class": Marx's View

Marx's analysis of capitalist development in his classic work *Capital* (1868) provides us with an understanding of the political economy of history. Marx is concerned in this work with showing us not only how the capitalist system operates but also how it began and how it continued to develop as a natural consequence of the economic forces that it unleashed in the world. The agent of growth was the capitalist class, a collection of individuals who often competed ruthlessly with one another but who nevertheless, as a group, were like-minded in the way they operated. Their interests and style of activity were relatively new to organized society in the eighteenth and early nineteenth centuries, although business people in many other countries during countless other times have acted in ways that resemble capitalist behaviors.

The capitalist class of Marx's analysis became fixated on the extraction of the greatest level of production and profit from the workers it had at its disposal, so as to *accumulate* money that they would invest repeatedly to acquire more wealth. The drive to accumulate was not mollified by any social or family considerations that formerly constrained typical business people, such as the social squeamishness that might accompany the employment of child laborers, the heartless demand for long days of work, or payment in wages rather than in kind (which left laborers to obtain their daily sustenance on the commodity markets).

Early capitalists were also hardened by their own fate should they fail in business and wind up in debtors' prison or in the employ of their competitors. They felt no moral or social obligation to provide for the welfare of their workers. If a worker's wage was not sufficient to care for his or her needs, the employer did not consider the matter of concern—unless it forced workers themselves to organize and demand higher wages. In the latter case, employers invested part of their expanding monetary resources in the hiring of guards, goons, or politicians, to force combatively inclined employees to comply with the capitalist class's conditions of work. In short, the capitalist class of Marx's analysis was untroubled by the social, religious, and moral failings of capitalism as long as these did not interfere with the fundamental goal of the maximum extraction of wealth from the production process and its accumulation as capital over time.

Common people during the European Middle Ages were not strangers to everyday suffering. However, they also did not live in a social world of values or norms that supported what later became the obvious excesses of early capitalism. Marx's analysis does not answer the question of how fundamental values could change to accommodate the new logic of capital. His work remains primarily focused on the economic and political shifts that resulted in the structural development, in western Europe, of a capitalist society—i.e., a society ruled by capitalist principles. Neglected in this analysis are the cultural adjustments that had to occur so that the new order could come into being and reproduce itself over time. The latter process, according to Marx and subsequent Marxists, occurred because capitalism created a world of *necessity* that compelled individuals, both workers and capitalists, to behave in the appropriate manner. But many other social theorists think the Marxian answer begs the question of how the social norms of accumulation came to dominate society. These thinkers appreciate the role of cultural factors more than do Marxists, who have tended to emphasize economic and political concerns in historical development. An important qualification and partial critique of Marx's work on capitalism therefore was needed to illuminate the cultural factors at work in capitalism. It was provided by Max Weber, a founding father of academic sociology at the turn of the century.

### Max Weber and Modes of Consciousness: The Forgotten Dimension of Culture

Weber, like Marx, was interested in explaining broad historical movements and changes. Unlike Marx, however, he treated the economy as merely one among several factors that served to develop society. He did not disagree with Marx or with Marx's understanding of capitalism but he sought to highlight factors in capitalism's development that were downplayed in Marx's analysis. Concerning broad sweeps of history, Weber was particularly inclined to emphasize the way modes of consciousness helped organize productive forces. In this concern, he was not unique. Marx, even before Weber—like all good German historicists—also focused on the role that ideas and values played in causing social change. Marx's interest was in what he called ideology—sets of beliefs that prevailed within particular historical epochs and that provided frameworks of understanding for social collectivities, particularly classes, in interpreting the events of daily life. In this sense, Marx's concept of ideology was essentially *political*. Conceptual universes that were used to "explain" the meaning of everyday life were, for Marx, frameworks that enabled social groups and classes, such as capitalists, workers, and landlords, to articulate political positions regarding the division of resources and wealth in any given social system.

Weber was also concerned with the role that states of consciousness played in daily life; but unlike Marx, he was more interested in the way individual ideas melded with group understandings. Thus, Weber was more focused on individuals and more abstract in his treatment of states of consciousness than was Marx, because Weber treated those states as autonomous, and as powerful causal factors of action in their own right.

When viewing the grand sweep of history, Marx focused on the struggle over wealth. When Weber looked at the same sweep, he was more intrigued by the way modes of thinking organized action into social forces and systems. Marx studied how a capitalist money economy forced individuals to become increasingly rational in their handling of productive resources and investment dollars so as to avoid being beaten in competition with more rational capitalists. Weber studied how rational thinking was increasingly apparent as an autonomous force in the organization of *every* aspect of modern societies, irrespective of the particular capitalist, i.e., economic, context. Weber considered "instrumental rationality" the most potent social force in the development of modern society. By this he meant *goal-directed thinking* divorced from tradition, religion, or emotion; thinking that was efficient and abstractly organized by rules. According to Weber, the historical development of society progressed from periods dominated by religious beliefs, traditions, and particular customs to the contemporary period, where social organization uses strict rational calculations of means to ends, abstract thinking that eschews emotions and religious beliefs, and the *efficient* deployment of rule-directed behavior.

The classic work of Weber in this regard is his writing on bureaucracy (1968 [1921]). For Weber, instrumental rationality found its greatest expression in the emergence of the state bureaucracies that organized German society at the turn of the twentieth century. Decisionmaking that was hierarchical, that was carried out without bias or emotion, that adhered strictly to the rules, and that held no special prejudice or value toward individual members of the public—these were the essential characteristics of the German bureaucracy. Weber saw this embodiment of instrumental rationality as a much-needed corrective to the chaotic world of the capitalist economic system. It was through bureaucracy, not the capitalist market, that the logic of social organization operated. Finally, although Weber believed that the strength of modern society lay in its harnessing of rational decisionmaking, he viewed the force of bureaucracy as increasingly troublesome. Instrumental rationality would "disenchant" the entire world and lead to an unfeeling society. By disenchantment, incidentally, Weber meant the reduction if not the elimination of important symbols and themes in daily life as well as in people's consciousness. In Weber's words (as quoted in Mitzman, 1969: 178):

> This passion for bureaucratization . . . is enough to drive one to despair. It is. . . as though we knowingly and willingly were *supposed* to become men who need

"order" and nothing but order, who become nervous and cowardly if this order shakes for a moment and helpless when they are torn from their exclusive adaptation to this order. . . . We are in any case caught up in this development, and the central question is not how we further and accelerate it but what we have to *set against* this machinery, in order to preserve a remnant of humanity from this parceling out of the soul, from this exclusive rule of bureaucratic life ideals.

## McDonaldization and Franchising

Weber's emphasis on the universal role of instrumental rationality in modern society is crucial to an understanding of today's consumer culture. This concept, which was neglected in the Marxian approach, has been used to great value by George Ritzer in his analysis of McDonald's fast-food franchising and its global success. Ritzer sees the production and sale of this product as ruled by the Weberian process of instrumental rationality. He identifies four key aspects of this ruling rationality, including efficiency, calculability, predictability, and control (1993, 2000):

> *Efficiency* is characterized by the effort to get from one point to another with a minimum of effort. . . . McDonald's systems of producing food and serving customers with minimal amounts of physical and temporal waste have become increasingly streamlined. . . . *Calculability* is an emphasis on things that can be quantified. In McDonaldized systems quantity takes priority over quality. . . . *Predictability* . . . creating predictable settings . . . scripting interactions with customers . . . predictable employee behavior . . . predictable products . . . and processes.

And in a later work, Ritzer writes, "Control through the replacement of human by nonhuman technologies is a major means through which predictability, efficiency, and calculability can be ensured both in production and in interactions with customers" (Ritzer and Ovadia, 2000).

The great success of McDonaldization in the United States has supported a global McDonald's franchising operation providing the same products and environments in various locations around the world. A McDonald's hamburger and French fries in Los Angeles are very much like those in Madrid, Spain, or in Tokyo, Japan. The store's environment and method of dispensing fast food are also the same in all of these locations. Ritzer (2000) shows how this successful rationalization of processes inspired literally thousands of other, similar fast-food franchises, including Burger King and Wendy's, as well as a host of similarly rationalized operations in other socioeconomic spheres, such as health care (in the form of managed care), higher education, and politics.

Despite Ritzer's enthusiasm for Weber's ideas generally, Ritzer does not pay much attention to the downside of bureaucracy (described by Weber as an "iron cage"), which left Weber feeling increasingly despondent and depressed until his death in 1920. As worldwide franchising of all kinds has developed, we also are increasingly aware of a countermovement among people in many countries who object to the McDonaldization of their lives. French farmer José Bové, whose act of protest is recounted at the beginning of Chapter 1 in this book, is just one of many who are involved in this international anti-McDonald's movement. In Chapter 6 we will examine similar contemporary reactions to themed store franchising and its negative effects on culture. As Weber so aptly put it almost a century ago, we are developing the tools by which we can "set against this machinery."

## The Transformation of American Society into a Consumer Culture

No one could claim that American culture prior to the 1920s was characterized by an emphasis on consumerism. During the early decades of the twentieth century, access to thematic elements in the organization of life was restricted to the relatively small class of capitalists, who for reasons of social status almost single-mindedly pursued the symbols of aristocratic ostentation via their conspicuous consumption. In contrast, the overwhelming majority of people in the United States were relatively poor. Most were employed in factories at low wages, and could not afford much in the way of consumer goods save the necessities of food, clothing, and shelter. They possessed a low social status, as signified by their lack of money and their social separation from the world of middle-class activities in education, art, family celebrations, and leisure. But because the overwhelming majority of Americans shared exactly the same status, symbolic wars among consumers jockeying for social position did not exist in this large group. The principal theme guiding consumption was the capitalists' aping of the landed aristocracy and their prestige symbols.

Between 1920 and 1960, however, several newly emergent forces began to transform the entire society into one organized around the process of consumption by the masses. This society provided the foundation for the themed consumer society of today. Among these forces were, first, the shift to what is called "Fordism" in industry; second, the growth of a middle class and home consumption activities organized around the theme of modernism, which is associated with Fordism; third, the uncontrolled economic collapse that occurred during the Great Depression; and fourth, the emergence of a mass advertising industry. Together these factors transformed capitalism to a system with a different social structure than that of the past, and, with that change, caused both the increasing economic emphasis on consumption and the use of themes in organizing everyday culture.

## The Advent of Fordism

In the United States, capitalist social organization had reached impressive heights by the beginning of the twentieth century. The country possessed a rich agricultural hinterland that provided an abundance of food, benefiting from a number of advanced industrial techniques of farming, including inventions such as McCormick's reaper. It also had a large labor force, continually replenished by immigrants, that adjusted well to the long hours of the factory regimen. Lastly, it had an expanding mass of developed land that allowed for the growth of cities, towns, and villages, providing new opportunities at every intersection for creative business ideas and enterprises.

Industrial society had developed to the point where businesses could produce an immense quantity of goods—everything from clothing to manufactured machines—on the mass assembly line. In this innovation of factory organization, individual craft manufactures were replaced by the piecemeal assembly of goods in mass quantities: Each operation was broken into separate tasks, and personnel were trained to do only a specific part of the whole assembly process; then each group of trained personnel who performed each particular, successive task were arranged along an assembly line. As the raw material of commodities passed from one work station to another, the goods were pieced together part by part. Workers at the end of the line finished the product and made it ready for consumer purchase. Within Fordist factories each laborer could produce a mass of goods in this manner.

The innovation of the mass assembly line, which Adam Smith observed in its early stages in the pin manufactures of eighteenth-century England, resulted in an explosion of commodity production. Mass quantities of relatively complicated producer goods—such as boilers, sewing machines, and farm equipment—as well as consumer goods, such as electrical appliances and clothing, were now readily available. The abundance of producer goods meant even more success for American capitalism because it enabled greater amounts of products to be produced. However, the presence of consumer goods presented capitalism with a dilemma—the "realization problem": Unless the goods could be sold, no profit would be realized. By the time mass quantities of consumer goods could be efficiently produced, World War I broke out. The industrial war effort ushered in the mass production of weapons—hundreds of thousands of bullets, rifles, uniforms, bombs, and even chemical weapons such as mustard gas. Despite this success, workers then earned a low salary that barely enabled them to afford the necessities of life.

The dilemma facing capitalism, its particular realization problem of the time, was straightforward: How could the economy move in the necessary direction of producing mass quantities of consumer goods, if the average worker could not afford those goods? The U.S. economy was poised, after World War I, at a point of great opportunity for expansion because of its developed manufacturing infrastructure and its large mass of disciplined workers. But without an increase in the ability of workers to afford the fruits of their own labor, it had nowhere to go.

Perhaps the most dynamic solution to this problem was offered by the accomplished entrepreneur Henry Ford. Ford did not invent the motorcar, but he single-handedly perfected its manufacture. He used mass assembly line techniques, selectively picked his industrial workers, and combined the two in large factories that could make mass quantities of cars. After the success of his "model A" car, which was purchased largely by the affluent middle class, Ford launched a new model at a more modest price level. This "model T" was meant to be a car for the masses. However, since the masses could not afford one on their meager wages, Ford faced a dilemma. He solved it by increasing the wages of his workers. Ford's idea was that mass assembly would work if the mass quantities of consumer products it produced were affordable. By raising the wages of his workers, Ford hoped to create a mass market for his own product. He also urged other capitalists to follow suit, so that society as a whole would move in the direction of greater consumption levels.

The use of technology (e.g., time and motion studies and the mass assembly line) to enhance efficiency in the workplace, and of social mechanisms (e.g., improving the purchasing power of workers) to enhance profits became known as *Fordism*. The term was first coined by Marxist philosopher Antonio Gramsci in the 1930s, and it was later popularized by the French political economist, Michel Aglietta, in an influential analysis of twentieth-century capitalism's success. Fordism, and Henry Ford's enterprise in particular, was remarkably successful. As Ford had hoped, many other large-scale manufacturers across the country followed his example in raising workers' wages. Workers were happier because they were earning more and could afford to buy more products; capitalists were happier because they were using the productive capacity of their mass assembly factories; and the society prospered and expanded in influence because of the greater wealth it held. Rather than dependency on an export-oriented economy, Fordism allowed countries to expand and develop by creating domestic markets for their goods. The key to success was the gradual transformation of workers living at levels of bare subsistence to consumers with more disposable income and with voracious appetites for new commodities.

The American romance with the automobile, which followed on the success of Fordism, almost single-handedly gave birth to several thematic elements that are the foundations for the so-called American way of life. Manufacturers advertised automobiles vigorously, because Americans had to be convinced to buy one for leisure reasons. Horses remained popular as modes of transportation for business deliveries and even for trolley commuter traffic within cities. Advertisements for cars appealed to the "freedom" of the open road, the excitement and comfort of automobile travel, and—not least—individuals' desire to possess this symbol of higher socioeconomic status. The private car was simultaneously a sign of success and progress—a dual signifier. In short, the automobile became a vehicle, through advertising, for new thematic elements of American culture, including attractive images of travel as freedom, of progress as the abandonment of traditional life, and of mechanical means as superior to other modes of transportation or consumption. By encouraging mass purchases of automobiles, Fordism created a new object of desire in the minds of the masses. The private car was a mechanical marvel, a sign of progress, of status, of freedom; it was the new confluence of desire and affordability for consumers in our society. It persists even now as the continual source of consumer thematic fantasies through advertising and the fashion of commodity changes; the link between the car and the consumer has not diminished in its intensity of desire in the past seventy years.

*Household Consumption and Modernism*

At the turn of the century, most people's homes were sparsely furnished, reflecting their limited purchasing power. This was true whether individuals lived in city tenements or on rural farms. Furnishings were largely heirlooms, hand-me-downs, or custom-built objects. As the number of middle-class people in the United States increased, however, new commodities destined for home use became more apparent. As it is to a certain extent today, the household then was the domain of the woman; and many manufactures aimed commodities at her needs. During the nineteenth century, household living arrangements were little different from what they had been for thousands of years. Women's domestic chores were labor intensive. Washing, cooking, and cleaning were backbreaking chores done by hand, utilizing washboards, wood or coal fires, and simple mops and brooms. Early industrial products designed for home consumption, such as the hand-cranked washing machine or the foot-operated sewing machine, were trumpeted as labor-saving devices. The advertising of that time promoted the value of such devices as a new norm of household organization.

One of the most powerful nineteenth-century innovations that led to the creation of a thematic environment was the department store catalog. The most famous was the Sears and Roebuck catalog, which contained hand-drawn illustrations of consumer products along with primitive advertising copy promoting these goods as objects of desire. These mail-order catalogs included everything from mass-produced farm machinery to clothing (such as suits available in any size) to "labor-saving" household appliances. They reached millions of American homes, subjecting them for the first time to the kinds of thematic appeals that later became characteristic of commodity advertising. The early mail-order catalogs converted industrial goods into *images*. The image was born of necessity, because of the nature of mail-order marketing. Yet, once it took its place alongside advertising copy (written appeals enjoining consumers to buy a product), the consumer universe of desire was driven by images and representations that tapped into cognitive associations that were pure symbols. The thematic environment began to emerge from this context. Desire was fueled not only by the images and the copy but also by the juxtaposition between image and copy—a powerful feature characteristic of advertising today, as Roland Barthes (1983) has observed.

During the early twentieth century, the taming of electricity and the invention of basic electrical technologies created a vast domain of new commodities destined for home use. All household appliances became electrified. Electrical refrigerators, sewing machines, vacuum cleaners, and washing machines are just some of the items that became necessities in the new commodified household. These appliances also fueled a peacetime expansion in American industry and capitalism. General Electric, Westinghouse, Singer, and Electrolux took their places next to the emerging giants of automobile manufacture—Ford, General Motors, and Chrysler—as major, "blue-chip" corporations. The larger the middle class grew, the more capitalism expanded and the more developed became the consumer-oriented economy; and that in turn produced the wealth that increased even more the size of the middle-class consumer market.

In Europe, during the early 1900s, as discussed in Chapter 2, several distinguished architects and designers working together, in reaction against the eclecticism of haphazard, Victorian-era design, produced a unified, geometry-based style called *modernism*. Industrial producers applied the modernist design methodology not only to the largest structures—that is, buildings and city planning—but also to the most intimate spaces of interior home furnishings. Modernism stressed clean designs that lacked symbolic appeals. The most important aspect of this movement was its unity of vision: It encompassed the entire spectrum of consumerism. As exemplified best in the works of the German Bauhaus design center during the 1920s, modernist designers reformed every piece of home furnishings, from kitchens and their appliances to living room and bedroom furniture, and even to the outside facades of homes. This unity of design principles from the inside to the outside was a distinguishing feature of modernism (see Lefebvre, 1974). In brief, modernist design created an entirely new and consistently orchestrated home environment that was also thematically linked to the design practices outside the home, which were producing the skyscraper concentrations of the industrial city.

Besides the newly designed surroundings, modernist culture also transformed the themes of consumer society. The movement was most associated with the ideas of "progress," of technological efficiency, of functionality of design, and of the concept of the "ensemble"—i.e., the concordant appearance of one object with another. The promotion of modernist designs changed the nature of advertising, especially that directed at homemakers. By the 1920s, the themes that were stressed involved technological progress and the fashion to "be modern," electrical and mechanical wizardry in the home, and newness as high status. These themes were played out in the burgeoning business of advertising via the newly emergent mass media, such as radio and magazines, in addition to the classic catalog mer-

*With the mass production of suburban living in the 1950s, housewives became the targets of advertisements for the modernist ideal—in this case, the all-electric kitchen. Photo courtesy of Corbis-Bettmann.*

chandising. Radio programming sponsors that manufactured soap or built washing machines combined their forces to entice listening housewives to consume the latest products in the interests of being modern. By the 1920s, then, the consumer society was characterized by a mass market of workers-turned-consumers; the commodification of the household and housing through modernism; the increasing use of the private car; the rise and powerful influence of the mass media, especially radio and magazines; the explosive growth of the advertising industry; and lastly, the production of fantasies creating the desire for objects through a thematic environment.

Finally, as discussed in Chapter 2, the creation of a mass market for domestic life, including the shift to suburbia, altered the role of adult women from that of home manager to houseworker. Women were targeted for the creation of new needs that were basic to the Fordist economy, which was producing electrical manufactured goods in mass quantities. Yet, as our emphasis on the problematic nature of capital realization suggests, compliance to the new marketing appeals by middle-class women was not automatic. It was necessary for corporations to create a mass market for their wares, and specific advertising appeals to housewives through the mass media accomplished the task. As Roger Miller (1990) points out, a significant influence in bringing about this social shift was a book published by Christine Frederick in 1929, called *Selling Mrs. Consumer.* Frederick was a disciple of the Fordist regulatory ideology propagated by Frederick Winslow Taylor, otherwise known as Taylorism, and she had adapted his "scientific management" techniques to the home environment. Frederick argued in her book that corporations producing domestic commodities should not view housewives as a monolithic market. Instead, they should treat them as market segments, each of which would be receptive to a different advertising appeal (Miller, 1990: 4). According to Frederick, there was a need to appeal more to images than to the intrinsic use-value of the new, labor-saving commodities:

> She [Frederick] advised advertisers to appeal to the less logical, more emotional aspects of female psychology, while at the same time educating women into the use of the new products of domestic technology. The strategies employed by Madison Avenue to exploit the new domestic market radically altered earlier practices utilized in different types of ad campaigns. Advertisements that previously had extolled the intrinsic quality, durability, and rich detail of products began to associate consumer goods with idealized images of life-style. After ideal roles had been promoted in media of sufficient circulation to assure their acceptance as general norms, it was relatively easy to create feelings of inferiority and guilt in women who fell short of them . . . . These feelings of personal inadequacy could be translated into consumer "needs," an explicitly ideological manipulation based on distorted forms of information exchange (Miller, 1990: 5).

A similar shift occurred in the direction of advertising appeals for other kinds of products and mass markets (Ewen, 1976; Williamson, 1978; Goldman, 1994). Such changes laid the groundwork for a truly qualitative shift in consumer mores after 1930. Prior to that time, products appealed to people because of their potential use-value. After the 1930s, the consumer's desire for new commodities focused on the commodities' image or symbolic value. I pursue the implications of this important observation in greater depth later in this chapter.

### The Great Depression

Another event occurred during the late 1920s that eventually sealed the fate of the formerly thrifty, subsistence-oriented American society: the Great Depression. This event and its aftermath erased all alternate lifestyles that had previously been untouched by consumerism due either to lack of money or to choice of values. A gradual restructuring followed the Depression, and the American society and economy did not really stabilize until the late 1940s.

The spectacular and most commonly noted feature of the Depression, the horrendous crash of the stock market on Wall Street in 1929, has been explained often as the failure of the investment institution to safeguard against overextended purchasing and the availability of easy credit. However, the greatest damage to the country—and, we might add, to the entire Western, capitalist world—was wrought not only by the fateful events of 1929 but also by the trend of subsequent years, when capitalism recovered at a level that had adjusted to mass unemployment, the frequent failure of farms and small banks, a timid stock market, and a stagnant GNP. During the early 1930s the slide toward economic ruin was halted, but at such a low level of business activity that financial disaster began to seem routine for most Americans.

When people spoke of "recovery" in the 1930s, they were not referring to the prevention of a further crash on Wall Street but to the restoration of the economy to its former robust level. The majority of voters believed the government could and should play a role in revitalizing the economy, and they elected the Democratic administration of Franklin Roosevelt, who had promised the government's help. The ideas that emerged then to help explain the nation's predicament and to guide its economic resurgence were first articulated in England, by economist John Maynard Keynes. Several years earlier, a crisis of capitalism had been predicted by socialist economist Michael Kalecki. As Keynes argued, there was nothing intrinsic to a competitive capitalist system that led it to stabilize around high levels of growth or employment. Once the shaky businesses were weeded out in every sector, the economy could function without disaster for many years at a *low* level of activity. To be sure, in this latter case, most people would be unemployed and most businesses would be bankrupt. However, Keynes showed that these effects did not necessarily portend the destruction of capitalism; capitalism would survive, but with a smaller productive capacity. Even though the social effects of the Depression might be lasting, the downscaled economy could "prosper" in its own manner.

Keynes suggested that if a society wished to reestablish equilibrium at a higher level of economic activity, it could not rely on the private sector alone. Government had to increase public spending in a way that would stimulate the expansion of the economy. This analysis and its public policy implications became the cornerstone of the Roosevelt administration's recovery plan. Simply put, the government began to spend so that more people would have money to spend, which it was hoped would in turn stimulate business, eventually leading to a higher level of economic activity and to more taxes, making up the losses from government spending. The private sector viewed the government as a "pump-priming" mechanism for the economy. It would spend money and go into debt, but it would so stimulate the economy that, in time, more people would be working and more goods and services would be produced. An increase in economic activity would, in turn, lead to greater tax revenues being collected and being available to service the debt. Although many Americans disbelieved this claim, many others believed it was true, and they supported government recovery policies.

One critical aspect of anti-Depression government spending was public policy aimed at putting more money in the hands of workers. If jobs were not available from the private sector, they would be created by the public sector. The unemployed would receive unemployment insurance to maintain their household income for a time; and if people could not afford consumer goods, they could tap into easy credit sponsored by the federal government. Through these and other measures, public policy provided people with more money, in the hope that they would spend and save more, thereby stimulating business and finance. Thus, the policies devised to achieve economic recovery relied heavily on consumerism. In the depths of the Depression, all workers—whether employed in the public or the private sector—were enjoined to do their share of spending to drive the recovery effort.

This period of U.S. history has had a lasting effect on Americans' economic behavior, changing the social norm from frugality to consumerism and debt-financed household spending. Through credit-based buying, especially in the housing market, people for the first time could go into debt without social stigma. The society viewed debt-financed consumption as good for the economy because it was a means of stimulating business. Furthermore, government programs made it attractive to go into debt. Banking acts of Congress that were passed to stimulate the economy made the interest on loans for homes and automobiles tax deductible. In particular, deductibility from taxes was a consumer incentive meant to boost the banking, automobile, and housing industries; but it also made going into debt to purchase homes and cars attractive.

Before the 1930s the "norm of saving" dominated consumer culture. People earned little and they viewed their lives as a long process during which they would work hard, live frugally, and eventually have enough savings to get married, raise a family, and perhaps buy a home. After the 1930s Americans were acculturated to the "norm of consumption," which encouraged people to spend and go into debt because of easy credit and the disappearance of the stigma attached to loans (since the latter, typically, were financed or sponsored by the federal government and contributed to the national economic recovery). By the late 1930s, when World War II broke out, many Americans were eager to obtain loans for the purchase of automobiles and single-family homes. These industries were leading the way out of the Depression. We will never know whether Keynes's policies and the Roosevelt administration's ideas would have eventually succeeded, because the outbreak of World War II, and the involvement of the United States in that war, became the single greatest Keynesian event of that time, as it led to government spending amounting to billions of dollars and the creation of millions of new jobs in support of the war effort. No matter what the driving force behind the economic recovery, however, a transformed culture remained after the 1940s, in which Americans adapted to the norm of consumption and eagerly anticipated going into debt to finance the purchase of cars and homes. The nation of savers had become a nation of consumers; and consumption had become a new American ideal that fueled the fantasy appeals of advertising (Galbraith, 1978).

## The Mass Advertising Industry

The need to stimulate economic recovery following the Depression and the need to stimulate consumption in order to solve the realization problem of capital are not identical needs. However, they worked together in a completely complementary way to create a nation of active consumers. In fact, permissible norms pushed the ability to consume beyond the margins of personal resources and included, by the 1940s, debt-financed household consumption. At the turn of the century, those who had sought a loan were socially stigmatized. By the 1940s, loans were commonplace, and even remaining in debt over the long term to finance a home was no longer shocking but conventional. Government programs like those created under the series of acts known as the GI Bill (designed to ease the transition of soldiers returning to civilian life) provided broad access to consumer credit and created millions of new consumers. Veterans could purchase a new home with a down payment of as little as $1.

As millions of people shifted to a high-consumption lifestyle, the advertising industry also shifted into high gear as the general purveyor of consumer fantasies and themes. Earlier I mentioned the important shift of advertising to the mass media outlets, especially magazines and the radio. The use of the mass media by advertising, and the media's positioning as the principal means by which commodities such as cars and home furnishings were promoted, resulted in the growth of advertising companies into a major American industry. In the early 1950s this industry was located principally in the area of Manhattan, on Madison Avenue above 42nd Street. From these offices, where thousands of specialists were employed in copy writing, art direction, and eventually, marketing psychology, professional practices were brought to bear on the production of consumer fantasies, the promotion of desire for commodities, and the manipulation of market demand for individual products.

American capitalism under Fordist arrangements had worked well in creating the necessary conditions for a mass consumer market. By the 1950s, however, corporate producers were competing fiercely with each other in every industry. Although most sectors of the economy still were controlled by a few firms—that is, most sectors consisted of *oligopolies*—considerable competition remained among these corporations for market share. The struggle for the consumer dollar was waged principally through advertising and superficial marketing ploys, because the competing products were quite similar. For example, take the "big four"—Ford, Chrysler, General Motors, and American Motors—that dominated the automobile industry during the 1950s (soon to become the "big three" by the 1970s, sharing market dominance with Japanese and German firms). Other, smaller companies, such as Studebaker and Hudson, were also competing for a bigger share. Each of these manufacturers produced similar types of cars—sedans, coupes, station wagons, and convertibles—for the private consumer market. Corporate brands and car names made the difference between consumer choices, and not the features of construction. Consumers could purchase a specific model type and have a choice of a six- or eight-cylinder engine, an automatic or manual transmission, and in some types of cars, either a two- or a four-door model.

Beyond the basic structural differences, consumer choice extended to include more superficial distinctions. For each manufacturer, models were divided in a completely superficial way among separate car divisions. Ford was split between Ford, Mercury, and Lincoln dealers; Chrysler had Dodge, Plymouth, and Chrysler divisions; and General Motors had hyperdifferentiated its products into separate lines based loosely on perceived price differences—Chevrolet, Buick, Cadillac, and Oldsmobile—each of which

*During the 1950s, modernist streamlining of automobile design merged with jet fighter forms to produce cars with futuristic fins, such as the Plymouth Fury depicted here. Photo courtesy of Corbis-Bettmann.*

appeared as different divisions. Second, cars competed with each other through differences in colors, trim, and design (the 1950s were famous for their fin wars). Third, although the engines and transmissions placed in different cars were similar, manufacturers gave their cars distinctive names and promoted them as competitively superior.

Using newspapers, magazines, radio, and later, television, manufacturers aggressively marketed these differences to consumers. As these corporations burgeoned in size during the 1950s and 1960s, their respective advertising budgets increased dramatically. Advertising became a multibillion-dollar-a-year industry, and the large firms established branch offices—mainly in Chicago, Kansas City, St. Louis, Los Angeles, and San Francisco. The intense competition among producers who were selling products that actually differed little from each other led to the increasingly intense plumbing of the depths of American culture for themes and images to which appeals could be made. The power of advertising—its unswerving pressure to create modes of desire in the individual consumer and its relentless scouring of the American psyche for symbolically meaningful appeals—formed the foundation for the themed environment of the present.

Early home market catalogs used copy to describe in as much detail as possible the advantages of using specific products. As I suggested above, these early appeals emphasized the use-value of commodities. Specifications and utility were the principal focus of mass advertising. But by the 1950s, following the Fordist marketing transformations in the 1930s, advertising had progressed beyond the specification of use-value to promote the product's image, its value as a sign of either fashion or progress—or occasionally, both. If all cars were pretty much the same from year to year, why would consumers want to buy new cars? Appeals now began to emphasize the value of "newness" more than the use-value of a new car. The "fin wars" of the 1950s erupted because cars were being differentiated by advertising according to their appearance and not by virtue of advantages in technological innovations. The same process operated in the domestic appliance market as well. In brief, by the 1950s, the multibillion-dollar advertising industry had shifted from informing the consumer about the use-value of products to *manipulating* the consumer by using symbolic or image-dependent appeals.

The manipulative techniques of mass advertising worked so well that people began to import them from retailing into other important domains. One clear example was the realm of politics. Before the 1950s, campaigns were waged through the traditional means of voter organization by parties and political "machines," and by the rhetorical competition among candidates, who went to considerable lengths to get exposure for themselves in an era dependent on trains and the radio. With the elections of 1960, it became apparent that politicians were turning to Madison Avenue for persuasive techniques and were basing some of their appeals less on rhetorical debates or ideological differences than on manufactured distinctions promulgated by advertising agencies. A number of books were published soon after, exposing this process—among them *The Selling of the President, The Hidden Persuaders,* and *The Image.* As a prelude to the appearance of a themed environment, the manipulative techniques of mass advertising spilled out to other social realms and began to dominate their processes of distinction as well. The concepts of "selling" someone or oneself, of "marketing" a person or idea, of "advertisements for oneself," and so on, began to control the logic of social relations in a variety of spheres—relations that were formerly based on the intrinsic self-worth of people and/or ideas—including politics, science, enterprise, and personal life.

*From Sales to Marketing.* In the nineteenth century, laborers worked in factories that manufactured commodities. They earned a subsistence wage that was just enough to cover the necessities of life—food, clothing, and shelter. They had no insurance, retirement funds, or opportunities to send their children to school so that they could better themselves. Today our social circumstances have greatly changed. During the twentieth century, the need to avoid another economic depression, government policies that propped up consumer spending, and the emergence of a commodity-oriented mass culture helped along by ubiquitous advertising, combined to produce profound social shifts that have made us all eager consumers. Today most workers are *relatively* better paid compared to the nineteenth-century world of subsistence wages, although there still is a big difference between the so-called "working poor," who have considerable burdens in rent, family expenses, medical and insurance expenses, and transportation costs, and the upper middle class, who own their own homes, have cars, possess retirement and insurance plans at work, and can pay for their children's higher education.

Writing in the nineteenth century, Marx believed all industrial workers were exploited. They sold their creative energies for a wage that they then exchanged to purchase their meager commodities. As he maintained, this exchange was one of individual creativity for a subsistence minimum of food and manufactured objects. For this reason Marx felt capitalism exploited the worker. In addition, he viewed the exchange relation of labor for a wage in the production of commodities as *alienating* to people. The world of "things," according to Marx, dominated the world of work, which resulted in the degrading of human labor to a mere thing itself.

Today, however, circumstances are different. A large segment of the U.S. population is working in service/information-processing industries. Creativity, or the human quality of achieving fulfillment in labor, is a principal criterion by which many employees evaluate their jobs and by which their performance is in turn evaluated by employers. Most often this takes the form of surveys of client or customer satisfaction, but it also involves the evaluation and transformation of work by credentialed professionals.

The well-paid segment of society purchases services and commodities without serious financial hardship, especially because they have been acculturated into accepting debt as a means of lifestyle pursuits. They value customer satisfaction and the realization of self through commodity purchases as much as, or more than, self-realization at the place of work. In today's society—unlike that of the earlier stages of capitalism, including the period of obvious exploitation observed by Marx—the creative power of workers in the "postindustrial" industries is exchanged for the creative power of workers whose job it is to please them. This relation exists also for the case of commodity purchasing from stores that value customer satisfaction. Thus, whereas nineteenth-century capitalism was dominated by a world of things that held power over "alienated" workers, the present period finds people in a postindustrial world where they exchange their creativity for the creativity of others. However, exploitation remains a part of the employee-employer relation in today's capitalist social system, especially in areas of the globe where manufacturing takes place under conditions very similar to those of the nineteenth century. In short, the concept of "worker exploitation" is still relevant, but it has been refined to account for the new realities of our present lives (Mayer, 1994). Furthermore, whereas Marx wrote about the problem of alienation as produced by the work relation, our society seems to have overshadowed Marx's dilemma. Alienation is rarely discussed today as a structural problem of society—that is, in the terms in which Marx and Marxism once framed the issue.

The most pressing problem in today's economy is less one of exploitation or alienation through either work or consumer purchasing than of how to constantly satisfy primed consumer desires with items that people will want to purchase in mass quantities. This is so because, as indicated in the previous chapter, the use-values of goods and services are uniform. People differentiate among competing suppliers less in terms of the use-value of commodities than according to their ability to assuage some desire created through effective marketing and advertising. As indicated in previous chapters, *symbolic* processes—including the desire for status, fashion, sex appeal, or power—controls the latter. Having established the structural conditions for the solution of its profit-realization problem and having successfully shipped manufacturing off to once-peripheral domestic places or global areas with low wages and limited unions, currently capitalism finds itself caught on the merry-go-round of a consumer culture that circles and circles over the same territory but requires ever new fantasies and modes of desire in order to maintain a high level of spending.

In the previous section I discussed how the emergence of mass advertising fuels the spending activities of our society through the production of desire. This activity is only one aspect of creating a mass consumer culture. Advertising must be coupled with efficient and timely marketing techniques. Marketing procedures encompass today not only the appeals made by advertising, such as those found on television or in magazines, but also appeals within the built environment itself—that is, in the suburban and urban landscapes, or the stores and malls that remain responsible for the realization of capital. The key economic relation of the consumer society is not the exchange of money for goods, as it was in the nineteenth century, but the link between the promotion of desire in the mass media and advertising, and the commercial venues where goods and services can be purchased. Store environments are but an extension of TV, magazine, and newspaper advertising. They provide material spaces for the realization of consumer fantasies primed by movies; rock videos; the record industry; commercial advertising; lifestyle orientations from religious, ethnic, racial, or class origins; and even political ideologies propagated in community discourse or at the place of work. The built environment operates not only as the fuel for consumer fantasies but also as the space within which mass marketing and purchasing take place. The central economic concern regarding the link between commercial venues and the supersaturated marketing culture of symbols or images is actualized through the production of themed environments.

*Marketing Practice.* The practice of marketing in the United States has gone from a rather straightforward affair involving the *distribution* of goods to potential customers that existed as a generic mass—otherwise known as "sales"—to a knowledge-based, purposeful effort at controlling consumer buying through scientific methods and management techniques. The latter is more commonly called marketing, since, unlike sales, it is targeted by companies toward specific consumer groups. Not too long ago, for example, many products were sold by door-to-door traveling salespeople who needed give little thought to the different types of consumers they might encounter. Among these products were brushes, cosmetics, encyclopedias, household appliances such as vacuum cleaners, and at the turn of the century, phonograph players. Although the once-ubiquitous "Fuller Brush Man" has passed into urban history, communities around the country are still hosts to traveling "Avon Ladies" or Mary Kay cosmetics sales people. In these cases, the sales pitch was a direct appeal to a relatively undifferentiated mass audience through oral or written discourse centering on the demonstrable *use-value* of individual products. Avon ladies or vacuum cleaner sales people, for example, went into homes to demonstrate their products—that is, they personally exhibited commodity use-value.

As consumer affluence increased, especially after World War II, and as large department stores and other commercial establishments appeared that catered to local customers, the need to sell door-to-door declined. In addition, as we have already discussed, appeals to the use-values of commodities were progressively replaced by appeals to *symbolic* values or the production of images of desire. Marketing, rather than sales, began to dominate the business enterprise because of recurrent crises in the realization of capital (especially during the Great Depression). Even the designers and planners of products—that is, the people who once led the production process of manufacturing and represented the projection of a product's future—had to work closely with company employees in charge of marketing. In truth, the placement of the realization problem of capital, rather than labor or manufacturing issues *per se,* at the center of business concerns, has also resulted in the rise of marketing as the principal aspect of corporate administration.

Marketing employs sophisticated psychological techniques aimed at promoting desire and at manipulating consumer needs; art and design aimed at the production of appealing environments and packaging; demographic analysis that identifies clusters of potential consumers; and advertising specialists, who have replaced door-to-door sales and catalog sales staffs with highly refined techniques of ad production and distribution. As many observers have noted, marketing procedure today cuts down the mass of consumers into individual "market segments" or clusters (Langdon, 1994; Weiss, 1988), using highly accurate demographic techniques and surveys. Specific appeals are then aimed at these particular segments.

Clusters are based on individual *differences.* They are often arrayed as oppositions, at least during the process of discovery and the production of marketing appeals. These categories include urban versus suburban residency; married versus single status; working class versus yuppie professional class; ethnics versus assimilated Americans; regional distinctions such as the midwest, the south, the northeast; differentiation by income bracket, in relatively small increments; renter versus homeowner; and a variety of other categories based on age, race, and life-course distinctions.

According to Michael J. Weiss (1988), a popular target marketing system has divided the U.S. population into 40 separate clusters. These can be found in all geographical areas of the United States and pertain specifically to consumer market types based on aggregate and similar lifestyles. Each market segment has been classified according to tastes in cars, magazines, leisure activities, food, TV habits, and preferred commodity purchases. These segments are reflective of combined factors such as income, education, stage in the life course, family status, urban/suburban location, ethnicity, race, housing status, and other demographic factors. Advertisers target these segments with appeals specifically designed for each cluster, often irrespective of the particular product sold.

Advertisers use two levels of appeals to consumers for distinct types of products. At one level, they aim marketing efforts at particular segments of the consuming public. Commodities are designed specifically to appeal to these segments. At another level, however, they still search for objects with mass appeal, that can cut across segments and realize massive sales. In the record industry, for example, different artists and types of music are designed explicitly for segments—rap, hard rock, soft rock, easy listening, top 40, Latin, romantic, punk, reggae. However, record companies also search for particular artists or bands that can attract various segments—such as Elvis, Madonna, Frank Sinatra, or Michael Jackson. It is often said about Madonna, for example, that the basis of her persistent popularity is the way she continually reinvents herself. Madonna is a mass object of consumption. The same thing could *not* be said, however, about rap singers or reggae bands, because the latter appeal to segmented markets and do not need cross-segment appeal.

When the philosopher Baudrillard criticizes nineteenth-century political economists for focusing on the production process as the key organizing practice of society, he does so by reaffirming the above shift in the importance of advertising. The rule of image over substance, of appearance over use-value, of manipulation over rhetoric and logic, all derive from the central role that the advertising industry plays in American life. The latter is a consequence of capital's need to realize wealth under oligopolistic production constraints with little actual difference among products. This substantive change couples with the structural shifts occurring in society as a consequence of adjustments to depression-era realities—especially the government's role in promoting the "norm of consumption"; the creation of a consumer consciousness in the working class; the commodification of our environment, including the commodification of the home; and the creation of ubiquitous social institutions for mass advertising and mass marketing. Along with structural changes came new sensibilities, such as the personal transformations in the self toward consumption as a domain of self-realization or the shift from home manager to housewife among middle-class women.

During the 1960s and 1970s, social commentators took note of fundamental changes in the United States with the coming of this consumer-oriented society (for example, see Galbraith, 1978). Before that time, organized labor questioned the quality of the labor process, and demanded higher wages and better benefits. Worker struggles with factory owners often involved a clash over social vision and the future direction of society. As labor bought into the consumer society and accepted the norm of consumption, their organized demands became confined to the quest for more pay under better working arrangements. As several observers have noted, this shift amounted to an acquiescence by labor to a society dominated by consumerist issues (Aronowitz, 1974; M. Davis, 2000). Thus, the assertion that contemporary society privileges consumption over production has credence at a variety of societal levels.

Currently, we live in a society much different from the world of industrial capitalism that existed prior to the 1950s. Movement toward a themed environment has progressed in sequence with the development of consumerist values and their respective social institutions, such as advertising, mass marketing, and the transformed role of the organized labor–capitalist relation. In the next chapter I shall examine closely the nature of the themed environment that consists today of a multilevel relationship between the restructuring national economy and a themed culture propelled primarily by the operation of symbols or images rather than the intrinsic use-value of material objects.

## Summary of Main Ideas

1. Companies compete for customers using signs when there is not much difference between their products (e.g., sneakers, soft drinks, and cars).

2. Today's economy places more emphasis on marketing and selling because it is harder to realize capital than to produce goods. Production is aided by the new global organization of labor and of finance.

3. Consumers are prone to stimulation of desire by symbolic appeals, even if price exceeds their budgets. Now easy credit makes up the difference.

4. Cultural critics such as Jean Baudrillard believe that the economy is dominated by consumer dynamics and the selling of goods rather than by the concerns of production that Marx identified.

5. Weber added to Marx's analysis of capitalism an emphasis on the role of culture. Weber viewed the development of contemporary society as a process in which goal-directed thinking or "instru-

mental rationality" came to dominate social organization. This mode of structuring activities is best exemplified by the phenomenon of bureaucracy, which Weber felt had as great an influence on industrial society as did capital accumulation.

6. Ritzer applied Weber's ideas on rationality to a study of "McDonaldization." Ritzer claims that the principles of the fast-food chain—efficiency, calculability, predictability, and control— have increasingly characterized the delivery of all sorts of consumer goods. Ritzer explains the phenomenal global success of franchising as a consequence of this rational organization. (The negative effects of McDonaldization are discussed in Chapter 6.)

7. Since the 1920s, American society has increasingly been dominated by a consumer culture as the forces identified by both Marx and Weber have played themselves out. Historical change is also the consequence of at least four main social processes and their effects on culture: the advent of Fordism; increasing household consumption; the Great Depression; and the growth of a mass advertising industry.

8. Attending these processes has been a change in the way goods are sold. Now companies use ever more sophisticated marketing techniques that include systematic consumer research coupled with symbolic and thematic appeals. These marketing techniques have melded with our society's culture and affect everything from music to politics to the delivery of health services.

# 4

# THEMED CULTURE AND THEMED ENVIRONMENTS

## The Themed Environment

The purpose of all commercial places, as we have seen, is the realization of capital, i.e., the selling of goods and/or services. These spaces cannot, however, make this function the prime focus of their appeal to potential consumers, who do not directly benefit from corporate profit making. Instead, businesses must disguise the instrumental exchange relation of money for a commodity as another relation between commercial place and the consumer. Our society bathes the consumer purchase in a benevolent light of nurturing and of promised self-fulfillment. Thus, the commercial environment, taken as a whole, has increasingly been designed as a sign itself, as some symbolic space that *connotes* something other than its principal function—the realization of capital through the stimulation of consumer desires and the promotion of sales.

By orchestrating selling as theming and by the strategic design of consumer environments saturated with symbols, the connotative dimension of marketing overwhelms other aspects. Furthermore, the increasing use of market segmentation to keep up with a highly differentiated consumer public, while most goods offered are little different in substance from their competitors, also contributes to the proliferation of symbol-filled environments and themed consumerism. Theming reduces the product to its image and the consumer experience to its symbolic content.

Connecting to advertising, the media, the phenomenon of celebrity, the compulsion of fashion, and the popularity of status markers that are also commodities, this process of theming and the ascendancy of symbols over substance increasingly characterizes American culture. Through the construction of hybrid environments such as eatertainment, shoppertainment, and the like, consumption is twinned with fantasy and amusement. Secondly, through mass advertising, themed environments promote themselves through deals, discounts, rebates, sales, easy credit, customization, and care—all part of the seller's marketing strategy for the daily seduction of the consumer. Finally, the reliance on well-known symbols also connects individual consuming to the general phenomenon of celebrity and links the consuming subject with spectacular individuals and activities that are venerated by society.

Presently, there are many kinds of hybrid themed environments. Restaurants promote specific images and themes, many of them linked to particular media celebrities; museums specialize in a certain genre of artifacts and advertise special exhibits with overarching themes; department stores sell symbols along with goods (e.g., designer clothing); malls adopt general design motifs; and theme parks proliferate as the preferred form of family entertainment. Even the interior of the home has been commodified through thematic devices and incorporated into the cyclical sphere of fashion. Some of these themed environments, such as home interiors or restaurants, are designed to be used on a daily basis—that is, they are part of our everyday life. Others are meant for special occasions, such as the theme park destination of family vacations or holidays. Let us consider some examples.

In what follows I shall emphasize the function of spaces as themed environments and pay special attention to the symbolic devices used to differentiate otherwise similar commercial places from each other. My discussion of motifed milieus is based on two propositions. The first is that due to increased competition, businesses increasingly use thematic and symbolic appeals in order to sell their products. In the past they relied more on direct demonstrations of the intrinsic use-value and quality of the goods they sold. In the second case, I suggest that although symbols and motifs also were used in the past by commercial establishments, businesses now are increasingly housed in built environments completely designed as themed spaces. These new consumer spaces typically consist of some overarching motif complemented by corresponding thematic details that together create a totally themed environment. People increasingly enjoy these symbol-filled milieus, such as large malls or spectacular Las Vegas casinos, for their own sake, as entertaining, fantasy spaces, and not simply as locations for the easy purchase of commodities. In sum, consumption today is characterized by the articulation of symbolic appeals, fantasy entertainment, and the value of image over substance.

A final dimension of the discussion to follow develops a subtheme of my argument. Along with the increasing reliance on theming have come reactions and resistance to its increasing domination of our culture. These conflicts come in a variety of forms, from outright declines of patronage because of terrible food, to community mobilizing against the opening of franchises, to a revolt of citizens against the bastardization of their culture by artificial and simulated themed environments. In Chapter 6 I shall return to these separate examples, when I consider the limits of theming and popular forms of resistance.

At present the increasing reliance on motifed spaces harkens back to earlier history when people lived within environments completely structured by cosmological, religious, or political codes (see Chapter 2). The important difference now is that our themed environments are imitations or *simulations* of substantive symbols. Today's signs possess superficial rather than deeply felt meanings. They are *fundamentally* disconnected from the use-value of the commodities with which they are associated. As pure images, their major source of inspiration is the fickle and rapidly changing fashionable world of mass advertising, television, and Hollywood culture. Thus, there is both a positive and a negative side to the proliferation of themed environments. In the former case, they have emerged as a qualitatively new source of entertainment in the history of human civilization. In the latter, their essential purpose of merchandising and profit-making, their control by *private* commercial interests rather than public ones, and their reduction of all meanings to superficial images, raises serious questions about the quality of our daily life.

## The Themed Restaurant

Until quite recently, Americans rarely ate in restaurants. The norm was to cook meals at home. Dining out was reserved for a special occasion. Eating at the local community diner was an exception, because it offered a substantial breakfast or meat-and-potatoes lunch for reasonable prices. Frequenters of diners were mainly people on the move, such as truck drivers, traveling salespeople and delivery men, or single adults, especially men who lived alone. The roadside diner was an important place during the 1930s and 1940s, at the first blossoming of our now mature automobile culture. Many of these structures were simple affairs that restricted their advertising to the daily specials. They counted on traffic and the sparsity of competition to bring customers their way. Nevertheless, a few of these establishments exploited advertising in competition for business, and some used thematic devices. One classic case was the original McDonald brothers' roadside hamburger stand, located on Route 66 just west of San Bernardino, California. The brothers embellished their simple diner with a large, bright yellow "M." Over the years, as the original stand grew into the multinational, multibillion-dollar corporation under new, franchise-thinking owners, this arched logo would undergo many stylistic transformations as it melded with the *theme* of the "McDonald's" experience (Ritzer, 1993).

Between 1930 and 1960, many similar examples of roadside hamburger stands developed and became thematic in conception, although none duplicated the success of McDonald's franchising. On the east coast a diner called the Red Apple Rest, located on a route that was well traveled by vacationers leaving New York City for the upstate Catskill Mountains, expanded into a thematic built environment. For a time, it was the most popular stopover point on the family trip between mountains and the city. In the midwest and parts of the south, the Stuckey Corporation opened franchised strings of roadside restaurants that offered pecan products, sugary confections, and the usual fare of hamburgers and fries to weary automobile passengers. Other examples of multipurpose roadside restaurants abound in the motorized American landscape. Currently, many gas stations double as "one-stop" convenience stores, servicing transportation with light shopping needs in a new version of the local roadside stand.

As Venturi, Brown, and Izenour (1972) observed, the diner is simply a shed adorned with symbols. The *decorated shed* became the forerunner for the themed restaurants of today. Competition among fast-food franchises or restaurants, coupled with increasing affluence and the new consumer norms that support frequent meals outside the home, have pushed eating establishments into the frequent use of thematic devices. Some restaurant chains exemplify totally themed environments. Typical of the trend are the dining places constructed by the Specialty Restaurant Corporation (Wright, 1989). They are often renovated structures belonging to failed factories, such as the Cannery Restaurant of Newport Beach, California. The original cannery operated from 1921 to 1966, processing seafood, until pollution from suburbanization forced its closure. The interior of the factory was gutted and converted into a restaurant. Instead of throwing out the original machinery, however, the designers recycled it as sculpture. Artifacts from the manufacturing process became part of the decor. Thematic elements unified around the motif of the local fishing industry—such as photographs, ship's compasses, and navigational equipment—were mounted on the walls. Employees dress in uniforms that evoke the 1920s. The elements of the cannery motif pervade the entire space, creating a totally themed environment. Of course, the current cannery is only a simulation—not a real fish-processing plant, but a fish restaurant *disguised* as a factory.

Most themed restaurants are synonymous with the image of their franchise chain, in both their exterior and their interior design. The use of themed environmental design, however, is so common today that even places with limited exterior signification often resort to fully themed decors for their interiors. I found one example of this phenomenon while searching for a place to eat in a suburban area outside Pittsburgh, Pennsylvania. I had been staying on a motel row between the city and the regional airport and was dissatisfied with the food prepared by the local motel restaurants. On a quick drive to locate a more promising place to eat, I saw a sign from the highway advertising the Hacienda restaurant inside a typical motel. I tried it less out of hunger than of curiosity. The place was fully themed in a mass cultural version of Tex-Mex designs. Earth-tone painted walls, Aztec printing on the menu, sombreros, cacti, painted chairs and tables, and hot sauce on the counter all combined to create that ambiance of simulated southwest America familiar from restaurants in Arizona, New Mexico, and places west. The suburban Hacienda offered a mode of Mexican cuisine that had been boiled down to its essential symbols in such a way that it was now transportable as a simulation to virtually anywhere. Indeed, I have eaten at similar places since then in Helsinki, Finland, São Paulo, Brazil, and Barcelona, Spain.

Perhaps the best-known fully themed franchise is the Hard Rock Café—a concept started in England by Peter Morton and Isaac Tigrett in 1971. Catering to young adults and serving comparatively simple meals centering on the staple of hamburgers and French fries, this restaurant chain has become so successful that it can be found in the capital cities of several countries; and recently, a Hard Rock Casino opened in Las Vegas. The thematic motif of this franchise derives from the rock music industry, including nostalgic elements from its origins in the 1950s. Two signature logos dominate the decor. The exterior of the restaurant is usually framed by a large guitar outlined in neon and has part of a 1950s Cadillac convertible embedded in one wall (the embedded Cadillac often extends into the interior as well). Inside, the Hard Rock Café franchises are decorated with both facsimiles and original memorabilia of the rock industry, including gold records, tour jackets, photographs, and the guitars of famous singers encased in special displays. Waiters and waitresses wear standard restaurant uniforms, and the menu is virtually the same whether you dine at the Café in London, Los Angeles, or Tel Aviv. The distinctive motif, fed constantly by the connection to the rock industry, is developed further by ambitious merchandising made available at all restaurant locations, featuring T-shirts, caps, jackets, and tote bags emblazoned with the name of the location and the Hard Rock Café logo.

Because the totally themed environment proved successful for the Hard Rock Café franchise almost thirty years ago, its form has been copied more recently by other operations. Today in many cities people can find a Harley Davidson Café, a Johnny Rockets 1950s diner, a Rainforest Café, Country Star Restaurants, Outback Steakhouses, a Fashion Café, and a Jekyll and Hyde Club (the latter is billed as "a restaurant and social club for explorers and mad scientists"). Despite the financial problems of some of these enterprises—for example, a projected "Baywatch" themed chain never materialized, for lack of cash supporters—schemes for new themed and franchised restaurants appear constantly. Some of the latest are Mars 2112, a chain that features a flying saucer that transports diners to their tables, and a joint venture of the Hard Rock Café with professional basketball stars, called NBA City.

Perhaps the most spectacular example is the chain called Planet Hollywood, launched in 1991 by Hollywood film producers Keith Barish and Robert Earl and including among its investors a number of movie superstars—Arnold Schwarzenegger, Sylvester Stallone, Demi Moore, and Bruce Willis. Like the Hard Rock Café, Planet Hollywood commodifies its connection to a popular culture industry, namely movies. Its walls are decorated with Hollywood memorabilia. Once inside a typical franchise, the customer can order virtually the same type of fare as at the Hard Rock Café—that is, basic American diner food. In fact, other than the themed environments of these two examples, there is little to differentiate them from any other local American diner existing virtually in every town in the United States. The *themed* environment makes the difference. Judging from the examples of the Hard Rock Café, linked to the rock industry, and Planet Hollywood, linked to the movie industry, the ordinary but always highly functional American diner is transformed into a successful *international* restaurant franchise through connection to a popular culture theme.

Recently Planet Hollywood has suffered from a lack of patronage and has begun to lose money. In April 1999 it defaulted on $250 million in notes and filed for bankruptcy. One of the repeated criticisms about the chain was that it had lousy food. As part of its reorganization plan, Planet Hollywood closed 9 of its 32 U.S. restaurants and kept only the most lucrative locations open. Fallout from this case has prompted other chains to place a greater emphasis on the quality of the dining experience. Apparently it is no longer enough to offer symbols or thematic connections to celebrity, without substance. Increasingly, the appeal of theming alone is viewed with suspicion, especially once the novelty of a new restaurant idea wears thin.

Other restaurant franchises that have not been successful commercially but that also use fully themed environments feature French village motifs, southwestern decor, New York City deli style, and a diverse deployment of nostalgia themes, such as 1950s "oldies"; country farmhouses; and ethnic symbols that are mechanically replicated, such as the quasi-Italian Olive Garden restaurants (more successful than most). A typical nostalgic themed restaurant is the Ruby Tuesday chain. I find it particularly interesting for its postmodern implosion of times and places that stretch over almost an entire century. The decor successfully integrates the many, varied referents in the exploitation of popular nostalgia. Its walls are lined with reproductions of ads and public signs from the 1920s, '30s, and '40s. The decor of the booths, however, reaches further back, to the previous century. The booths are illuminated by a remarkable display of imitation Tiffany lamps (originally dating to the 1890s) and stained glass windows. The nineteenth- and early-twentieth-century implosion is complemented by old-fashioned ceiling fans and hanging plants arranged in the style of the Victorian era. Lastly, no Ruby Tuesday restaurant would be complete without its authentic-looking, simulated plastic "tin roof." Eclecticism and a dizzying postmodern pastiche, rather than historical accuracy, define this experience.

Along with these more dramatically themed environments, famous franchises such as McDonald's, Kentucky Fried Chicken, and Burger King stylize and abstract their identifying logos into equally pervasive motifs that add to the array of signs and symbols within the built environment. One case of abstraction is the recent alteration of the Kentucky Fried Chicken logo to the stylized letters "KFC," which the company reproduces as part of

*Chi-Chi's restaurant, Buffalo, New York, an example of the simulated adobe-style hacienda that signifies Mexican food. Photo by the author.*

the decor and as a logo in packaging. More comprehensive examples can be found in the mass production of virtually identical interiors by the McDonald's corporation, capitalizing on the many thematic elements it has produced in advertising over the years, such as the cartoon cast of characters associated with "Ronald McDonald" and his "friends" (Ritzer, 1993, 2000). These signs, along with the McDonald's interior, are found around the globe. Anyone familiar with the McDonald's restaurant in their local hometown can also successfully negotiate the one in the Ipanema section of Rio de Janeiro, Brazil, or the several locations in Paris, France, Tokyo, Japan, and London, England. Because the names of franchises like Kentucky Fried Chicken or McDonald's are so famous, promotional advertising develops the name itself as a corporate theme that functions along with the efficiently designed fast-food interior scheme as a total environment.

The marketing of a restaurant as a thematic environment also deploys aspects of merchandising to attract customers. Part of the economics of these chains involves the sale of merchandise such as hats, jackets, and T-shirts. Planet Hollywood and Hard Rock Café outlets often locate their merchandise counters at the entrance to the eatery. It is estimated that the

*Hooters restaurant and highway sign. Photo by the author.*

more successful chains make approximately 25 percent of their profit from the sales of clothing and other merchandise in addition to food. Fast-food places such as McDonald's and Burger King often run promotions by selling popular culture items that have some tie in to mass entertainment media—for example, a newly released Disney film for children, or the series of Star Wars movies. Even when not engaging in special promotions, themed restaurants carry through their coordinated designs down to their napkins, plates, cups, and table decor. They spruce up menus with restaurant symbols or logos, much as medieval manuscripts were illuminated by graphic embellishments. Often eateries that lack exploited advertising symbols nevertheless bring their decor into concordance with the type of food they serve. Diners offering ethnic foods, such as Greek, Jewish, or Italian specialties, include dishes from those cultures along with the standard American fare, and commonly have ethnic signs mixed in with generic decorations on tables and menus. In short, when it comes to food, theming is everywhere.

Despite the mixed fortunes of themed restaurants—some unabashed successes and some obvious failures—the economics of theming remains an important profit incentive in today's business environment. Put simply, the price of theming for a customer can be arrived at easily by comparing the cost of a typical hamburger and French fries at a fast-food outlet with the same dish at a themed restaurant. I have conducted this comparison many times and have found that the price is most commonly double. So, the cost of theming adds 100 percent to the cost of the food at a non-themed, fast-food diner.

Another way to understand the economics of themed restaurants is by examining their costs and profits. Information from the new NBA City flagship states that the restaurant cost about $10 million to construct, with each additional location in the chain estimated to cost between $8 and $10 million. Expected revenue from the first year of operation is $15 million from a projected 1 million patrons (Schneider, 2000). Of course, location means a lot to profitability. The chain of Rainforest Cafés follows a selective, comparatively less ambitious scheme of limiting the number of their outlets to lucrative locations. They had 29 stores worldwide in 1999. Their eatery at the MGM Grand Hotel in Las Vegas makes $50,000 a day, and their branch at Disneyworld clears $35 million yearly (Edwards, 1998).

In recent years there has been a backlash to much of this superficial theming. Already mentioned is the criticism of bad food, leveled against several popular chains. Increasingly the attraction of eatertainment hybrids has declined in part because people have grown more reluctant to pay for theming. According to one report:

> Flashy theme restaurants always ranked as a given in any developer's plans to fill massive amounts of retail space in just-as-flashy urban entertainment complexes in downtown Philadelphia. No more. The industry of themed and hyperthemed 'eatertainment' restaurants, such as Planet Hollywood and the Rainforest Café, formerly darlings of Wall Street, have taken a battering both in the market and in their national images. Store closings and plunging stocks have replaced news of lucrative IPOs and celebrity launchings, most recently with news of the Fashion Café's folding and Planet Hollywood's desperate attempts to reposition itself (McCalla, 1999).

In response to this trend, the themed eatertainment chains have not only renewed their emphasis on the quality of food and the overall dining experience but have also altered their locational strategies. Today, franchises often decide not to locate in the centers of cities that are frequented by tourists, because that is both a highly competitive and an unreliable market, and instead favor sites in large suburban shopping malls (McCalla, 1999: 2; Hodson, 1999). In short, themed restaurants have become more of a suburban phenomenon in recent years and have melded with another aspect of theming, the symbolically motifed, fully enclosed shopping mall.

## The Themed Mall

Malls, just like the restaurants I have discussed, vary regarding the extent to which they carry through thematic designs. Yet, they too increasingly use overarching motifs and coordinated symbolic schemes in total environments. As we have seen, restaurants compete with each other for cash customers. Malls, however, first emerged in competition with the downtowns of cities. Their direct competition was for many years the large department stores located in the center of the metropolis. Consequently, they had to advertise themselves as a *place* to go, and they still do. This kind of advertising for a particular space or location is increasingly common in our society, as all places compete for tourist and consumer dollars.

As a particular destination, malls require some overarching means of identification. Consequently, they often adopt an image meant to attract consumers who have a choice of where to do their shopping. There is another reason why malls adopt a unified image. Whereas the central city remains a public space that allows free interaction among a variety of people for any number of purposes, the mall is a highly regulated, *private* commercial space that is expressly designed to make money. This instrumental function of the mall—aimed at realizing capital—must be disguised because it would not be attractive to consumers. As a result, almost every mall has an overarching motif that attempts to convey its uniqueness and desirability as a destination *for its own sake*. As with restaurants, the exterior mall theme is a simulation, a facade; but as a motif it also sets the symbolic tone for the interior.

There are several motifs commonly adopted by malls around the country. One type, "ye olde kitsch," is exemplified by the Olde Towne Mall located in Orange County, California. The interior space contains a pedestrian path lined with artificial gas lamps and park benches. Each store facade presents an image of an old-fashioned emporium of the past. Even the mall security office is signaled by a "Police" sign in nineteenth-century-style graphics. The conformity between overarching mall motif and the particular facades of interior stores is characteristic of the totally themed environment. The latter is rarer among restaurants, as we have seen, and more common among malls, Las Vegas casinos, and theme parks (discussed in Chapter 5).

Another frequent motif is "high-tech urban" (Gottdiener, 1986). Malls of this type are several stories high. They have skylighted ceilings that recall the Parisian arcades once studied by Walter Benjamin. They strive for a clean, modern look that accentuates chrome, large plate-glass windows, and flashy neon signage. Perhaps the most famous high-tech mall is the Galleria in Milan, Italy. This mall became so popular as a means of marketing commodities that many mall developers in other countries copied its form. The United States alone has many large malls called "The Galleria"—one in Houston, Texas, one in Buffalo, New York, one in Glendale, California, and so on. The original galleria, however, is the Palazzo Vecchio in Florence, Italy, which was constructed during the Middle Ages. A galleria is a two-story building with a large interior space and with the second story open to the interior space. The original galleria was an open space without a roof. Galleria malls in the United States are always large, enclosed spaces that are several stories high.

Malls have been very effective as commercial spaces. They account for over half of all retailing sales in the United States. In many metropolitan areas, competition from malls has been so severe that it has forced downtown shopping districts out of existence. Buffalo, New York, for example, has several large suburban malls ringing the central city, but the last department store located downtown closed in 1995. During the 1960s, suburbanization and mall development were so devastating to central cities that the latter required heavy infusions of cash from federal government renewal programs to float schemes that would bring their customers back. Few of these efforts were successful.

Despite their commercial accomplishments, malls are now locked in fierce competition with each other, especially because their customers can commute to a variety of alternatives. As a result, owners have resorted to thematic appeals both in the outer design of the mall and in advertising, to attract business. Typical of this process is yet another Galleria, located in Riverside, California, a medium-sized city 50 miles east of Los Angeles. Riverside had a one-story mall built in 1970 that serviced the local area. As the community gained affluent residents over the next few decades, the mall could not compete with more fashionable, upscale places in Orange County, such as the large South Coast Plaza, less than one hour away. In 1990 a consortium of developers invested $100 million to transform the Riverside Mall into the Galleria. The new mall is two stories high and contains over 120 stores, including four large, "anchoring" department stores. It has a cinema and a dual-level parking structure that can accommodate almost 10,000 cars. These specifications are typical of the large, suburban shopping mall.

The most important aspect of the new Riverside Galleria was the advertising campaign for the mall itself as a competitive location. This campaign used thematic elements in its core appeal to customers who had forsaken local shopping for the flashier sites of the Los Angeles basin. According to the local paper:

> Riverside's regional mall reopens tomorrow with a new theme, new promise and new stores. . . . The lofty marketing theme for the grand re-opening of the Galleria is 'Reaching New Heights.' But the subliminal message could easily be 'Reaching New Customers.'. . . . The Galleria Gurus are confident that their dolled-up, classed up, two-storied showcase will lure Riverside County shoppers who had defected to the hallowed malls of Orange County (Lucas, 1991: 1).

Besides creating pressure on cities with competitive retailing locations, malls often use symbolic design devices that expressly recall the central city through simulations. That is, malls have always competed with the urban downtown, but recently suburban malls have attempted to replicate these downtowns in design motifs, re-creating a simulated "urban" environment. First malls destroyed the inner city's monopoly on retailing, then they proceeded to co-opt the very image of urban life itself for their themes. According to one of the leading southern California architects of malls:

> In essence, the difference between what malls are trying to look like now versus what they were trying to do 10 years ago is that now they're trying to create more of a street scene with a variety of store fronts and architecture. . . . And they're also trying to create an interplay of store merchandise from store to store—which is like a department store with different kinds of merchandise in each section, only now you would consider the whole mall as a large department store and each store is one of those separate departments. . . . Behind this kind of mall design is the idea of going back to the old sense of community, where there used to be the general store where everyone met and knew each other's name (Knaff, 1991: 4).

In at least one case, fierce competition has produced a mall that advertises itself as an "anti-mall." Located in Orange County, California, this shopping area, also known as the Lab, caters to young adults who find no use for typical mall stores such as Waldenbooks or the Nature Company. Instead of these mall standards, it features retailers known for their alternative clothing or accessory styles. In addition, while many malls around the country discourage teenage loitering, this anti-mall welcomes it and offers places to hang out. Other mall owners are also aware of segmented marketing (discussed above). They aim for a mix of stores that will appeal to different class and status groups.

Suburban malls changed the nature of retail competition by adding the dimension of space to the marketing equation. In the past, when central city department stores dominated all commerce, only individual stores themselves had to advertise. Once suburbanization reached a mass level, after World War II, and malls were introduced as retailing outlets dispersed within the larger metropolitan region, the downtown of the city became only one location among several alternate destinations for shoppers. Each retailing center, suburban or urban, had to compete with every other center as a specific destination of commuters. Besides advertising that expresses competition among stores, therefore, mall advertising also expresses competition among the alternate locations of retailing centers. The latter type of promotion takes the form of thematic appeals, especially for malls that project a special image of their own. Lately, even central cities have begun to advertise themselves to shoppers. Thus, *spatial* competition leads to a greater use of themes, and the success of certain malls leads to a preferred form that is a self-contained, total environment, such as the galleria. In addition, because of place competition, there is a tendency over time for malls to become bigger and bigger so as to offer more store possibilities to potential visitors. This process of greater reliance on theming as a consequence of increased locational choices and spatial competition is also characteristic of other destination-based businesses such as theme parks, vacation places, and other tourist attractions around the globe.

The largest mall in the United States is the Mall of America, located in Bloomington, Minnesota (on the outskirts of Minneapolis), which opened for business on August 21, 1992. In many ways, this "megamall" is, in fact, a separate small city. Developers pushed the total environment of the galleria a step further by constructing a closed but immense interior space (sometimes called a "hyperspace" because of its size; see Jameson, 1984). The Mall of America covers 78 acres and contains over 4 million square feet of floor area, including 2.5 million of actual retailing space. It houses more than 400 specialty shops and 4 large department stores, a 14-screen movie theater, nightclubs, bars, 9 areas of family entertainment, over 22 restaurants, and 23 fast-food outlets. But that is not all. At the center of this three-story complex, beneath an immense hyperspace of skylights, mall develop-

*The Mall of America: a three-story view. Photo by the author.*

ers located a seven-acre theme park, Camp Snoopy, which is run by Knott's Berry Farm of southern California. The park has trees and bushes, a controlled climate, 23 amusement rides including a roller coaster, 14 places to eat, and high-tech virtual reality simulations. At the entrance of this interior theme park stands a two-story-high balloon statue of Snoopy, the cartoon character, an image that can be seen from most locations within the larger mall itself.

Promotional literature for the megamall states that it is as big as 88 football fields—twenty times the size of Rome's St. Peter's Basilica, and five

*The Mall of America: Camp Snoopy at the center. Photo by the author.*

times that of Moscow's Red Square. According to its Canadian developers, the megamall site in Minnesota was chosen among several alternatives in various states because of key factors, including the presence of 27 million people in the surrounding region and an average household income above the national average. In addition, local governments put up over $100 million in transportation upgrades for the surrounding area, including the construction of large, multistoried parking ramps.

The Mall of America cleverly ties its overarching theme to the grand symbol "America." Developers made up the exterior facade in stars and

*Mall of America floor plan.*

stripes and red, white, and blue. Its patriotic decor can mean so many things to so many different people that it serves as a consummate mass marketing device. Ironically, the original developers of the mall were Middle Eastern immigrants to Canada, but that did not prevent them from feeding an "all-American" simulation to the hungry consumers of the Minneapolis–St. Paul region. The interior of the megamall articulates the polysemic patriotic theme, with other themes shaping the major shopping sections. Many of its restaurants have individual themes. Most are chain franchises, such as Hooters (featuring scantily clad waitresses), Tony Roma's (a chain of rib restaurants), Ruby Tuesday, Fat Tuesday, the Alamo Grill (southwest food), the California Cafe (a simulation of southern California style), and Gators (another diner food chain), among others. Each of these themes relates to the others only in the loosest possible sense, as a part of the tapestry of American folklore simulations.

Retail space within the mall is subdivided into four main areas: North Garden/Main Street USA; West Market; South Avenue; East Broadway.

*The food court at the Mall of America is typical of the fast-food, cafeteria-style eating areas found in large malls. Photo by the author.*

Each area resorts to the old standby simulation—a recapturing of urban ambiance in a varied version of the city street scene. It seems, so far, that malls cannot escape from their main competitor—the downtown, truly public space of the classic central city. The mall's inaugural brochure describes the North Garden area as follows: "This lushly landscaped, serpentine walk extends from the venerable Sears to the eagerly awaited Nordstrom. With plant-covered balconies, wooden trellises, gazebos, bridges and airy skylights, North Garden is Main Street, USA" (Mall of America, 1992: 10). Why North Garden is like a typical main street of this country is not at all clear from the above description, but the mall's promoters make that connection anyway.

The second area, West Market, is a simulated representation of a European-style marketplace: "From Nordstrom to Macy's, West Market bustles like an old-fashioned European marketplace. You'll make your way past a variety of carts, street venders, shops and eateries to the fancifully painted shop fronts" (p. 11). In the description of the third area, South Avenue, the urban metaphor continues: "This upscale promenade between Macy's and Bloomingdale's just might become the Rodeo Drive of the Twin Cities. Its sophisticated storefronts recall the great shopping streets of Europe" (p. 12). With this description we now reach the realm of mixed references and geographical confusion. First compared to the shopping street located in the city of Beverly Hills, California—Rodeo Drive—South Avenue, which is named for its directional location in the Mall, is then described as recalling streets of Europe. It is possible to ask at this point whether South Avenue is that distinct from West Market and whether, in fact, the entire Mall description as recalling or representing a type of place or specific "placeness" of some kind, merely exists as advertising discourse with no real basis in reality. In short, this mall's interior is a simulation with the distinctiveness of place produced more by discourse than by real design differences.

This characteristic can also be illustrated by East Broadway, the last area of the Mall. Promotional discourse from the brochure defines the experience for the consumer in what might otherwise be mistaken for a mere extension of other areas: "From Bloomingdale's to Sears, this upbeat district features sleek storefronts, bright lights and the latest looks from the hottest shops" (p. 15). At last we have escaped the European street. The locale we find ourselves in, however, is just as amorphous in description and as hard to pin down with any degree of certainty. It is clear, in fact, that the ambiance of the Mall of America is produced less by careful recreation of place than by the use of symbolic decor specifically to fit in with the style of stores located in each of the four sections. Thus, the two large department stores, Sears and Nordstrom, dominate North Garden; West Market contains several small shops and places to eat besides the department stores; South Avenue is denoted as the "upscale" section of the mall, with the most expensive stores; and East Broadway possesses shops specializing in glitter, current fashions, and more youthful clothes.

Despite the overreaching metaphors of promotional materials aimed at connecting the mall with urban spaces in real cities, the actual decor is only a thinly veiled disguise for an immense indoor commercial area. This is also true of other malls. The grand themed environment of the mall functions as a sign-vehicle that aids this space's role as a container of many commercial enterprises, because it is also attractive as a desirable destination itself. What makes the Mall of America different are its large scale and the overabundance of family entertainment opportunities it offers, including the seven-acre theme park. It represents a consummate linkage between retailing and the effort to attract families in competition with the downtown of the city. These multiple functions are now typical also of other commercial spaces. The mall is a shopping/family entertainment/eating/leisure/cine-

*The self-regulation of crowds within the central space
at the Mall of America. Photo by the author.*

ma/quasi-communal space. Commercialism, and not the overarching themes of the classical city—i.e., religion, cosmology, or politics—dominates its form.

## Airports As Themed Environments

When commercial air travel was first introduced in the 1920s, the emergent industry benefited from the still-new romance of flying. Airlines had to compete with the more popular (and more affordable) modes of transportation at the time, especially the railroads. Early air carriers competitively stressed the special treatment of passengers by stewardesses, the availability of in-flight meals, and the comfortable seats. Then, airports were rather humdrum affairs. After World War II, however, when air travel had become a generally accepted mode of long-distance transportation, the design of air terminals became an important part of the transportation industry. For some time air travel was relatively expensive; but by 1960, declining fares due to price wars combined with a burgeoning consumer demand from the growing middle class to produce a *mass market* for commercial air transportation. Airport authorities and commercial carriers both turned increasingly to the use of themes in promoting their respective services, doing all they could to glamorize flight.

In the United States, unlike other industrialized countries, it is the local municipal authorities that build and run airports; however, terminals are the property of individual airlines. The latter can do little to affect the decor of the entire complex, but they do have control over their own service space. Few airports have been built since World War II, but there have been many terminal renovations. The most impressive postwar airport constructions were Kennedy International in the 1950s, Dulles Airfield in the 1960s, the Dallas–Ft. Worth complex in 1974, and the Denver International Airport, which opened in 1995. Terminal renovations, in contrast, have occurred frequently, in response to advertising needs and competition from other airlines. In addition, airport terminals renovate in response to the needs of local authorities for more revenue. Lately, both terminal and airport renovations have increasingly resorted to themed environments in order to improve their competitive positions or to adjust to new technologies of flight.

For example, in the 1970s the major carriers introduced wide-bodied jets. Up to that time airports had handled smaller planes. Because these new jets required more room, terminals across the country had to renovate. At that time, O'Hare airport, outside Chicago, was the busiest in the nation. As at other airports around the country, expansion at O'Hare necessitated the construction of new concourse spaces linked to the old central terminal. Each airline, however, had to renovate its own concourse spaces, because each was responsible for its own terminal. United Airlines launched an ambitious redevelopment scheme that included the construction of two concourses, B and C, within the United terminal area—but separated, unfortunately, by the expanse of the airport runway. They constructed an underground tunnel that connected the two concourses and solved this dilemma. United's problems, however, were only beginning. The main issue facing the airline was not only how to construct the underground connection but also how to design the linking space to attract customers and encourage them to overlook the inconvenience of the relatively long trek between the different concourses.

At an early stage in facing this marketing problem—in what seems to have been almost a reflex action—the airline invited the Walt Disney Corporation to help design the tunnel space in a user-friendly fashion that included dioramas along its walls. In other words, the airline immediately decided to solve its marketing problem by using a themed environment produced by the acknowledged master of theme parks. However, the original architect of the terminal renovation, Helmut Jahn, objected on aesthetic grounds and convinced United to commission an undulating light and music sculpture, which was more abstract in design, to fill the tunnel space. The proposed work of art used an organic theme of growth and continuity as its foundation. As one architecture historian notes: "In the [proposed] model, undulating walls of glass flowed with light reflected from a colored wall behind. . . . The glowing glass wall continued to flow up into the ceiling in a structure resembling the trunk and branches of trees, and the space was capped by a series of brilliantly colored tubes running the length of the tunnel" (Bruegmann, 1989: 8).

After construction, many travelers strongly criticized the tunnel environment. They objected, in particular, to the type of computerized music played along its length. The effect of the lights and music was quite startling to passengers who had come to expect unobtrusive decor in their travels. For a while the underground design was a controversial topic in local newspapers and also in United business meetings. Eventually, United changed the music and adjusted the light sculpture to more average tastes, but not before a good deal of negotiations and controversy.

As this case shows, themed environments are not always instantly embraced by consumers. Despite their growing popularity as a marketing solution, they can be irritating to customers. Airports in particular seem to have their share of problems with the design of renovations, perhaps because they are combined private and public facilities that can mix the worst of both worlds—local municipal politics and corporate wrangling over marketing schemes. Recently, the city of Denver abandoned its municipal airport and built a larger one 23 miles east of the city at a cost of $3.2 billion. The new Denver International Airport was plagued with many construction and polit-

*A view of the Jeppesen terminal at Denver International Airport, silhouetting the
ambiguously symbolic design. Photo courtesy of Corbis/Bettman.*

ical problems before its opening in 1995. Additionally, it has its share of signification problems. A great deal of money was invested in the unusual
Jeppesen Terminal Building, which is constructed of thirty-four spires and a
white, tensile fabric roof. Seeing the structure from a distance, it is difficult to
say what it is meant to symbolize. Consequently, the airport authority has
had to work overtime to define the meaning of the design. According to
brochures available at the airport, "The white peaks of the Jeppesen Terminal,
visible from several miles, are reminiscent of the Rocky Mountains." So far,
this grand architectural scheme has been unveiled to mixed reviews. As in the
O'Hare tunnel case, perhaps the story of the Denver design awaits a new
round of negotiations regarding its symbolic content.

Airports differ from themed environments in another important way.
Although all interior commercial spaces require sign systems to steer customers through the environment in the most functional fashion, airport
interiors must perform this task in an exemplary manner. Passengers disembarking from flights and requiring a change of planes must be able to
negotiate the space of the airport terminal with ease and rapidity. The sign
systems of terminals, therefore, are quite explicit in their *denotative* content. They announce, point, direct, guide, and provide up-to-date informa-

tion on flights and flight statuses. Perhaps the best way of appreciating the important role of airport interior signs and spatial design in this purely functional sense is by reflecting on the scale of passenger traffic. By the late 1970s, many more people passed through airports than lived in the local city that contained them. The total number of annual passengers in 1979 was greater than the entire U.S. population (see Gottdiener, 2001). For example, more than ten times the number of people passed through O'Hare airport, outside of Chicago, and Stapleton, in Denver, during 1979, than lived in either Chicago or Denver, respectively. Similar proportions are found in the traffic in and out of other major airports as well.

Air terminals use electronics, fast-resolve TV screens, and computer-generated graphics and information displays to provide timely information to passengers. Graphic designers are employed to create large, readable signs that guide passengers to the appropriate gates. The flight information displays, which are computer generated, and other graphically designed sign systems, must perform three main functions. They must direct and orient passengers; identify locations of flights, ticket counters, airline companies, baggage claims, bathrooms, and ground transportation; and provide information on arrivals and departures (Hart, 1985: 132). Well-marked airline terminals, above all, should facilitate embarking, disembarking, and transfer to connecting flights. Their success in these tasks is due largely to properly functioning sign systems.

Despite these functional needs, air terminals also strive for a themed experience. At first architects stressed the central terminal building and its ticketing facilities in their schemes. Most commonly they chose a theme that recalled the waiting rooms of the great railroad passenger terminals of the past. In these early designs the airport building was conceived of as an extension of the nineteenth-century transportation experience. Over time, functional requirements and aesthetic tastes both changed. In the 1960s, Kennedy International Airport stressed its role as the gateway to the world. Each of its major terminals was isolated on a connecting roadway, designed separately, by various architects. One of the most impressive buildings of the time was the Trans World Airlines (TWA) terminal, which was designed by Finnish architect Eero Saarinen, who later also crafted the look of the main terminal building for Dulles International, outside Washington, D.C. The TWA terminal at Kennedy embodies the expression of flight. Long, arching concourse tunnels swoop down and away through a large central interior space that serves as the ticketing, baggage claim, and restaurant area. The central space is framed by full-height, expansive windows that

*The terminal building at Dulles International Airport. Note the symbolic architecture suggesting flight. Photo courtesy of Corbis/Bettmann.*

allow views of the runways and bathe the interior in natural light. Saarinen applied many of these ideas also in the design of Dulles International. There, too, the central terminal building was emphasized in the airport design, replicating the analogy with the nineteenth-century train station. Dulles carried this analogy to an extreme by centralizing all airline ticketing and baggage claim functions within the large terminal. As a result, embarking and disembarking passengers were required to take a second means of transportation, an airport bus, to their respective planes before they could either fly or claim their baggage and leave the facility.

By the 1980s, the railroad terminal theme had become obsolete. One reason was the technological advance of wide-bodied jets, which now predominate in long-distance airborne transportation. The new planes require more space to maneuver and dock in and out of flight bays. Another reason was the realization that with a greater volume of air traffic, many passengers were using airports to transfer from one flight to another. Consequently, the preferred, developed space changed from a terminal/ticketing area that recalled the nineteenth-century railroad days, to expansive concourse areas. The concourses are the arteries that allow the free flow of passengers from plane to plane, ground transportation to flights, or plane to baggage claim to home. Unlike terminal spaces that centralize people and functions within one area, concourses can range across linear space, spreading out to accommodate wide-bodied jet flight bays—and, as it happens, intensive mercantile activity.

The 1985 conception of United's facility at O'Hare dramatically exemplifies the new type of terminal design. Although a tunnel connects the main concourses, the terminal buildings themselves are airy structures recalling the Parisian arcades of the nineteenth century, allowing natural light to filter in. Passenger perambulation is facilitated by moving walkways, and expressive but functional sign systems guide people to their desired destinations. Whereas the older terminal style contained a more static crowd congregated around ticketing and baggage checking activities, the grand concourses of the newly renovated terminals are areas of constant flows and urban-style pedestrian traffic. At Denver International Airport, the floor space is allocated to three expansive concourse-terminal buildings, in which air travelers spend most of their time.

In many ways, the new, concourse-oriented terminals are reminiscent of the massive interior spaces produced by mall construction. It was, therefore, not surprising when the two functions—air transfer and retailing—merged through conscious design. Actually, airports have served as retailing sites for some time. International travelers, in particular, can obtain commodities without paying import taxes, provided they purchase them in duty-free shops. After World War II, when propeller-driven planes were still standard, several airports around the globe, such as at Shannon, Ireland, nurtured duty-free shopping. As flight equipment and transfer patterns changed, different airports became hubs for passenger traffic and also capitalized on duty-free shopping. Due to the ease with which people can cross borders in western Europe, some of the best developed airport shopping areas arose in terminals on the continent. The bustling nodal points of Frankfurt International in Germany or the Zurich airport in Switzerland are two examples of airports that have extensive concourse space devoted to duty-free shopping. These retail outlets resemble large American supermarkets, with shopping carts and laser scanning at checkout.

Always the basic design of airport retailing relies on the broad expanses created by concourse-oriented terminal development. Moving along the extensive pathways to and from planes, passengers become consumers with time on their hands. Shops hoping to capitalize on the need for diversion line the broad concourses, advertising their wares. In form this array resembles the fully enclosed shopping mall. In sum, today's facilities are combined airport/malls (see Gottdiener, 2001).

Within the confines of the United States, airport retailing was a neglected activity. Even when extensive concourse renovation began, as in the United facility at O'Hare, the sidelines were dedicated to rather unimaginative, utilitarian shops selling newspapers, limited snacks, alcohol, local knickknacks, or traveler aids such as luggage and drugs. During the late 1980s, however, several airports began to take the lessons of duty-free retailing to heart, and expanded their commercial functions within renovated concourse spaces. One of the most expansive projects was the transformation of the Pittsburgh airport into an airport/shopping mall—an operation acknowledged as "the leader in airport retail" (Johnson, 1995: F-2). Officials invited upscale retailers common to suburban malls to open stores within the terminal structure, and many did. This airport now contains 80 restaurants and retail shops. By agreement, prices are kept at the same levels as at other area malls. Therefore, the airport acts as a mall and attracts local shoppers who have no immediate interest in air transportation. Sales have been impressive, averaging almost $7 for every boarded passenger in 1994 (Johnson, 1995). Pittsburgh's success has inspired other airports to become shopping meccas. LaGuardia Airfield in New York City, for example, recently completed a renovation of its main terminal and concourse areas to accommodate an extensive shopping space. Here as elsewhere, the mall form is followed because it fits so well the shape of the terminal concourse.

The new Denver International Airport also boasts many shops and mall-type retailing outlets. In this case, the design of a combined airport/mall was pursued from the start of construction, rather than as an innovation during subsequent renovation. Each of the three concourses has several levels that offer a considerable variety of consumption alternatives. Concourse A, for example, has four restaurant/delis, snack shops, apparel stores, a children's museum, and banking services. Concourse B has seven restaurants, a fast-food court, more specialty apparel stores, gift shops including the franchise chains the Nature Company and the Body Shop, and a chiropractor's office. Concourse C contains four restaurants, five apparel/gift shops, banking facilities, and an "airport family fun center." More shops like these are also found in the main terminal building. Unlike the Pittsburgh airport, which is easily accessible from the city, the facilities at Denver International are aimed directly at the large volume of passenger traffic anxiously anticipated in the future.

The expansive concourse spaces created by the new air terminals are not only exploited by retailers. In Nevada, where gambling is legal, airports are mere extensions of casino spaces. The McCarran Airfield in Las Vegas, Nevada, for example, has slot machines located in every available place throughout the concourse area. It is possible to engage in traditional casino games of blackjack or slots without ever leaving the terminal. Bathroom facilities in major airports have also recently been renovated to include showers and baby changing tables. Airport cuisine, once restricted to the most basic forms of food and drink, now provides an impressive array of food choices due to the location of eating facilities along the new concourses. Terminals and concourses at O'Hare, for example, provide mall-type food courts that are home to several different kinds of commercial eateries, including varied ethnic foods: Mexican, Chinese, Italian, and delicatessen. An extensive dining selection is planned for the renovated Los Angeles Airport, including major chains such as Kentucky Fried Chicken and also smaller but well-known franchises, such as Wolfgang Puck and Panda Express.

Increasingly, then, the mall and the airport merge in design. With this conjuncture, the same thematic dynamics discussed in the case of malls also applies to the new retailing places in air terminals. These enclosed, themed spaces capture the pedestrian mode of urban street culture for the purposes of commerce—even in places such as airports, whose primary function is air travel. In short, airports are interesting themed environments not because they overwhelm us with highly coordinated themes, as do restaurants such as the Hard Rock Café, but because they are overendowed with sign systems. Airports are extreme cases of semanticized environments. They require functional sign systems to guide people to and from planes and local streets. As transport hubs they facilitate multidimensional traffic movement with easy-to-decipher, graphically denotative sign systems. But there is a second dimension to their symbols. Within the airport interior, signification processes have altered with the architectural shift from an emphasis on waiting room and ticketing spaces—the old railroad metaphor—to airy, well-lit pedestrian concourses that facilitate the changing of flights. These spaces are overlaid with a second semantic field deriving from consumer retailing and mass marketing. Here the airport space has been transformed into a type of shopping mall. As such, the interior built environment intersects with the consumer culture propagated in mass media advertising and commercial marketing, with its cornucopia of signs and sign systems (Gottdiener, 2001).

## Theming and Hybrid Spaces

This chapter has focused on themed environments encountered in daily life. An important common characteristic of these commercial spaces is their multifunctionality. As local destinations they attempt to attract as many customers as possible by melding various services with entertainments. These hybrid forms include the modern shopping mall, which is also a theme park and restaurant/cinema center, the airport that is also a shopping mall, and the themed restaurant that is also a fashion merchandising center and entertainment space.

Recently, commercial multifunctionality has been extended to cinema complexes, which are often stand-alone environments inside shopping centers located in the sprawling complex of suburban regions. Canadian firms have been particularly innovative in designing new variations of these hybrid spaces. Giant multiplex screen centers now offer video arcades, restaurants, themed lobbies, coffee shops, and even party rooms for rent. Describing one of these complexes, a reporter (Warson, 1998) wrote:

> The flying saucer shaped Colossus Theater located near Toronto has 18 screens and 4,800 seats and includes an IMAX 3-D screen along with a stand-up bar for about 200 patrons. Famous Players Corporation has the Colossus and also a round cinema called the Coliseum. The fourth weekend after the first one opened in Mississauga, Ontario [just outside of Toronto], it was the highest grossing movie theater in North America.

According to the same report, the theater grossed an average of $1.3 million (Canadian) per screen, or $5,100 (Canadian) per seat. The Canadian national average is $1,000 (Canadian) per seat. In 1998, "more than 8,000 children attended more than 322 birthday parties and patrons spent 8,500 hours or 354 full days playing interactive video games" (Warson, 1998).

Multifunctionality is a marketing strategy for commercial developers in suburban regions. New shopping centers also include cinema multiplexes, restaurants, hotels, and offices for rent. In this way, such developments compete for local patrons among the sprawling population of the expanding metropolitan region, which adds alternative locations for spending money on a regular basis. According to one developer (quoted in Warson, 1998):

> "Just as with food courts, restaurant-plexes and movie multiplexes, if there is enough of a choice, the project itself will become a destination, and the entertain-

ment selection will be made upon arrival. . . . We're doing more urban entertainment centers than theme parks these days. They're destinations mainly for the 18 to 35 year olds that have more money to spend and know what they want to do without necessarily knowing why they head for a particular place."

In short, the ever-expanding metropolitan regions within which most people live create a kind of spatial anomie regarding consumer and entertainment choices. Spatial competition among alternatives creates hybrids that combine theming, entertainment, and commercial products. The draw of being able to accomplish more than one consuming task at once while also being entertained makes these newly developed complexes irresistible for many suburbanites, and contributes in no small measure to the further decline of the central city, which historically was the original multifunctional space.

## Summary of Main Points

1. Commercial establishments increasingly resort to overarching themes, constructing fully themed environments as a way of luring customers.
2. The symbolic aspect of goods overshadows their intrinsic use-value in our culture.
3. People enjoy symbolic fantasy places as entertaining environments as well as places of consumption.
4. Along with the increasing appearance of themed spaces, there is a growing negative reaction ranging from complaints about the quality of food and the poor dollar value, to the adverse effects on real cultures and meaningful symbols.
5. Restaurants are increasingly themed and franchised. Some of the most successful are linked to modern media or popular culture industries, such as rock music or Hollywood films.
6. The retail merchandising of products such as T-shirts and caps is an important source of profit for franchised, themed restaurants.
7. Recently, themed franchise chains have encountered serious financial problems.
8. Increasingly, shopping takes place in gigantic suburban malls that are themed environments. The motifs commonly found within these consumer places borrow heavily from city street scenes, although the competition presented by many of these same places

previously had driven commercial businesses within the city center out of existence.

9. Theming and large size is a consequence of the increasing place-competition among all alternatives within the expanding metropolitan regions, in which almost all Americans now live.

10. The largest mall in the United States has a 7-acre theme park at its center. This hybrid space combines shopping with family entertainment.

11. As air travel has become progressively more common, new airports resort to overarching themes in ways evoking new mall construction.

12. Airports are good spaces in which to observe the active role of sign systems.

13. More and more airports offer mall shopping and other hybrid functions, such as business conferencing. Like the large malls, they also take advantage of the symbols of urban pedestrian street scenes to exploit arcade-type shopping.

14. Themed commercial environments that must compete with massive metropolitan regions progressively offer multiple services. These new hybrid spaces are malls/cinemas/restaurants/theme parks/conference centers and places of family entertainment.

# 5

# THE LAS VEGAS CASINO,
# THEME PARKS, AND
# THE GENERAL TREND
# OF THEMING

Several academics have written about themed environments since the first edition of *The Theming of America* was published (Hannigan, 1998; Ritzer, 1998); but their work misses the internal cultural dynamics of theming. John Hannigan's book *The Fantasy City,* for example, is based on the premise that theming is an urban phenomenon, an assumption that I believe is erroneous. Theming is a general aspect of our culture, with the production of motifed environments increasingly being chosen to address the global aspect of declining profits in commercial enterprises. Now spatial competition exists between all locations, within the metropolitan region and throughout the world. Themes have become a way for all businesses and destinations to differentiate themselves in the hope of attracting customers, often by entertaining them. Suburban as well as central city venues are involved. By missing the generalizable nature of theming and the role it plays in making all locations attractive, writers focusing on the issue of "city" development fail to explain the growing problems of spatial inequality and discriminatory access, which overlap with and intensify traditional forces of economic inequality in society (these issues are addressed more thoroughly in Chapter 7 of this book).

One way of illustrating the more generalizable aspects of this phenomenon is to consider places that are not part of our daily lives (unlike the places discussed in the previous chapter). Tourist and leisure destinations that involve trips that are special occasions also attract people to locations around the globe that are known for their exciting elements of fantasy and theming. Las Vegas is an excellent example of this more spectacular dimension to theming, because it attracts over 30 million tourists a year (Gottdiener, Collins, and Dickens, 1999). More significantly, the most successful area of this tourist destination is not the city of Las Vegas itself but the suburban district known as "the Strip," which lies in Clark county. Today, when most people fly to Las Vegas for a vacation, they are really going to the metropolitan area just outside the city limits.

## Las Vegas Casinos

Almost a quarter century ago, three architects—Robert Venturi, Denise S. Brown, and Steven Izenour—published a spectacularly prescient book, *Learning from Las Vegas* (1972). In their exhaustive study of the Vegas architecture of that time, they identified a new design phenomenon, namely the rejection of modernist architecture that ignores symbols in favor of building that emphasizes signs and symbols of all kinds. According to the authors (and as I have discussed in Chapter 2), modernist architecture actively avoided the use of symbols and instead emphasized austere, blank walls of glass and steel, and simple, abstract geometric shapes like the tall rectangles of the flat-roofed skyscrapers built in central cities for decades. As Venturi and his associates observed during their visits in the late 1960s and early 1970s to Las Vegas, architecture there represented a thorough rejection of modernism. It was built, in fact, as if modernist doctrines had never existed.

The Las Vegas casino environment is a multidimensional system of signs. Both the built forms and the messages conveyed are highly developed and articulated as intentional symbols. Signs are everywhere. They direct traffic off the main interstate highway to the streets on which the various hotel/casinos can be found. They advertise individual casinos and their attractions, such as food and headliner entertainment. The signs also amuse through computer-generated electronic light displays. What caught the eyes of Venturi and his associates in the 1960s is this amazing contrast between the rather austere, businesslike environment of the large city, with its one overarching theme of modernism (that is, of "being modern"), and the explosion of light, sound, and symbols in the garish milieu of Las Vegas casino facades. What was true three decades ago is even more so today, as one new casino/resort after another tries to outdo the competition in the extent of its theming.

The function of the Las Vegas themed environment is straightforward: to seduce the consumer. Las Vegas is a multidimensional experience of seducing pleasures—money, sex, food, gambling, nightlife. Las Vegas constitutes a specialized space. It is one of several global "pleasure zones," like Monte Carlo and the French Riviera (*Monte Carlo* and *Riviera* are also the names of Las Vegas casinos), the Greek islands, Rio de Janeiro (the name of another Las Vegas casino), Disneyworld, Marienbad, and the Taj Mahal. According to Venturi and associates, "Essential to the imagery of pleasure-zone architecture are lightness, the quality of being an oasis in a hostile context, heightened symbolism, and the ability to engulf the visitor in a new role: vacation from everyday reality" (1972: 53).

At one time this themed excess was meant to capture potential gamblers passing by on the old highway from California, now Interstate 15. But today's neon and fantasy facades are less oriented toward automobile traffic and more designed as tools in the competition for a larger share of the more than $5.7 billion total annual revenue from tourism. In this sense, casino theming fights the competition located elsewhere, including other pleasure zone destinations around the world, as well as within the Las Vegas metro region itself.

Because of the relentless competition among individual casinos, the building exteriors are blanketed with highly developed motifs and symbolic displays that express some of the most vivid fantasies of American culture. Advertisements for Las Vegas casino-resorts develop these themes through elaborate signs, sculptures, and three-dimensional light-and-sound shows. Fantasy motifs are developed through language, images, neon, and other design elements that *connote* a specific theme. As in the case of the themed mall, the metaphorical relation is declared both as a particular set of connotations by the design of the exterior or facade of the casino/hotel and as a unifying motif exploited within the interior. For example, Caesars Palace Hotel and Casino has an exterior designed as an immense Roman villa. This motif is carried forward throughout the interior by design elements that always refer to a fantasy version of Rome. Even the cocktail waitresses wear a uniform that recalls that style. To be sure, theming at Caesars Palace is a simulation that not only anachronistically mixes Greek and Roman elements together but that also reflects Hollywood ideas more than classical inspiration. Yet the fantasy effect is unmistakably powerful, and Caesars remains one of the most successful projects in Las Vegas history, despite its location miles from the center of the city, on the Strip.

Nearby Caesars is the Mirage Hotel and Casino, another place with a totally themed environment. This highly successful destination develops several motifs. The dominant one is "tropical paradise"—a seeming contradiction with the casino's name (*mirage* signifies a desert phenomenon). But in Las Vegas no one seems to care about such nuances. The Mirage develops its motif through both exterior displays and interior design.

This complexity of fantasy simulation, and the rapid-fire transmission of distinct messages that simultaneously denote specific forms of information, such as the contents of a meal and its price, and connote thematic associations, such as the invitation to participate in an entertaining space, are communicated by the literal signs of Las Vegas both to the cars passing along the interstate and to the local pedestrian traffic on the Strip. In recent years the latter has become a true urban street scene (see below).

The Las Vegas gambling economy is situated within structures that are combinations of a casino, a hotel, and often also a family-oriented resort. Most of the spectacular resort-casinos are located on the north-south route of Las Vegas Boulevard or on the Strip outside the city, because of the need for sprawling space and to avoid city taxes (see Gottdiener et al., 1999). The downtown area, or "Glitter Gulch," is dominated in contrast by casinos specialized in gambling, and by adult-oriented hotel/casinos such as the Golden Nugget, which exploit the original theme of Las Vegas as a wide-open town in the Wild West.

Every casino in the city and on the Strip possesses a distinct theme, some overarching code or ideology reflecting a desirable fantasy of American culture. The varied thematic devices, borrowed largely in execution from Hollywood sound stages, create an emergent system of signification through difference. Even the buildings themselves function as one large sign. Each differentiated casino, as a separate theme, standing juxtaposed against other casinos, produces an overarching intertextuality that is the grand text of Las Vegas, a system of difference at the level of casinos themselves. This grand text is not intended to convey any particular message but instead becomes the profusion of signs that is the total environmental experience of Las Vegas. As owners alter individual casino themes, or when they build new casinos, the system of difference also changes and the Las Vegas experience becomes more varied and deeply modulated. This is especially true of the Strip, because it has been the scene of intense building since the 1980s. With each new addition trying to outdo its neighbors on this single length of roadway, a new environment of theming has been created that is so spectacular that it now overshadows, both in money earned and in tourist attention, the city of Las Vegas.

Starting from the southern tip of Las Vegas Boulevard, or the Strip, and working northward, for example, the following casinos and their overarching themes are juxtaposed. The Mandalay Bay is furthest south and displays an exotic Polynesian/Hawaiian fantasy theme. Outside, on the grounds, the Mandalay Bay features a swimming area of sand beaches, palm trees, and an enormous wave-making pool. Going north on that side of the street are two spectacular hotels—the Luxor, an Egyptian pyramid fantasy, and the Excalibur, a medieval castle and King Arthur themed environment. Just north of this complex, across Tropicana Boulevard, is the New York–New York Hotel and Casino, which features a simulated miniature version of Manhattan within its interior, complete with famous landmarks and shops. In sum, on the western side of this intersection of the Strip and Tropicana Boulevard, we have the close proximity of a simulated and architecturally condensed version of New York City and an equally simulated rendition of King Arthur's medieval castle, Camelot. The approximately one-thousand-year difference between these two fantasies can be bridged by a short walk across the street.

On the eastern side of the Strip, facing the Excalibur, is the Tropicana Hotel and casino, one of the older Vegas casino-resorts, with its highly articulated tropical/Polynesian theme. Going further north across the street, we arrive at the largest casino-hotel in the world, the 5,005-room MGM Grand, with an illuminated lion near the entrance. This complex elaborates the theme of Hollywood glamor and MGM memorabilia. On that same side of the street and continuing north is the recently refurbished and greatly expanded Aladdin, with an Arabian Nights theme, one of the oldest fantasy allusions present on the Strip. Next and up the street is Bally's, which exploits the ambiance of continental luxury and a Monte Carlo–type setting. Directly adjacent to Bally's is a new addition built by the same company—the Paris casino-hotel, which reproduces in simulation the milieu of Paris, France, complete with a 2/3-scale Eiffel Tower that people can access and ascend.

Across the street from the Aladdin once stood the Dunes hotel-casino, which also exploited the classic Las Vegas Arabian theme. It was demolished in 1993 to make way for a larger, more profitable project. The space is now occupied by the multibillion-dollar flagship of the Steve Wynn empire, the Bellagio Hotel, Resort and Casino. An upscale attraction that features high-quality dining, expensive designer shopping, and first-class room furnishings, the Bellagio is fronted by a fake lake (a half circle that is barely a few feet deep)—a simulation of Lake Como, in the Bellagio region of the Italian Alps. The area is the site of a spectacular water fountain and sound show that erupts regularly in front of the hotel complex and draws a crowd.

Crossing Flamingo Road on the western side, just north of the Bellagio, we encounter the Caesars Palace complex, which has undergone several expansions. The Palace modulates the overarching themes of Caesar's Rome and classical Italian architecture, with a bit of ancient Greece thrown in for good measure. Across the street, heading east, are the Barbary Coast, with its theme of old-time, nineteenth-century San Francisco, and the Flamingo Hilton (Bugsy Siegal's hotel), which retains its twin themes of continental luxury and Hollywood glamor. Above the Flamingo are the Imperial Palace, which has Asian thematic elements, and the Holiday Inn Motel. Across the Strip toward the west is the giant Mirage complex, which exploits both Hollywood glamor and tropical paradise themes. The Mirage has a spectacular nightly display outside the building—an erupting volcano—for the benefit of passersby on the Strip. The volcano light-and-sound show is repeated every 15 minutes. North of the Mirage is the casino-hotel Treasure Island, with its Caribbean pirates theme. It too offers a nightly repeating show outside the building, of a battle between two ships within an artificial Caribbean lagoon. This display is spectacular in scale, and it features live actors.

Across the way from Wynn's Treasure Island, we find the multibillion-dollar Venetian Hotel and Casino, which was built on land made vacant by the implosion of the classic Sands Hotel in 1998. The Venetian is, perhaps, the most successful new hotel on the Strip. Gigantic in size, it features a second floor that is given over to a brick-by-brick re-creation of the Grand Canal of Venice. Almost a mile long, it is lined on both sides with mall-type shops. The canal—like the Bellagio's Lake Como, a simulation that is no more than a few feet deep—features authentic gondolas that offer rides to tourists. A central area provides a simulation of St. Mark's Square, minus the pigeons and garbage, situated beneath a fifty-foot-high ceiling painted to look like the sky. So popular is this combination mall–Venice simulation that it attracts an estimated 100,000 visitors a day.

Walking toward the city, we find the Desert Inn, the most famous resort-casino, which features a professional golf course and an old-fashioned Arabian Nights theme. Across the Strip, the Frontier Hotel introduces a Wild West, cowboy theme for the first time and allows a thematic segue into the downtown, with its overly endowed Wild West–themed casinos such as the Golden Nugget, Binions Horseshoe, and the Four Queens. This cowboy motif was originally exploited as the thematic referent for the old

*The MGM Grand entrance, Las Vegas. Photo by the author.*

Las Vegas, and it once symbolically marked the entire casino experience, before the extensive Strip development of recent years abandoned it for more spectacular, simulated consumer fantasies.

Before entering the downtown area, we encounter several other large casinos. On the west side of the Strip, next to the Frontier, is the Stardust, an immense hotel/motel complex that expresses a limited association with Hollywood glamor. Heading north we find the Westward Ho casino, which exploits the downtown cowboy theme, and the gigantic Circus Circus complex, with an obvious circus theme that includes the performance of live circus acts, and a family-oriented amusement park. On the east side of the street are several small hotel-casinos and the Riviera casino-hotel, which utilizes a continental, Monaco–French Riviera theme. North of it, on Sahara Avenue, we find the Sahara Hotel, another Arabian fantasy thematic attraction that has also been recently renovated.

Graphically illustrating the competition for customers through the use of symbols—which are the essence of the new, themed economy—this juxtaposition of motifs produces a spectacular interaction of signs all along the Strip that is itself an attraction. Standing at the corner of Tropicana Avenue, for example, one can see in a single gaze the tropical themed Tropicana Casino, an immense golden lion at the MGM Grand entrance,

*The sphinx in front of the Luxor Casino and Hotel, Las Vegas. Photo by the author.*

*The Excalibur Casino and Hotel, Las Vegas. Photo by the author.*

*Kon Tiki Village, in the back lot of the Hotel Tropicana, Las Vegas. Photo by the author.*

the medieval edifice of the Excalibur castle, the spectacular high-rise towers simulated by the New York–New York Hotel and Casino, and the giant simulated sandstone sphinx and slate pyramid of the Luxor. Within the same field of vision one can also see an implosion of ordinary, mundane signage—tall gas station signs with their corporate logos, gigantic casino signs advertising food and showcase entertainment, bus stops, parking lot signs, and advertising for various products on walls and fences.

With the new construction of spectacular themed casinos at the southern end of Las Vegas Boulevard has come escalating density in pedestrian

*Las Vegas street scene. Note the postmodern implosion of symbols from ancient Egypt, the European Middle Ages, Polynesia (stone heads), and contemporary America (cars). Photo by the author.*

traffic. Las Vegas as a whole has become a theme park. The activity of casino-hopping has taken on a new cachet and relevance, as the built environment produces signification through thematic differences. Pedestrians, who in years past never ventured far from their casino of choice because of hot weather and limited attractions, now derive obvious pleasure from walking among the casinos along the Strip in this new symbolic space. Hundreds every hour of the day make their way from the spectacular edifices at the southern end, especially the Luxor and the MGM Grand, several blocks north to the spectacular Venetian and the Eiffel Tower of the Paris Casino on one side, and the Mirage/Treasure Island complex on the other, with its spectacular exterior light-and-sound shows. In short, not only has the Strip become a theme park but it also has developed features of an urbanized environment in that it nurtures and draws out pedestrian traffic from within the casinos themselves. This is certainly a new phenomenon, and it has led the central city of Las Vegas to strike back with its own, controversial pedestrian mall attraction, the Fremont Street Experience

(Gottdiener, Collins, and Dickens, 1999). The latter, unlike the Strip, has been only marginally successful.

A final characteristic of Las Vegas involves the role of thematic elements in the development of the gambling economy. In the abstract, the gaming-based economy of Las Vegas is not much different from other cities that have undergone restructuring during the deindustrialization of advanced capitalism. Its employment base is overwhelmingly dominated by the service sector, like those of Washington, D.C., Boston, New York, and other large cities. Yet the gambling basis of Las Vegas sets that city apart from these other service-oriented economies. Competition through signs and image-based differentiation exploits the symbolic value of products rather than their use- or exchange values. As the former type of competition comes to define the economy, we progress toward a postmodern culture where sign-value dominates all transactions (see the discussion of Baudrillard, in Chapter 2).

Until recently, Las Vegas themes have drawn from a narrow but increasingly diverse repertoire of sources. The earliest casino fantasies borrowed from associations with casino gambling around the world (e.g., the Wild West, Monte Carlo, or Riviera motifs) or adopted a somewhat hokey Hollywood version of the Arabian Nights fantasy. More recently, casino designs have plundered the past by resurrecting the themes of medieval Europe, Rome, and ancient Egypt. Other casinos drew more directly from exotic fantasy motifs such as the popular "tropical paradise" theme. All of these symbolic appeals are quite common to our popular culture. It is interesting to speculate where Las Vegas environments might be going in the future.

From recent developments it seems that casino-resorts are definitely drawing most directly on an urban motif. The casino re-creations of New York City and of Paris, the simulation of Venice at the Venetian, and the equally impressive simulation of the Lake Como district at the Bellagio are excellent examples of urban street re-creations for the purpose of shopping and entertainment. These examples suggest that the urban ambiance and street culture of the large, historically significant central city, rather than depictions of popular fantasies, is the preferred direction of new casino planning. In this sense, proposed thematic environments aim to capture both the scale of the city and its unique culture of pedestrian space, where chance encounters, specialized commercial shopping, restaurants, and the street milieu of the urban walker intermingle. This is all very much like the way malls function as well.

Because this type of city culture is on the decline in the United States within actually existing urban places, this more recent trend for Strip casinos is quite ironic. With advancing suburbanization, as central city districts themselves die, they are recycled as images and themes for Las Vegas casinos and large suburban shopping malls, as we have seen. One can say, then, that Las Vegas casinos help keep urban culture alive in a certain fashion. The city itself has become a theme. New York, Venice, and Paris are represented by casinos simulating New York, Venice, and Paris. As discussed in Chapter 7, this shift to image and simulation in our culture of leisure has negative as well as positive aspects.

## The Theme Park

Restaurants, malls, and even airports are environments that people use every day. Commercial establishments as a whole have experienced increased competition for customers because of alternate locations that are now easy to reach. Retailing and restaurants, in particular, are no longer dependent on the central city, especially its department stores, ethnic neighborhoods, or business districts. Commercial activities can now be found throughout the ever-expanding metropolitan regions, drawing customers from among those who are able to commute to and from preferred consumer locations, work, and home. As we have seen, with intensified competition has come an increasing reliance on the use of themed environments. By using architectural and retailing elements that appeal to shoppers, built forms such as malls have achieved a commercial success rivaling that of central business districts. The mall is not just a location for buying commodities, however. It is very much a *place,* an important space, just like the downtown central city area that draws people to it for a variety of reasons.

The most spectacularly successful themed environment is Disneyland, in Anaheim, California, followed closely by the much larger Disneyworld in Orlando, Florida. The Disney theme park form is the most popular attraction on earth. It has been exported to Japan and France and has influenced both the construction and the operation of similar themed amusement parks the world over. Most recently, Disney-style amusement areas have been altered for use in urban and suburban development because of the success of overt, obvious theming in attracting customers to retailing and housing. Unlike the symbolic forms encountered in daily life, however, the theme park remains a destination that people choose for special recreational breaks, especially for planned family vacations. When most visitors go to Disneyworld, for example, they do so as families who have flown in from another area and have arranged hotel accommodations for the duration of their visit.

What was so remarkable about the original Disneyland that produced the global mass phenomenon of the popular theme park? We might guess that corporate advertising and the close link between Disneyland and the many films of the Disney Company fueled the popularity and acceptability of the images and fantasies upon which the park experience is based. Walt Disney used merchandising in tandem with his cartoons as early as the 1930s. The Mickey Mouse watch was already a popular consumer item then—a fact that attests to Americans' long-standing familiarity with Disney images. In addition, as discussed in Chapter 2, theme parks have important antecedents in world expositions and state fairs, whose entertaining features the present attractions exploit. Surely these factors are a major part of the success story. However, at the time of its construction, in the 1950s, Disneyland provided an encounter for its visitors that was so unique and compelling that it became a new form of commercial enterprise. People not only visited the park for the rides or merchandise that it offered—as they do state fairs—but also for the park space itself. Experience of Disneyland's *entertaining* environment is its own reward, as is true also of the large, fully enclosed mall and of other successful, hybrid environments that mix a social activity with a themed, designed space that also entertains (such as shoppertainment, eatertainment, leisuretainment, and the like).

## Disneyland

By the early 1990s, more than 300 million people had visited Disneyland— many more people than the present population of the United States. Built on a 160-acre former orange grove, the original Disneyland opened in 1955 at a cost of $17 million. Then many critics argued that the park would not succeed because it did not possess the typical amusement rides, such as a Ferris wheel. But Disney, who went into debt to build the attraction, was not offering a collection of rides. His park was a fantasy environment. This latter aspect became one source of Disneyland's success. As an architectural critic observed: "It is an almost faultless organization for delivering, against cash, almost any type at all of environmental experience that human fancy, however inflamed, could ever devise. Here are pedestrian piazzas, seas, jungles, castles, outerspace, Main Street, the Old West, mountains, more than can be experienced in a single day's visit" (Banham, 1971: 127).

Another aspect of Disneyland's success is the way the park experience fits into and reinforces the merchandising effort of the Disney Corporation. Walt Disney was one of the first businessmen to create a consumer market exclusively for children through the retailing of toy products based on his cartoons and movies. Although most people's incomes during the 1930s were relatively low, Disney had already begun at that time to merchandise successfully spinoff items based on his cartoon characters. As one historian has noted about the social significance of Disney's early efforts in the 1930s, "By cross marketing toys and movies Disney was able to convince critics that movies were not harmful to children, while *persuading children* to gain satisfaction through shopping" (Heller, 1994: A9).

Both parents and children enjoyed the Disney creations at the movies. As the scale of merchandising increased, people around the globe became familiar with Disney characters and spinoff products. By the 1980s, when Disneyworld was built in Orlando, Florida, the themed elements of the park's experience were ubiquitously familiar. According to one writer: "Struggle as we may, it's impossible for Americans to discover Disneyland. The first visit feels like a trip back. From whatever angle, nothing looks fake. Fabricated, yes, fake, no. Disneyland isn't the mimicry of a thing; it's a thing" (Carson, 1992: 17).

Over the years Disneyland has attracted its share of criticism (see Sorkin, 1992). It is reviled for its crass commercialism, for the very merchandising from films that is the basis of its early success, and for its alleged escapism and simulation (see Baudrillard, 1973). To be sure, one of the most penetrating criticisms notes the consummate skill with which the park planners engineered both crowd control and crowd movement. As Carson (1992: 18) observes:

> Militaristic the place isn't; it's hard to be martial in pastel. But militating, certainly. As you queue in those ingenious waiting lines, or stroll in obedience to a traffic flow whose engineering you never register, or take on bric-a-brac at concession areas designed not as breaks in the continuity but proofs of it, what you and your 10 or 20 thousand cohorts are performing is a huge, choreographed, aesthetically quite arresting species of close-order drill in mufti.

Besides its share of criticism, Disneyland has also attracted the admiration of some important city planners, such as James Rouse, the developer of many commercial themed environments and of the new town of Columbia, Maryland (Gottdiener, 1995: 103). According to Charles Moore (quoted in Carson, 1992: 20): "People often use Disneyland as a synonym for the facile, shallow and fake. It just doesn't wash. This incredibly energetic collection of environmental experiences offers enough lessons for a whole architectural education in all the things that matter—community and reality, private memory and inhabitation, as well as some technical lessons in propinquity and choreography."

Some observers have even commented on the *utopian* nature of Disney "town planning." They note that its physical infrastructure performs remarkably well, especially given the large numbers of people visiting the park daily. As we shall see, the Disney Company recently entered the housing development industry itself. Whatever its appeal to architects and designers, we know that Disneyland over the years has had a profound impact on the construction of themed environments across the country by blending common mass culture symbols and an appealing physical design. Let us examine this phenomenon more closely, because of its great influence.

*The Structure of the Park.*   The theme park known as Disneyland has a definite structure that is also replicated from Disneyland to Disneyland, whatever the global location. The area is fronted by a large parking lot in which visitors must abandon their cars as their very first act upon arrival and become pedestrians. At the entrance they purchase tickets that allow them full access to the rides inside. The grand entrance of the park itself is a simulation of Main Street America and represents Disney's idealization of the small midwestern town where he grew up. Main Street is a bisecting road that serves as the gateway to the rest of the park, and along its contours retailers sell assorted Disney merchandise. Disneyland contains four separate realms, three representations of towns and an open air center that features food and entertainment. Each realm represents domains developed by the Disney Corporation in films and television shows over the years: Tomorrowland, a sophomoric representation of futurism; Frontierland, the scene of old Disney successes, such as Davy Crockett, and a representation of the early days of American settlement; Adventureland, a series of escapist fantasies ranging from Tom Sawyer rafting to jungle safari cruises; and Fantasyland, the virtual site of Disney cartoon fantasies and animated films. Fantasyland also contains the mock Matterhorn mountain and Sleeping Beauty's Castle (which could as well be Snow White's or Cinderella's). The castle, which commonly serves as the distinguishing feature or sign of Disneyland as a whole in publicity images, is located at the end of the gateway road (Main Street).

The three mock towns of the park consist of the area around Main Street; New Orleans Square, which is an open-air minicenter that features food and is the site of some more popular park rides, such as Pirates of the Caribbean; and Toontown, which was added to Disneyland after the success of the film *Roger Rabbit*. Amusement rides are distributed all around the park area, within each realm and minicenter. The landscape is upgraded from time to time by the addition or subtraction of attractions. For example, ten years ago the upper left area of the park consisted of the realm of "Bear Country," which was dedicated to simulated amusements representing country and western culture of the "Hee Haw" variety. Market studies revealed that this area was the least frequented by park visitors. It is now gone, having been replaced entirely by Toontown. Despite this change, and the periodic replacement or additions of rides, the classic Disneyland form remains roughly the same. Disneyworld, in Orlando, Florida, contains a larger version of this scheme, as well as additional amusement areas, such as the immense Epcot Center, with its villages of the world, rides, and exhibits.

*Analysis of the Park.*   Disneyland has been analyzed and interpreted many times and in many places. According to Michael Real (1977), for example, the success of Disneyland is the result of the success of Disney cartoons, films, and television shows. Visitors are primed by years of familiarity with Disney images before they enter the park and participate in its themed environment. In this sense, Disneyland is an extension of the media culture in the same way as the mall experience is an extension of the mass consumer culture of advertising, marketing, and retailing. In contrast, Marxist critics make note of the way the park's environment is saturated with corporate references. Major franchise chains run the food concessions, and the rides are "brought to you by" corporate sponsors. It is even possible to offer an analysis of the various sections of the park as signifiers for phases of capitalist historical development (Gottdiener, 1995: 113). Thus, Frontierland can be interpreted as a reference to the stage of predatory capitalism; Adventureland, as a representation of colonialism/imperialism; Tomorrowland, as state-financed capitalism, or the military-industrial complex; New Orleans Square as a signifier for venture capital; and lastly, Main Street as the period of family and mercantile capitalism.

In the latter interpretation, the sections of Disneyland represent snapshots in a capitalist family album, documenting the different manifestations of its political economic development within separate historical times and various social contexts. Societal experiences from the history of America that are part of our common culture provide the fantasy themes for the sections of the park. These include the folklore of frontier days; the Hollywood images of adventure in the wake of colonialism, such as the film *The African Queen;* the adolescent fantasies of spectacular careers in technology; the military and space exploration that are pumped up by school science fairs; and the more mundane comfort of familiar commercial centers, such as Main Street, USA. The Disneyland experience, therefore, depicts a popular version of American history (Heller, 1994: A8).

There is, however, much more to Disneyland than a simple array of fantasies derived from the development of American political economy. The classic form of the park is arguably the most successful themed environment in history, judging by the number of visitors around the globe and the manner by which other themed amusement parks have imitated the designs of Disney. I contend that there are two sources for this success in the planning of the space. The first involves the special vision that Walt Disney brought to the design of park elements, based on fantasies of his midwest adolescence. The second involves a contrast between the experience of the park itself and the area surrounding it—namely suburban America (originally, suburban southern California).

## The Vision of Disney

According to the vision of its originator, who drafted the structure of the park in the 1950s, Disneyland provides adults with a return to childhood and children with an idealized version of community. As the plaque dedicated at the opening on July 17, 1955, states: "To all who come to this happy place: Welcome. Disneyland is your land. Here age relives fond memories of the past . . . and here youth may savor the challenge and promise of the future."

Material from several biographies of Disney (Schickel, 1968; Thomas, 1977) reveals that he sought to recapture memories of his own youth by designing a space containing the fantasies of his childhood, including a recreation of the type of small midwestern town where he grew up. The material framing of this fantasy invocation uses Main Street as the gateway to the park experience. As Carson (1992: 20) notes, "It was only a quarter-century before 1955 that Sinclair Lewis had excoriated the conventionality that Walt now idealized. His novel's title, of course, was *Main Street*."

In the previous section of this chapter, I suggested that we can trace the fantasy or thematic bases for the separate realms of Disneyland to stories associated with the development of U.S. capitalism. Interpreted in this way, Disneyland functions as a type of American history. However, we can also read the park structure in the more personal way that Disney himself intended. If its origins lie in the desire to recapture youth, then the various sections of the park can be read as aspects of children's play. Adventureland, for example, becomes the realm of childhood games such as cops and robbers or cowboys and Indians. It is the backyard space where play came alive for children acting as superheroes and comic strip characters. Frontierland, in contrast, is the realm of the boy scouts or summer vacations to national parks and the homes of folk heroes. Tomorrowland represents the world of science and industry much as it is presented in science fiction literature, inspiring grade school children to envision themselves in spectacular careers in technology. Finally, Fantasyland is quite literally the realm of dreams, fables, and bedtime stories that are the cultural fodder of children the world over. Many of Disney's movie and television themes came directly from the realm of classic children's stories—Snow White, the Three Little Pigs, Cinderella, Pinocchio, and so on.

In short, then, Disneyland can be interpreted both socially and personally. The first reading relates the themes of the separate realms to historical periods in the development of our society as depicted in popular culture—that is, not as historically accurate history, of course. The second shows how Walt Disney actualized through the production of a material environment the desire to recapture elements of his lost youth. Disney's confidence that the public at large would also find enjoyment and entertainment in a themed space drawing on childhood memories has been borne out often by the continuing success of Disneyland and its replications around the world.

## Disneyland Versus Suburbia

Theme parks are not city-based phenomena. They emerged in suburban regions as the majority of Americans took up residence there after World War II. As already noted, any visitor to a theme park (except those imitating jungle safaris that involve live animals) must abandon the private auto and experience the environment as a *pedestrian.* This status stands in sharp contrast to the everyday one of being a commuter in an automobile- and train-dependent world of suburban or urban life. In suburbia the car is a necessity and walking is discouraged by the layout of housing subdivisions that rarely, if ever, offer pedestrian paths. It is not stretching things to say that suburban housing developments are hostile to pedestrians (Langdon,

1994). Because most visitors to the park come from the areas outside the central city, their experience of the communion of the crowd is a rare occasion. Suburbanites also find a classic *urban* experience of this kind at malls. Lately, as crime levels have risen in the city and new lifestyle changes, such as cocooning, now characterize the routines of urban residents, even the latter seem to enjoy the unfettered, crime-free pedestrian environment of the theme park.

When high crime threatens enjoyment of city public spaces, malls and theme parks are desirable substitutes for that same experience. It is also for this reason that, despite the apparently infinite possibilities open to Las Vegas casino developers for the pursuit of new fantasy themes, they seem to gravitate back toward megastructures that replicate central city spaces, such as the Venetian, Parisian, or New York–themed casinos discussed in the last chapter. People miss the open and free city and the thrill of pedestrian status within the crowd. Some observers have likened this experience to eroticism (Barthes, 1970–1971) or to the unabashed joy and freedom of serendipitous encounters (Lefebvre, 1974).

Second, Disneyland-style theme parks offer a contrast in the serving and eating of *food*. At home, in everyday life, food is designed for subsistence and nourishment. Meals are planned and budgeted. But families eat together only when they can all be in the same place, at the same time—a usually difficult chore, given the complexity of everyone's schedules today. At the theme park, food is part of the celebration. It is festival or state fair food. People can buy things to eat any time and at almost any location within the park. They are never far from food. They eat snacks while walking—a classic joy of city living. Compare this to a freeway commuter who is munching on a noontime fast-food burger or burrito with one hand while menacing traffic in all the other lanes. In addition, most theme parks offer a cornucopia of food choices, although none of them may be up to gourmet tastes, much less to acceptable nutritional standards. Along with the expected fast-food franchises, themed environments often offer variations on ethnic dinning, and other exotic treats. Of course, the prices for all this enjoyment are quite high compared to those in food outlets outside the park.

Experiencing the park also transforms *family relations*. At home the father rules and the mother manages. Adults define the agenda of daily life. Children exist within a social world of parent expectations. At the park, things are different—even reversed. The kids most often define the routine of the park visit. They direct their parents to the attractions they would most like to see. Whereas the home tends to be adult centered in its structuring of behavior, the theme park is child centered.

Fourth, in our daily lives *entertainment* is strictly defined by the available time we have after work and family chores. Most people do not leave home in the evening during the week, but are instead found in front of their television sets, if they have the time to watch. Mass media entertainment, in addition, is a spectacle. People sit passively and view commercialized programming or videotapes. Our society even has a name for the person who engages frequently in this behavior—"couch potato." At the park, entertainment is a festival, not a spectacle (Debord, 1970; Lefebvre, 1971). The urban experience of the crowd is active and constantly surprising. Beyond the rides and amusements, both the park and the people in it are also sources of entertainment.

Fifth, *clothing* in everyday life is highly regimented both by fashion rules and by institutional norms. Jobs require their own special styles, and children in school are slaves to the conformity of their peers' mode of dress. The work uniform is usually constraining for men and women who have to "dress up" to pursue their respective careers. At the park, dressing is for leisure and play. People appear as tourists. Some can even be seen wearing stylized merchandise sold at the park, such as funny hats or mouse ears.

A visit to a theme park also provides people with the illusion of escaping from the demands of their own *economy*. At home they are hemmed in by the realities of capitalism: the need to work, to budget, to save. Everything one desires has a price. At the park, once visitors can afford to purchase the expensive ticket, which runs over $20 at most parks, they then experience the *illusion* of cornucopia or a visit to the classic "land of cockaigne" where everything is "free." Disneyland used to have one charge for entering the park and then a scale of charges for each of its rides. It was no doubt assumed at the time that people would balk at paying one large sum at the start of their experience, and so the ultimate cost of a day at the park was hidden by this pricing mechanism. Over the years, however, public pressure and a different style of marketing prevailed. The fee structure was changed to a single admission at the entrance. As noted, however, this onetime charge is not cheap. A family of four can expect to pay more than $100 to enter. This expense seems not to deter the average American family one bit, judging by the unparalleled yearly customer levels for Disneyland and Disneyworld; and it does have the added merit for park officials of keeping the poor out.

Finally, the park experience involves a nonquotidian encounter with *architecture*. Here the built environment itself is a form of entertainment.

Each structure provides its own fantasy. The park itself is architecture that entertains. At home, in contrast, places of work lack symbols, and the home is principally a sign of status, lacking the kind of richly endowed themes characteristic of places like Disneyland.

In sum, theme parks are fun. They entertain. In addition, they provide visitors with definite and enjoyable contrasts to their daily lives. Much of this experience is the result of recreating an urban-style environment in a safe and nonthreatening but also very commercial atmosphere. However, the theme park as developed by Disney and others also offers people sharp contrasts with the constraints, regimentation, and normative burdens of their everyday existence. A park visit is a holiday from the quotidian responsibilities of adulthood. Children lead the way, all rides are free, the ordinarily forbidden fast foods are the normal mode of nourishment, and even mouse ears can be worn without evoking negative reactions from others.

On balance, then, I believe Disneyland has succeeded not so much because it recreates the experience of youth alone, nor because it materializes the myths of capitalist development as a celebration of American society's fantasies, but largely because it liberates people from the constraints of everyday life, especially life that yearns for the freedom and serendipitous possibilities of urban culture (see Cohen and Taylor, 1992). This latter feature, coupled with the holiday aspects of food, clothing, and leisure, is what makes the park so successful, and it has led to conscious imitation in countless other themed parks across the country. It is also these dimensions that explain why Disneyworld, in particular, is the single most popular vacation destination in the world.

### Beyond the Disney Experience

Much attention has been paid by academics to the Disney themed environments, and rightly so. Many critics of Disneyland and its offshoots consider the Disney Corporation the perfecter of theme parks but fault those parks for being products of Hollywood glitz and east coast corporate profit-making mentalities. They adopt a critical, elite perspective that finds only consumer manipulation behind themed facades and only corporate greed behind the proliferation of themed environments (Sorkin, 1992). Largely this view is true; but like other reductionist criticisms of American culture, it is only partially true. As we have seen in previous discussions, there are many elements that converge to create an emphasis on a meaningful environment in daily life. These factors create multileveled experiences and symbolic milieus. Our discussion of Disneyland, in particular, illustrates the way in which Disney's nostalgic yearning for a lost youth and for the intimate scale of midwestern small towns articulated with the goals of a large corporation interested in profit. The need of producers for the realization of capital does not enter the public's perception of their own experience. Instead, the act of consumption—with its connections to fantasy and symbol—and the quest for meaning characterize the everyday experience of themed environments. Commercial themed environments succeed not because of corporate will alone but also because places like Disneyworld are entertaining.

The satisfaction of this experience is grounded also in a more visceral connection—namely the satisfaction of the individual's desire for a sense of community, for pedestrian communion in public spaces. People seem to crave the street-level intimacy created by many themed environments, which is lacking in ordinary life, due to the destruction of public space through suburbanization and the terror of urban crime. The fact that this latter need is satisfied through the activities of the very same profit-making enterprises that exploit themed environments should not obscure its fundamental role, along with the quest for meaning, in the way humans structure everyday life. In this sense, although it is a long way in social development from the simple but redolently symbolic ancient city of Athens to the high-powered retailing and entertainment complexes at the Mall of America or Disneyland, the two different environments are both extensions of the human need for a material environment that signifies and has meaning.

As a means of amplifying this idea, let us examine the case of country and western singer Dolly Parton and her prospering theme park Dollywood, located near the small Tennessee mountain town of Pigeon Forge, in the foothills of Smoky Mountain National Park.

## Dollywood and the Generalized Need for Themed Environments

The name of this theme park is an obvious, conscious attempt by Dolly Parton to play off the well-known Hollywood sign as a signifier for her own pet project. In keeping with this intent, the Dollywood management has skillfully imported to the "down home" area of Pigeon Forge all the corporate aspects of running a successful theme park, perfected by generations of Disneyland-style establishments. The significance of Dollywood is that its very success and scale testify to the generalizability of themed appeals and of the techniques of consumer manipulation. As perfected by Disney, the themed park environment is thoroughly transportable to virtually any milieu and seemingly any group with substantial financial backing. When social critics search for mass media and corporate cultural conspiracies while exploring the causes of the themed environment phenomenon (see Sorkin, 1992; Hannigan, 1998), they miss the more important point regarding the seemingly universal applicability of theme park engineering to a variety of cultural contexts. In this connection, it is interesting that Dollywood recently announced its negotiations with Japanese investors for a Dollywood park in Japan—a culture as far removed from the Appalachian symbolic universe as one can probably get on this earth. Apparently, inspiration for meaningful milieus everywhere derives increasingly from the canned culture of Hollywood, popular music, and television.

The Dollywood theme park consists of 400 acres, with 93 of these having been developed as of 1994. Originally this land was occupied by Silver Dollar City, a locally geared attraction featuring Smoky Mountains/Appalachian crafts, owned by Jack Herschend. Most of the park at this point was undeveloped. In the 1980s, Parton teamed up with Herschend, lending her name to a new venture that would develop the park's national appeal as a tourist attraction. Because Pigeon Forge is close to her birthplace, Parton was very familiar with the area and had many relatives still living there. Besides her name, she, like Walt Disney, also brought a personal vision to the proposed theme. Parton sought to enshrine her own rags-to-riches story, as a small-town Appalachian girl born into poverty (her father was a poor tobacco farmer) who had become an international celebrity via a singing career that crossed over from country and western to popular music. The original focus of the proposed park was the Dolly Parton Museum, featuring re-creations of her birth home, artifacts from mountain culture, and extensive video, audio, and printed displays from her career. Around this shrine, Parton and her partners created a general theme that articulated with the local Smoky Mountain culture. The park features folksy, down home, country attractions pumped up by marketing and promotional techniques perfected by the Disney Corporation, including Disney-style regulation of customers—"no litter, no alcohol, no bare feet on young 'uns" (*Travel Weekly,* 1986).

Pigeon Forge, located on former Cherokee hunting ground, has a population of only 2,800. It lies along the route to the Smoky Mountain National Park, the most-visited national park in the country. It is also not far from the metropolitan area of Knoxville, Tennessee, and other larger towns that have thriving motel businesses due to their proximity to recreational areas. Parton's original proposal was for a 9-acre, $5 million expansion of Silver Dollar City. In a meeting with the local town board and state politicians, her new corporation persuaded the city to spend $600,000, and the state, $1.6 million, in public funds for infrastructure improvements including new streets and sewer lines. The park opened in 1986, with attendance at 10,000 a day. By 1993 the annual number of customers was over 9 million. Original ticket prices in 1986 were $12.95 for adults, and $9.95 for children between ages 4 and 11 (admission for children under 4 was free). By 1994 the down-home pricing system had graduated to $23.99 for adults, $15.99 for children between 3 and 11 (free for children under 3), and $20.99 for senior citizens. This most recent price structure places Dollywood squarely in the same cost range as Disneyland in Anaheim or Universal Studios in Burbank, California.

Dollywood is still evolving and does not have the defined, timeless structure of Disneyland. It combines typical country state fair elements with the features of a fully actualized amusement park. It offers a variety of country-style foods (the number of restaurants and fast-food places continues to increase), craft demonstrations, and simulated Appalachian cultural artifacts and scenery. The major draw of the park is Parton's connection to the world of popular music. Big-name country stars play in several venues, and lately Dollywood has been exploiting popular music as well, such as a 1950s "oldies" revival. The park's only competitors in the region, with regard to the quality of musical attractions, are in Branson, Missouri, and Nashville, Tennessee. In summer 1992, twenty-five top names in country music performed at Dollywood.

Dollywood is no Disneyland, and lacks the latter's well-developed fantasy worlds. The park consists of a prior existing attraction based on Appalachian home crafts and an overlay of Dolly Parton's personal rise to fame and her connections with the commercial world of country music and Hollywood. Nevertheless, as it develops and its separate realms evolve into sharper relief, it has acquired its own special appeal as a family vacation destination.

At the level of merchandising, however, the park managers have borrowed much from the Disney Corporation. Dollywood's first restaurant was called Aunt Granny's—an excellent example of redundant semiotic naming that doubles the message of nurturing. Aunt Granny's featured country cooking, including some of "Dolly's very own recipes." Most food places featured beef and pork barbecue, ham and beans, hamburgers, and southern fried chicken. More recently, pizza was added to the list of affordable foods, and a more upscale restaurant, the Backstage, was built to cater to the increasing numbers of urbanites attracted to big-name country and

*Map of Dollywood*

western entertainment. The park now boasts 35 separate retail stores, including several that cater to imitators of Dolly's style of dressing. In 1991 the Dollywood Corporation proposed to build a 12,000-square-foot exit shop. According to officials of the park: "Nobody will be able to leave the park without going through this shop. We'll have a sampling of merchandise from all the shops in the park here" (*Amusement Business*, 1991).

The park management also has extended the times of the year when they could be open for business. No longer just a summer attraction, Dollywood is now open for a fall crafts festival, a winter carnival or "Smoky Mountain Christmas," and a spring attraction. In 1989 the park underwent a $10 million expansion to incorporate a Victorian-themed village that is open the year around.

At Dollywood, merchandising and advertising synthesize the two distinct codes of Appalachian mountain culture on the one hand, and glitzy show-business signifiers on the other. Parton never ceases to inject homespun rhetoric into her public announcements of new attractions. After unveiling plans for a new, multimillion-dollar expansion called "music road," Dolly commented, "I am hoping for a really good tobacco crop to pay for all this" (*Amusement Business*, 1992).

The business logic of Dollywood is also pure corporate Disney. Although few patrons of Disneyland derive a deeply meaningful experience from the re-creation of midwestern small-town life and the youthful fantasies of boyhood games represented by the Disney universe, Disneyland as a theme park has proved its ability to continually entertain millions with its blend of simulated amusements. No doubt a few customers of Dollywood derive a deep, meaningful experience through contact with its simulations of Appalachian culture. But most are drawn by the combination of country music attractions with the easy availability of ham and beans, barbecued ribs, and southern fried chicken—a mix also overlaid by Dolly's special appeal as just "one of the folks" despite her $100 million fortune. Using these elements Parton's park seems firmly established as a packaged amusement in the Disney form, if not in content.

## Disney in the City: Tourism and Themed Environments

Theming has been utilized most often by individual enterprises caught in competitive environments, as a means of attracting customers where the actual products being offered do not differ greatly from one seller to the next. Designer clothes and Las Vegas casinos are good examples. Recently, a separate kind of economic condition has also led to theming. Since the 1970s central cities have reeled under the impact of social forces that have stripped away both a middle-class population once residing there and an industrial manufacturing economic base that gave urban communities jobs, revenue from taxes, and general social stability. As a consequence, cities have had to search hard for new ways to make money. Beginning with the 1980s and increasingly so today, many cities have looked to the expanding presence of tourists as a means to acquire wealth. Local urban economies have shifted from their previous emphasis on manufacturing—an emphasis belonging to the pre-1980s period—to an almost singular focus on promoting tourism and commercial activities that attract upscale consumers to the downtown area. In all of these aspects, themed environments figure most prominently as part of the overall urban recovery strategy.

New York City today is perhaps the best example of the above change in economic emphasis. Under the aggressive leadership of Mayor Rudolph Giuliani, the center of Manhattan, Times Square, became the focal point of an ambitious redevelopment scheme that now serves as a model for other inner-city areas left in dire straits by urban decline. For decades, the stretch of territory between Broadway and the 9th Avenue Port Authority Bus Station complex could have been closely compared to a particular circle of hell. Off-limits to decent folk, this stretch was the scene of low-rent porno theaters, sex shops, and flophouses. Hookers, pimps, junkies, and homosexual cruisers lined the streets at all hours, plying the flesh trade. Giuliani's all-out war against these breeding grounds of street crime evoked controversy and accusations of gestapo-like tactics against the sex trade and the homeless, as well as objections from some who yearned for the perpetuation of this deviant zone (see Delaney, 1999). Despite almost fifty legal challenges to the condemnation of buildings and the steamrolling renovation activities, the project moved forward with rapidity—particularly once the Disney Corporation signed on. During the 1990s a complete transformation occurred that turned the Times Square area and the former nether regions of 42nd Street into a premier tourist attraction. This effort was so successful that by 1999 New York City had surpassed Las Vegas as the nation's number-two vacation destination (Orlando, Florida, is still number one).

This remarkable change was spearheaded by the Disney Corporation, which opened a merchandise store at the corner of 42nd Street and Broadway, and renovated a theater to showcase Disney-produced musicals such as *Beauty and the Beast.* The complex was designed by the famed architect of simulated, themed environments, Jon Jerde, who also created Universal Studio's CityWalk and downtown Las Vegas's Fremont Street Experience. To effect the renovation of the area, the City of New York created a limited public-private partnership directed by a new municipal concept, the Urban Entertainment Development zone, which mobilized almost $2 billion in joint public- and private-sector funds. Themed restaurants attracted to the site include the ESPN Zone and the All-Star Café, both with sports-oriented motifs, and nearby, a Harley Davidson Café, a Mars 2112 franchise, along with the staples—Planet Hollywood and the Hard Rock Café. Both Disney and the World Wrestling Federation (WWF) opened merchandising stores, adding to the already hyperactive motifed merchandising of the themed restaurants. In a rather bizarre turn of events, once the entire complex had been finished and was proving a success, the National Rifle Association proposed a themed restaurant of its own for the 42nd Street area; but the project immediately generated stiff resistance from native New Yorkers.

Times Square's special combination of themed restaurants (many of which are connected to media industries) with the retail merchandising of trademarked goods produced by other corporations, and with themed, fantasy environments designed by architects adept at simulation, may be the envy of other cities longing for downtown renewal; but it also has raised concerns that are now growing. Some observers worry about the "Disneyfication of the metropolis" (Warren, 1994)—that is, the sacrifice of authentic urban culture, locally owned stores, unique subcultures, and street life to the corporate sanitizing of entire city sectors through the construction of simulations that owe their thematic appeal to Hollywood and other media industries. To be sure, the renovation of Times Square has turned it into a popular draw for tourists and has helped propel New York City upward in the ranks of preferred visitor destinations. But a growing number of people now recognize that positive aspects of their local culture—a certain sense of the city that is created only through unorchestrated, lived activity in the truly unhindered street scene of urban existence—are pulverized and swept away by all that neon, media merchandising, and theming. Opponents ask: How different is the "new" Times Square from architect Jerde's other project, the totally simulated CityWalk at Universal's Burbank movie studio? In short, Times Square may be an unqualified commercial success, but is it *really* New York City? When tourists visit, are they not in essence going to Disneyworld rather than to New York? The increasingly troubling questions associated with commercially themed and simulation-infested urban redevelopment schemes will be discussed more fully in Chapter 7.

## Celebration

Ever since the opening of the original Disneyland in the 1950s, the Disney Corporation has been lauded in some circles for its imaginative town planning. In the 1990s, the Walt Disney Company entered the realm of land speculation and housing development, betting that it could turn a swampy part of Florida into cash. Using thematic elements of small-town life that are now associated with the fashionable "new urbanism," they built the community of Celebration, which comprises both moderately and expensively priced single-family homes. The small-town theme is reinforced by the community's special, unifying symbol. As described by reporter Karal

Marling, "The official Disney-designed seal for Celebration shows a little girl on a bicycle zipping along a pretty tree-lined street in blessed safety, her ponytail streaming out behind her in the Florida sunshine" (Marling, 1999: B-9). Thematic elements were strictly engineered into the homes and backed up by a rigid plan book that guided property owners in the selection of permissible individual touches to their houses. The entire effort had the effect of reinforcing conformity to the most minute aspects of theming and simulation in the regulation of daily life. Celebration is not a themed environment that people visit and then leave, savoring the entertainment value of the experience. Celebration is a themed and simulated environment within which people live. In Marling's words:

> This visual consistency is a strong selling point for the upscale houses, of course, but it is also an irritant: the 'porch police' are apt to visit those with an un-communal taste for purple polka dots on their draperies. Because the look of Celebration cries out for dormers, the builders supplied them, but because dormer spaces don't fit into the plan of a contemporary American home, they are fake ones, with the windowpanes painted black.

Several books have appeared about Celebration, cataloging the discontents of living there, despite the best efforts of Disney planning (Frantz and Collins, 1999; Ross, 2000). Along with the pioneer "new urbanism" community Seaside, designed by Duany and Plater-Zybeck, also in Florida, Celebration represents an alternative to the more commonplace suburban mode of living. Within the latter mode, people tend to have minimal thematic elements attached to their homes. The new style sells housing by advocating the additional appeal of participating in a thematic environment that is supposed to offer a greater degree of personal and family happiness. Although there is no evidence that greater happiness results from residing in overtly themed housing spaces like Celebration and Seaside, the hunger of middle-class people for more meaning in their personal lives will no doubt support similar development efforts.

## Extensions of Themed Environments

### Corporate Extensions

As our discussions of Dollywood and Times Square show, the theme park technique is highly mobile, being applicable to a variety of contexts. As a mode for the realization of capital, it is exportable to other countries and cultures exposed to our popular culture. Because American mass cultural forms—particularly those produced by Hollywood and the rock industry—are found around the world, fantasies and simulated environments based on them are universal. Theme parks, unlike malls, restaurants, and other commercial ventures, are popular as profit-making enterprises because they do not need to sell a product, only an experience. They market attractions to potential customers, and they channel visitors through the space by careful engineering and crowd control. The fact that in most cases they are also successful in selling merchandise and food makes them powerful moneymakers.

This book has argued that the increasing use of themed environments is the consequence of increased competition for consumer dollars during the present period of highly mobile shoppers, alternate consumption locations, and increasingly diverse lifestyle choices. The preceding discussions of theme parks, Las Vegas casinos, and urban redevelopment schemes, however, demonstrate an additional aspect of the shift to themed environments. The mall form and the open-air theme park form recreate the ludic and entertaining elements of urban street culture in a safe, controlled, and commodified environment. They confer pedestrian status on people and thus allow participation in the crowd. This highly regulated "public" experience within theme parks and malls, nevertheless, seems quite enjoyable for its own sake. Along with participation in fantasies and symbolic milieus, therefore, the new shopping and consuming spaces also provide people with a controlled, crime-free, entertaining crowd experience. When these milieus are coupled with retailing, as in the new mall airports, they also allow individuals to realize their consumer selves, which have been primed by hours of television watching and exposure to mass advertising (see Chapter 6).

Some American corporations have turned underutilized urban resources or abandoned factories into theme park developments. The Auto World theme park in Flint, Michigan, unveiled after manufacturing left that city due to the deindustrialization of the American auto industry, was an unmitigated failure. However, other examples have been more successful. The Hershey Corporation in Hershey, Pennsylvania, developed land adjacent to its chocolate factory into a large theme park. It contains four roller coasters and the tallest wet slide in the country, as well as nearly 50 other amusement rides. In addition, Hershey Park contains an 11-acre zoo and special rides designed just for small children. In 1996, admission tickets cost $20.95 for adults and $14.95 for children between the ages of 3 and 8. The beer maker Anheuser-Busch has developed a theme park concept called Busch Gardens. Like other amusement areas, this one contains rides and various other entertainments and attractions for families. Busch Gardens has locations in Virginia and Florida. Tickets for the latter in 1995 were $30.50 for adults and $25.50 for children ages 3 to 9.

In another recent development, the mall form with its themed restaurants and retailers has been imported onto university campuses. A recent report notes the following:

> They stood eye to eye and nose to nose for almost 40 minutes, exchanging heavy talk, soulful looks and angry glares outside Mrs. Fields Cookies at the food court entrance. . . . It was the kind of minor mall world melodrama that plays out all the time whenever kids gather over their Whoppers, Pizza Hut personal pan pizzas and Freshens Premium Yogurt—everywhere from Tysons Corner Center in suburban Washington to the Galleria in Dallas and Phipps Plaza in Atlanta. The only difference was that this was no shopping center, it was the student union at Boston University (Applebome, 1995: 16).

The report goes on to contrast this scene with the one at Harvard University, across the Charles River, where students prefer the elite facilities of elegant dining areas such as Dunster Hall. "No one expects a Jack in the Box or a Taco Bell in Harvard Yard, though even Harvard will offer an upscale grazing emporium on campus this fall that includes a familiar name or two" (Applebome, 1995: 16–17).

According to those interviewed, campus administrations find the mall form a promising way of raising revenues. The University of South Carolina, for example, constructed a fourteen-store shopping center for its students and faculty over ten years ago. Recently, other campuses also have seen the virtues of blending a university environment with the commercial attractiveness of the mall. As this report argues, "Increasingly, the culture and values of the mall are coloring the culture and values of the university. . . . Let's face it, Main Street America doesn't exist anymore. Mall America exists. Why should collegiate life be the last bastion of something that doesn't exist anymore?" (Applebome, 1995: 17). As elsewhere, franchising of food and retailing takes over commerce because of the success of the mall form—the enclosed, themed space of quasi-public communion. But like the "new" Times Square, this "happy" space is in reality a thoroughly commercialized and commodified environment.

Themed environments are being imported into other commercial ventures as well. Many metropolitan areas of the country have experienced difficulty, for example, in keeping their professional sports teams happy in recent years. To maximize their profits, the owners of teams want larger stadiums and more fan attendance. Some cities have responded by creating entertainment complexes that are easy to commute to from the suburbs and are attractive to customers. These complexes, which resemble mall or theme park milieus, are built either within or adjacent to stadiums. Baltimore, for example, redeveloped a sports complex called Camden Yards for the city's baseball team, the Orioles. The complex includes entertainment facilities. Recently, New York City proposed to renovate Yankee Stadium as a "theme park" in order to keep the Yankees happy. According to one report (Purdy, 1995: B–1), there would be "stores and restaurants around the complex and . . . new roads leading to new parking garages at the ball park. . . . Estimates of the project's cost are as high as $600 million, making it the most extensive and expensive strategy for keeping the Yankees in the South Bronx that has yet to be presented."

In this case, as in those previously discussed, a single social activity that attracts a mass of people—professional baseball—is intertwined with an organized and diverse form of commercialism including the mall with its array of stores and food outlets. This latest development should come as little surprise because of the already high degree of merchandising in professional athletics today. In fact, the increasing exploitation of the fans is now the principal way for team franchises to make their money (see Bramlett and Sloan, 2000).

## Commercial Theming Turning Back on Itself: Themed Rock Concerts

If theming is now the powerful means by which commercial interests increasingly compete for the marketing of their products, then it should come as no surprise that the techniques of theming can also be used by the commercial sources of themes. One of our examples, the rock music industry, has been cited as the originator of the most popular themed restaurant chain, the Hard Rock Café. Every event in the industry, every popular product—a new record or a new artist—becomes a way of attracting customers who are seeking a rock-themed eating experience. But like other industries, rock music is also a highly competitive economic sector. Consequently, every group, every artist seeks its own distinctive theme by orchestrating its appearance and attitude to appeal to a mass audience. Themes literally saturate the rock music industry. Hair styles, faces, figures, clothes, desirable consumer objects, and musical genres are all carefully combined to contrive an association with desirable lifestyle symbols.

One effect of this thematic competition is the recent emergence of touring rock concerts that employ elaborate simulations and themes. Examples of this latest trend are the multimillion-dollar, Hollywood-style stage sets constructed for the most recent concert tours of the Rolling Stones and of U2. But megastars who command a large enough audience to sell out a concert are rare. Most of the industry consists of rock groups with smaller followings. Now record companies have discovered the fully themed concert tour as a useful device for appealing to a particular market, which can be targeted with a strategic assembly of select groups. Over the last few years the number of themed concert tours has grown as a consequence of their success in attracting a mass audience. The various participating bands receive unprecedented exposure for their music (Seiler, 2000).

As of the summer of 2000, the following themed tours were in progress: Smokin' Grooves Tour (hip-hop), OzzFest (heavy metal), H.O.R.D.E. Fest (counterculture, hippie music), Lilith Fair (a now-defunct tour of "women's" music), the Warped Tour (skaters, punks, ska), Lollapalooza (the alternative music festival), and more recently, the Y'all-apalooza Tour (country and western music). In sum, the record industry, long the source of theming for other enterprises, has discovered the power of theming for its own marketing purposes in an ever more competitive business environment.

## Sex Tourism

At a certain level, rock music sells the body. Music videos mix muscles, hair, skin, dress, and sexual innuendo to sell records. Because sex sells, as every advertiser knows, it is not surprising to learn that it is also an industry. With the rise of global tourism, in fact, people travel not only to experience fake, simulated environments constructed by Disney-style "imagineering" but also to enjoy the special treats that come from an encounter with an "exotic" culture. In most cases, these exotic tourist destinations are located in the third world and have a long history of crushing poverty that has left many of the local people in desperate circumstances. For socioeconomic reasons (relating to patriarchy, feudalism, and the absence of humanitarian welfare provisions), many tourist destinations are the sites of an active sex trade.

Overseas tourism is invariably themed because hotels and resort complexes use decor and architecture to tie their environments symbolically, if not strictly superficially, to the local culture. People seeking a vacation abroad have their choice of locales, each of which offers a trademark brand of thematic association—Polynesian motifs, Asian delights, African mystery, and Caribbean partying. Working hand in hand with the corporate makeover of third world destinations for the tourist industry is an equally flourishing sex trade that also is often themed.

Beverly Mullings describes a number of examples of Caribbean-based tourism that illustrate this phenomenon. As she demonstrates, sex tourism, like the more general phenomenon of vacationing in exotic places, exploits the fantasy associated with dark, "native" women that exists in the minds of middle-class white males from industrialized countries. "Fantasies associated with travel to the unknown, combined with common-sense theories regarding the naturally libidinous appetites of 'native' women, served to justify sexual practices by European males that would have otherwise been considered morally transgressive in Europe" (Mullings, 2000: 231).

In parts of Asia notorious for their sex trade, such as Thailand or Korea, most of the individuals caught in the business are young women. Mullings points out that the case of the Caribbean is different. As depicted in the Hollywood film *How Stella Got Her Groove Back,* the islands offer a range of sex services that cater to women as well as men. According to Mullings, the images used to market the Caribbean to mainlanders in the United States and Canada trade on fantasies of sun, sea, and sand in exotic locales. To this mix is added the extra element of a possible sexual encounter for both men and women. As each island destination has its own associated themes, so too is the sex trade differentiated among distinctive thematic appeals. For example, Jamaica, with its male subculture of "Rent-a-Dreads," and Barbados, with its "Beach Boys," cater to middle-class women on vacation. Men prefer the dark-skinned, poverty-stricken young women of Cuba, known as *Jineteras,* the mixed-race "Sanky Pankies" of the Dominican Republican, or the light-skinned African Caribbean women in the former Dutch colony of Curaçao, known as *Sandoms.* As Mullings points out, "Although potential consumers may dream of erotic encounters with exotic humans in far-off lands, these fantasies are dependent upon a whole battery of producers to become reality" (2000: 234). The socially constructed, "exotic" erotic visions possessed by travelers from Canada and the United States who frequent Caribbean locations for vacations that include sex are also dependent on themes that are culled from media influences such as Hollywood films, magazines, and television programming.

### Representing the Unrepresentable

So far we have discussed themed environments that represent aspects of our culture that are also found elsewhere, such as in the movies, popular music, or the familiar signs of food and retail franchising. For Disneyland and Dollywood, in fact, success of the park environment is based on the linkage between historical aspects of American culture and the glitzy world of show business. In all cases, symbolic motifs are designed to simulate common fantasies, popular conceptions of history and of exotic locales, nostalgic glorifications of local culture, or idealized conceptions of lost youth. All of the themed environments based on these sources are simulations—artificially recreated milieus, designed for the purposes of entertainment and commerce and demonstrating little interest in accuracy of historical detail or other content. Disneyland's Main Street, for example, is a cartoon-like simulation of a small midwestern town's main street; it is *not* a real main street. However, real midwestern town main streets still do exist, and some may even bear a resemblance to popularized simulations.

Recently, as thematic competition has increased in the commercial world of restaurants and fast-food franchises, malls, parks, and other roadside attractions, several cultural experiences that are not commercial enterprises also have become themed environments. When a memorial to the veterans of the Vietnam War was proposed in the 1970s, an image was recalled of the typical war memorial that can be found not only in the United States but in many other countries around the world. One or more idealized, muscular, and heroically scaled soldiers stand as statues over some dedicated plaque that commemorates a battle, a war, or those who sacrificed their lives for their country. Sometimes this basic form is abstracted and further articulated by metaphor, as in the classic Hellenic statue *Winged Victory*, a monumental figure of a draped, winged woman (her head is missing) brandishing a sword, which stands in the Louvre, in Paris. Another example of this genre is the similarly scaled and metaphorically abstracted monumental figure of Mother Russia that stands as a memorial to the battle of Stalingrad.

The Vietnam War Memorial in Washington, D.C., designed by an actual refugee from that war, Maya Lin, bears no resemblance at all to this traditional type. It is a long, relatively low, black marble wall that zigzags its way along one side of the park that links the U.S. Capitol building with the Lincoln Memorial. Inscribed on this stark wall are the names of Americans who died in Vietnam. Since its unveiling, this memorial has become the most profoundly emotional of all Washington places, eclipsing even the solemn cemetery at Arlington and the themed monuments to our greatest Americans. The Vietnam War Memorial is perhaps the first successful built environment that represents the unrepresentable. It exists as a direct line

*The National Vietnam War Memorial, in Washington, D.C., has become a model form for representing the unrepresentable. Its design has been imitated at similar memorials in the United States and elsewhere in the world. Photo courtesy of Corbis/Bettmann.*

between the grim reality of too many deaths on the one side and the anguish of military survivors or relatives of the deceased on the other. No image, no picture, no video, no music—in short, no simulation—can represent the agony of that war; the stark wall alone represents the unrepresentable.

The Vietnam War Memorial is not a theme park or a mall. It does not provide its visitors with the urban-style experience that is at the core of many other themed environments, as we have discussed, nor does it serve as a link between popular cultural forms, such as Hollywood, and the mundane aspects of everyday life. Yet this memorial is one of several recent themed milieus designed to evoke a human drama that cannot be captured in images, music, or words. It has been so successful as an expression of the unrepresentable that recently its vision has been copied in several monumental memorials. In June 1995, on the 50th anniversary of the Battle of Okinawa, a memorial was unveiled that resembles the one in Washington, consisting of several low-lying walls of marble arranged in parallel, engraved with the names of the 250,000 soldiers and civilians who died in the bloody battle. The land-use design of this memorial evokes the same ambiance as the Vietnam wall. More recently, the German government announced plans for the construction of a memorial to the European Jews killed by the Nazis in World War II. The winning design for the memorial consists of a gigantic monolith with the authenticated names of the 4.5 million Jews and gypsies who were killed in concentration camps. The wall motif, therefore, has become the principal means of representing unrepresentable, monumental tragedies of recent times.

The National Holocaust Museum, which is located not far from the site of the Vietnam memorial in Washington, D.C., is another highly successful venture of this kind, aimed at representing a horrific event. Built with private funds on publicly dedicated land, the Holocaust Museum is, first, a museum—that is, a repository for artifacts that deal with the Holocaust experience of European Jewry. Its designers, however, have orchestrated the viewing of the museum in a way that makes visceral connections between the Holocaust and the museum experience itself. At the entrance to the Holocaust Museum, visitors are given a pass with the number of some unfortunate Jew (or gypsy) who died in the camps. The museum's interior was designed to personalize the experience of the Holocaust in other ways as well—through photographs of ordinary families, pictures of children, exhibits of articles of clothing, of village settings, home interiors, in short, of the normative everyday life existence of fellow humans. Other parts of the museum are more intrusive. One section represents the Jewish residents of a particular town decimated by the Nazis. Bare brick walls recall the ovens of Auschwitz. Visitors are guided along through these and other mini-environments within the museum. In the end, however, the public confronts the ineffable. The domed roof covers a large vacant space, the empty void left by the destruction of European Jewry. Like the Vietnam memorial, all that is left is to imagine alone the unrepresentable anguish and horror of the transforming experience.

The Jewish extension to the Berlin Museum, like the National Holocaust Museum in Washington, D.C., was designed by Daniel Libeskind to represent the unrepresentable. The centerpiece of the Berlin museum extension is its division by a blank concrete wall that, like the barrier of the Vietnam memorial, traverses the space in lightning-bolt fashion. The facade is all that is necessary to suggest the unthinkable events and allow feelings to flow (Feireiss, 1992; Broadbent, 1994). According to Geoffrey Broadbent (1994: 2), the wall circumscribes a space that uses the simplest form of representation, iconic imagery, to invoke the Jewish presence annihilated by the Nazis:

Libeskind started with a map of Berlin, that is to say an icon, marking onto it addresses of those Jews he saw as essential to the city's cultural history. . . . Having plotted their addresses, Libeskind connected these by lines which have an elon-gated Star of David. Across this space is the lightning flash. . . . Since almost all the Jews were deported from Berlin, their possessions destroyed or looted by the Nazis, there was nothing much Jewish to show in the Museum. The 'void' itself is his major exhibit.

Recently, there has been talk in academic circles of other possible attempts to represent the unrepresentable—a trend that contrasts with the thematic simulations and virtual reality re-creations increasingly charac-teristic of our culture. A suggestion has been floated, for example, that a national museum should be built in the United States to commemorate the experience of slavery. Americans of late clearly have been concerned with symbolic commemorations of contemporary events that defy human pow-ers of representation and depiction. At the same time, the popular culture simulations in malls, theme parks, and the like are widely criticized as superficial, false, and idealized representations. However, most people pre-fer to be entertained by themed spaces rather than confronted by some awesome tragedy of human experience. Simulations carry us away to the fantasy worlds that most of us seem to crave—places where we are free to shop, eat fast food, and spend time with friends and family. Yet the less-welcome symbolic representation of the unpleasant and unrepresentable—in museums, through art, and in national gatherings such as the recent piecing together of the AIDS quilt on the lawn in front of the White House—seems inevitable. Even these less-comforting themed environments appar-ently fulfill a human need.

## Summary of Main Points

1. Theming is not a city-based phenomenon. It can be found throughout metropolitan regions worldwide—wherever there is competition among spatial locations for customers.
2. The Las Vegas casino environment is a multidimensional system of signs. Every hotel-casino is themed with the most spectacular symbolic motifs, supported by displays of neon and by Hollywood simulations.
3. The fantastic diversity of themed casinos on the Strip, including a number of outdoor staged spectaculars that occur at regular inter-vals, has attracted casino-goers to the streets in record numbers. This urban, pedestrian street culture is new to Las Vegas and has

redefined the experience there. In the past, people generally stayed within the casinos and only traveled by car.

4. The most spectacular and successful fully themed environments are the Disney theme parks—Disneyland in California, and Disneyworld in Florida. Abandoning the old Coney Island–style amusement park in the 1950s, the Walt Disney Company has relied instead on theming in an obvious and extended way to attract visitors. Disney theme parks connect with media productions and a long history of merchandising to create their market, which is extensive. These links among themed environments, media, and commodity merchandising constitute a formula that has also been used with success in other themed businesses.

5. As theme parks, Disneyland and Disneyworld provide visitors with an intense personal experience that contrasts greatly with people's daily life. Although this difference is based on fantasy and simulation, it contributes to the parks' success.

6. The Disney theme park formula has been replicated by other spaces, such as Dolly Parton's Dollywood, in Pigeon Forge, Tennessee—proof that the themed environment is a form that *potentially* can be used almost anywhere.

7. Disney-style themed environments, with their strong media and merchandise connections, have appeared in cities that are in need of economic revival, such as New York's Times Square.

8. Disney-style theming is also the basis of a new style of housing development, exemplified by the community of Celebration, in Florida. Unlike other examples of themed environments so far, Celebration is a space where people live instead of just visiting temporarily. Life there, according to several recent books, has mixed reviews; but this new style of single-family housing development will no doubt be copied elsewhere.

9. There are additional ways in which themed environments are used by our society. Theming occurs in franchised parks like the Busch Gardens, in university shopping malls, and in professional sports complexes.

10. Theming has increasingly been used in rock concert tours, such as the last U2 tour, to maximize audiences and profits. Themed tours of bands lumped together by genre, such as Lollapalooza and the Warp Tour, are also increasingly common marketing tools, used toward the same purpose.

11. Theming is used in sex tourism, where body types and gender differences are the basis of marketing and commodification. Tourists interested in cheap, exploitative sex choose locations around the world on the basis of these body type and gender themes.

12. A special kind of theming has emerged (with some notable successes) that attempts a representation of what cannot really be represented. Maya Lin's Vietnam memorial and the Holocaust Museum, both in Washington, D.C., are two examples.

# 6

# EXPERIENCING THEMED ENVIRONMENTS AND ORGANIZED PROTESTS AGAINST THEM

## Themed Environments and Personal Self-Realization

This book has argued that theming is increasingly used by businesses faced with intense competition in economic sectors with products that are essentially similar, such as tourism, casino gambling, restaurants, theme parks, and mall shopping. For individual users, the same built spaces present themselves as novel, entertaining, and fashionable. Usually the milieu signifies an attractive invitation to participate in a structured fantasy, such as that offered by the Mars 2112 restaurant, where customers are transported to their tables in a flying saucer. Once seated, they can enjoy the more mundane treats of hamburgers and French fries, which are offered by nearly every eating establishment. Theming and structured fantasy make the difference in the commercial attraction of one place versus another; and these same elements also contribute to an increase in the price. Families consider the purchase of a ticket for a theme park, no matter how costly, as the price of entertainment, and they factor it into their budgets when they depart on vacations. For the giant corporations that run them, in contrast, the theme park ticket is one source of profits, along with the sale of merchandise and food. Consequently, any themed, commercial environment is always at the intersection of enjoyable or desirable personal experience and the corporate activity of moneymaking. In a sense, I could argue that both producers and consumers are satisfied by the experience. However, as I shall discuss more fully below, as theming and Disney-style attractions have taken over more of our environment, protests and criticisms also have followed.

The difference between the ways owners and users of themed environments view these built spaces is compounded further by the polysemy of signs. As with any signifying object, the sign means different things to different people. Individuals experience themed places in a host of ways. Perhaps children are much more enthralled with the experience than adults. But the question of who enjoys fantasy theming most has yet to be answered by social researchers. A study of how people relate to the milieus I have discussed in previous chapters would need to survey children along with adults; the young and the old; men and women; native-born Americans and foreign tourists; people with families, and couples without children; and groups as opposed to single individuals. The polysemic array of interpretations for any given themed experience might be quite spectacular. This range of meanings that exists for any signifying object is why I am very skeptical about claims for a single, definitive interpretation of any particular themed milieu—an activity that is increasingly common in academic circles.

Polysemic ranges of interpretation can be understood through the concept of the code or ideology. Individuals belonging to localized cultures possess certain overarching codes for interpreting their experiences based on their daily life. When people visit a themed milieu, they draw on the ideology they know best to interpret that space as enjoyable and meaningful. Thus, successful environments appeal to a variety of cultural orientations. They utilize polysemy to give the mass of consumers alternative ways of enjoying their themed experience. Visitors to Dollywood, for example, might find certain aspects of the milieu more entertaining or enjoyable than others. The crowd of visitors will resonate culturally with different aspects of the park experience. This occurs because their personal interpretive codes fit some attractions better than others. Disneyland, for example, as conceived by Walt Disney, offers something attractive to every segment of mainstream America. He succeeded remarkably by exploiting the already existing markets for Disney products established in films, television, and ubiquitous marketing.

Malls work in the same way. The variety of stores and the variety of goods within stores connect with the most common consumer codes or lifestyle choices in the population. Chain store marketing, which operates nationwide, controls mall merchandising. Each outlet may appeal to particular segments, but those limitations are chosen very carefully, with one eye trained on the mix of other stores within the large malls. People's experience of the mall becomes a selective mode of behavior motivated by resonance with those images and commodities, with which they are already familiar through mass-market conditioning by TV, advertising, magazines, and movies, much in the same way as the Disney themed environment works. The same can be said of successful franchises like the Hard Rock Café, because everyone likes some aspect of rock music.

All themed environments strive either to appeal to the largest possible audience or, unambiguously, to an intended market segment. The Harley Davidson Café aims for the young adult market, with an emphasis on motorcycle decor, and it succeeds despite a limited menu and disappointing food quality. Dollywood distinctly advertises its simulated "country" roots. Las Vegas casinos repeat tried-and-true themes from American popular culture, even as they rummage through the dustbin of Hollywood fantasies for new ideas. Because of this wide coverage of average consumer tastes, themed milieus—like the proliferating product lines of major consumer goods industries—are designed intentionally to allow polysemy. Through the very act of consumption, each individual brings his or her own baggage to the interpretation; but every commercial milieu that desires success strives to be relevant to many different kinds of people. The great American melting pot, for example, is on display each night, walking down Las Vegas Boulevard.

Individuals function in society through different roles. Adults spend much of their time as workers, and that is one source of identity and self-fulfillment. When they engage in recreation or leisure, they assume a different role—that of consumer. As noted, increasingly it is the activity of consumption that most people turn to for self-realization. The conditioning of mass advertising through television, magazines, and the like, becomes actualized when people enter the themed, commercial space. Indeed, the latter are extensions of the former. That is, themed, commercial environments and our consumer-oriented mass culture are integrated through the structure of consumption. According to Lauren Langman, "Although there have been historical antecedents in the distribution of goods, malls cannot be thought of apart from the mass mediated images of television that stimulate and soothe at the same time" (1992: 40). A visit to a theme park, a mall, a themed restaurant, or a Las Vegas casino enables people to actualize the consuming or commodity-desiring self that remains latent during the work-a-day world of daily life. This other self has already been created by years of conditioning from advertising and image-driven media. Within commercial spaces the consumer self is triggered by the stimulus of a milieu whose themes are integrated into the larger media culture.

Where, exactly, can people actualize the consumer part of the self? Where can they encounter the perfumes, clothes, hats, desires, fantasy obsessions, and images that they have been longing for? Increasingly, the answer is within the quasi-public space, the ersatz urban pedestrian culture of the controlled, manipulated, and thoroughly commercialized themed environment. For this reason these spaces are increasingly the sites of personal self-realization in our society. We are compelled to visit the mall for shopping or the theme park and casino for a vacation, because it is within these environments, after many years of media conditioning, that we feel most like "ourselves." The popularity of theming is due, in no small measure, to the way we personally connect with the new consumer spaces and find them entertaining.

## The Personal Experience of Themed Environments

Several years ago I was invited to give some talks in Brazil. My first stop was Rio de Janeiro. My hosts arranged for me to stay in a small apartment in the section known as Ipanema, adjacent to the beach. The area was quite lovely. A bakery was located directly across the street from my apartment. On my very first morning in Rio, I went there for my breakfast. I did not speak any Portuguese, but felt confident that I could execute the transaction. This bakery was very impressive. It occupied a large space with a huge counter area displaying an incredible variety of baked goods. There were many breads to choose from. All of them had just been baked, because that unmistakable smell of freshly made bread saturated the warm, moist morning air.

I stepped up to the counter with full confidence and caught the attention of a clerk, a middle-aged woman. She looked at me with an open, anticipating expression. I pointed to the piece of bread I wanted and took out some Brazilian money. She began to speak rapidly. I could not make sense out of anything she said. I kept staring at her and then pointed again at the bread while waving my money. She spoke again and began gesturing. I assumed she was now getting angry, because of her gestures. Her words fell on my untrained ears, deaf to Portuguese. As she spoke and gestured more violently, the realization grabbed me swiftly that I was not getting any bread that morning at all, at least not from this place. I was now totally tuned out to all the sounds she was making, and I began to sketch a mental picture of some nice Brazilian supermarket that I hoped was just down the street, with open aisles and shelves filled with prepackaged loaves of bread—the exact kind that I would never, under any circumstances, ever contemplate buying, were I back home in America.

Through my busy mental picture-making, a waking dream of supermarket bliss, I happened to notice that her gesturing had a focus. All the time that she was talking to me and getting increasingly frustrated, her hand motions seemed always to point in the same direction—namely, directly behind me. When that realization finally penetrated my understanding of the interaction, I turned around immediately and noticed a man in a small booth at the back wall, who was laughing at me. Propelled both by the intensity of the woman's gesturing and the pleasant smile of the man, I walked quickly to the booth and then noticed that he was behind a large cash register. The clerk yelled over to us with some necessary information and this cashier repeated the phrase. I still did not understand any Portuguese, but handed him some money. He took what he needed and handed me back some of my money plus some change. He then rang up a sale and handed me a receipt, gesturing that I should return to the counter.

When I turned around with the receipt in my hand, I saw the woman clerk's face. It was beaming. She seemed so relaxed—or should I say, relieved. She watched my every step, like a mother with a baby learning to walk, as I went back to the counter. There the woman proudly handed me the bread I had wanted, wrapped in a paper bag, and took the receipt from my hand. A few minutes later I was back in my room, drinking coffee and eating the still warm, freshly baked bread.

There are, no doubt, many travelers to places with a different language or customs who have had similar experiences. My interaction almost failed. Were it not for the very hard work of the bakery clerk, I would have left that place to search for an American-style supermarket. The interaction was placed in jeopardy not just because I do not speak Portuguese. Clearly, had I known the language, I could have bought the bread quite easily. A significant part of the transaction, however, involved familiarity with the *method* of buying bread in that place. In this particular shop, you go to the cashier first and pay your money, and then you get your purchase. This is a complete reversal of the usual method of buying, back in the United States. My lack of familiarity with this reversed method—probably a practice of all large bakeries in Rio, if not throughout Brazil—threatened the completion of the purchase.

Every built environment presents itself to the user as a series of obstacles. These are overcome in two distinct ways. Firstly and primarily, language is deployed in sign systems to facilitate use. The latter can be either spoken or written discourse. Most public places have explicit, graphic sign systems that guide visitors to their respective destinations and facilitate interaction. An airport, for example, could not function without its intricate and easily readable sign systems, including the automated and continually updated information monitors listing departures, arrivals, and gate numbers. Mall sign systems mark parking places, entrances, instructions for finding particular stores, and so on.

Secondly, users must have some familiarity with the built environment they visit. Even without knowledge of a specific language, there is some greater understanding of interaction that must come from experience. I was lost in the Ipanema bakery, both because I could not understand the language and because I was unfamiliar with the method of negotiating that space. However, I had purchased goods in a store before. I had some competency as a consumer with past experience. I knew that no matter how strange the environment seemed, I needed to pay someone and obtain my purchase from someone, somehow. This basic knowledge and familiarity with the practice of consumer purchasing was the foundation of my eventually successful transaction. Once through it, furthermore, I could, and did, buy bread there as effortlessly as the cariocas that morning.

Familiarity with the sign systems of a themed environment enables users to select a method for the negotiation of the space and, therefore, the satisfaction of their consumer desires. This condition is basic to the success of any commercial place. When encountering any experience, our success requires work (Garfinkel, 1967; Livingston, 1987). We must read the signs of the environment and interpret them. We must follow the cues given to us by others in interaction and behave normatively. If we fail to understand the signs, or if we respond in unexpected ways, we call attention to ourselves and jeopardize not only our ability to function in the environment but also our well-being in the event that others respond to us as a threat (see Goffman, 1959, 1963, 1971, 1974).

Successful interaction in public environments requires an effort from all those involved. Part of that effort consists of taking the sensory cues of our experience and sculpting them into a comprehensive form. This kind of work is not self-evident, nor is it always successful (Garfinkel, 1967;

Heritage, 1984; Livingston, 1987). It often involves considerable creativity. Take, for example, the case of the woman clerk in the Ipanema bakery. She sweated to make her sale. Only by adding to her spoken language a set of gestures that eventually stimulated me to "turn around" did she snatch the interaction from the brink of complete failure.

In many ways, visits to foreign lands provide the best examples of the basic work required by all of us in every successful interaction (Cohen and Taylor, 1992; MacCannell, 1976). The tourist must, above all else, learn the methods of negotiating everyday environments. At home these techniques have long since passed into the unconscious, being programmed into our bodies so that our ways of moving, walking, and talking all seem "natural." Only when we visit a foreign environment do these "taken for granted" gestures become problematic. They then require reexamination for appropriateness. Hence we dredge them up from our unconscious and deploy them as a set of repertoires in the negotiation of the new, foreign space. The work of tourism is the reexamination, relearning, and creative improvisation of methods for successful interaction. The tourist's negotiation of the unfamiliar environment is also illustrative of the kind of work we all must do that is often taken for granted in our daily lives.

When we enter any themed environment, we become very much like a tourist. Malls, theme parks, casinos, and themed restaurants are all engineered to produce a special effect that stimulates our desire to spend money. They call forth that part of our identities that revels in the act of consumption. We switch from the more ordinary mode of relating to the world—perhaps as a worker, student, or parent—and enter a more focused sense of self that seems at once special and deliberate. This consuming self, like the tourist self, is only one of the many roles we can play; but as new consumer spaces increasingly have come to characterize our everyday environment, it is more and more the way we relate to the world. At home, when we watch television, advertisements supply us with artfully conceived suggestions. Desire is further primed by the sign systems of magazines, films, and daily media programming that saturate their subjects with the aura of consumerism as an expression of status and celebrity. Once we hit the mall or a restaurant like Planet Hollywood, we have little will left to resist these major influences that compel us to consume, and we are even entertained by the experience. Through the spending of money, we realize our consumer self and achieve satisfaction, however fleeting, in the purchase of commodities. This mode of gratification also defines our participation in theme parks and gambling casinos. These themed milieus swath their visitors in perfectly engineered enticements, directing our behavior toward the spending of more money, and making us like it.

## Segregation, Surveillance, and the Disappearance of the Public Sphere

A focus on the personal, interactive level in the encounter with themed environments helps us understand the critical link between these spaces and the influence of the larger, mass culture on the individual pursuit of self-realization. An exclusive concentration on the "phenomenology" of shopping, however, would lead us to ignore the ways in which the larger social context structures the opportunities in society for personal fulfillment. Several factors in the social context have an impact on themed environments, including the processes of segregation and surveillance. In addition, the rise of commercial, motifed spaces must be considered against the backdrop of the general decline in our society's public sphere—in other words, the decline in the available opportunities for a public life.

### Class, Race, Gender, and Spatial Segregation

On December 14, 1995, Cynthia Wiggens, a young black woman who happened also to be a single mother, exited the bus that took her to work every morning. She was employed at the immense, upscale Walden Galleria Mall in the suburbs adjacent to Buffalo, New York. Cynthia lived in the inner city, like many other poor working African Americans. She had gotten used to the fact that bus transportation was relatively slow and sporadic, especially during the Buffalo winters. Besides these limitations, however, city buses were not allowed to enter the mall area. Every morning she was discharged by city transportation across from the mall entrance, on the other side of a busy, seven-lane highway that she had to cross in order to get to work. On this particular morning she didn't make it. A 10-ton dump truck hit her as she was crossing the road, and she died soon after. According to an account in *Time* (Barnes, 1996: 33), "Often during the day, charter buses would pull into the Galleria parking lot and disgorge shoppers from as far away as Canada. But the city bus wasn't allowed on mall property."

In the investigation that followed, it was determined, much to the embarrassment of both the mall developers and city officials, that the plan for the immense suburban shopping complex intentionally avoided accommodating city buses, thereby making it difficult for residents of the inner city not only to shop there but also, in the case of Cynthia Wiggens and others, to work there. According to *Time*, such actions amounted to "bus-route discrimination." In fact, malls are commonly perceived as aiding the patterns of segregation in our society, simply because most malls are located in the suburbs. Without proper public transportation, they are unapproachable by the less affluent who do not have cars.

An interactive focus on the phenomenology of environmental experience in consumer spaces, as in the work of Erving Goffman (1971), can overlook the way in which these places filter people according to the patterns of class, race, and gender segregation. Class distinctions do operate in malls, although often in subtle ways (Gottdiener, 1995). Shops selling similar merchandise are often stratified according to the range of prices. Clothes, shoes, or sportswear can be purchased within a large mall at several alternative stores, each of which carries commodities geared to specific household budgets as well as particular lifestyles or fashions. At a typical galleria, the consumer can buy a men's suit, for example, for $150 or $1,500.

Class distinctions based on prices at the mall are reinforced by the symbols and themes of different stores. Some project the idea of a fashionable bargain through sale signs and special discounts and promotions. Others justify higher prices by stressing quality. Often the latter is signified through upscale-sounding product names, such as the "Essex" collection of ties, or the "executive" line of business suits. Designer names and celebrity endorsements are used for the same effect. Department stores will even internalize the variation according to household budget segmentation by offering several different lines of commodities that range in price.

The last observation recalls the discussion in Chapter 3, on market segmentation as the dominant mode of commercial sales. Our society not only discriminates against people through class and racial distinctions but also commodifies that discrimination through differences in sale price. Furthermore, this commodity sales bias is compounded by the spatial inequalities of our sprawling regions. Metropolitan areas, for example, are already segregated, in that racial and class distinctions operate through the prices of housing. Although it is unlawful in this country to discriminate against people on the basis of race, class, or gender, prospective buyers or renters of housing can acquire only what they can afford. It is not against the law for builders to develop entire sections of suburbia at a relatively high price, without a mix of housing stock. In fact, most community zoning and building codes demand it. Thus, the law in housing sales—namely that potential buyers must be treated equally—is negated by the segregation of housing according to level of affordability—which is legal, even though it results in inequality. The outcome of such practices in the housing market is the discrimination and segregation of the population in space by class distinctions.

Theme parks reinforce patterns of segregation in our society in a similar way. Because they can charge admission, they can filter out visitors who cannot afford the experience. Theme parks are not public spaces; they are commercial ventures. It would be against the law to prohibit individuals' entry to a park on the basis of race or religion, yet it is perfectly within the law to discriminate against anyone who cannot afford the cost of entry. As indicated in Chapter 5, most theme parks, even the "down-home" Dollywood, are quite expensive. A family of four will spend well over $100 just for admission. A holiday visit to Disneyworld is an exciting experience for an average family, but its cost can rival a European vacation of the same duration. On my many visits to Disneyland in Anaheim, California, I rarely saw the same admixture of people belonging to different classes, races, and ethnic groups present in any of the downtown city spots, although large numbers of middle-class Asian tourists might give someone the impression that the park is a place of diversity.

Our society is segregated by class, race, and space. Part of that pattern is produced by the costs of things and part by the way the housing market operates through inner-city and suburban distinctions that have an economic and a social, interactive basis. The crowd of consumers at most themed malls, restaurants, and parks reflects those patterns of discrimination. Often, despite the successes of new themed developments heralded by cities, these areas are difficult to reach unless people have access to cars. In short, there is an inherent bias against true public access to waterfront developments, regional malls, and other themed, fantasy-oriented consumer milieus that are not easily accessed via public transportation.

Perhaps the only exception to the rule among symbolic milieus is Las Vegas. I have described that city previously as one large themed environment, with a new style of urban fabric created by the casino-to-casino contrast. It also appears to be a true "workers' paradise" like that dreamed of by hundreds of Marxist revolutionaries, because so many of its visitors are quite ordinary in their circumstances, because there is a vibrant pedestrian street culture, and because there are bargains everywhere in food, drink, and lodging.

In addition to class- and race-based filters, the experience of the themed environment is filtered also through the optic of gender. Most places, for example, reflect male values in the larger society by celebrating machismo and peculiarly male fantasies. For example, Las Vegas casinos often celebrate male modes of entertainment, such as the many "girlie" shows (regardless of their disguise under conventional signs of show business). Western motifs glorify the pumped-up period of the frontier era. Treasure Island provides a spectacle of warring pirates. Excalibur is a simulation of medievalism with its brotherhood of gallant, fearless knights. And so on.

There are, however, exceptions to this domination by male fantasies. In its invocation of the glory days of Hollywood filmmaking, the MGM Grand highlights Dorothy and her visit to Oz, adding a feminine touch to the spectacle of machismo everyplace else. Can we also consider, as the gendered fantasies of females, the "hunk" performers who headline many casino shows? Are the topless chorus lines mainly for the men? Even if they are not, however, they do engineer women simply as sex objects. More graphically, the backstage, less visible part of Las Vegas, its environment of sleaze sex and peep shows, constitutes a male-dominated space that commodifies women in the basest terms. Consequently, male-oriented activities characterize the space of Las Vegas and its rich environmental imaging (see Gottdiener et al., 1999).

Malls, theme parks, and even restaurants can also be read as gendered spaces. Obviously, the activity of shopping is associated more with women than men (Oh and Arditi, 2000). Thus, in contrast to Las Vegas, malls may be spaces dominated by the commercialized fantasies of women. Women may negotiate these places in ways different from those of men. The activity of shopping itself is structured in terms of gender differences.

And just as the MGM Grand may serve as an exception in the realm of casino spaces, there is also a theme park that stands out because of its attention to female desires. As described in the previous chapter, Dollywood derives much of its thematic expression from the life of Dolly Parton, its owner. Her "rags-to-riches" story, which is highlighted by the park environment, is a narrative representation of female mythology for a society dominated by male-oriented popular cultural forms.

Some visions and fantasies engineered into themed environments might slight the female point of view, but this is not the main point I wish to make. If we consider the mall, for example, from a female perspective, we must account for its apparent gender neutrality. The mall space is designed to get every visitor, young and old, male and female, to spend their time and their money, much the way a Las Vegas casino is set up, but through a different experience. The gender issue of the mall space is not one of alleged discrimination against women but simply of the difference in the experience between men and women. Every themed environment presents a gendered filter through which people experience the space. A phenomenology of the themed environment must account for this gender difference in experience.

## Surveillance

Writing about developments in Los Angeles, Mike Davis (1990) called attention to the increasing use of surveillance and belligerent defensive measures built into the new landscapes of suburbia, especially malls. Although one might disagree with his analysis (which suggests a conspiracy of the middle class against the poor), the facts he has recorded are accurate. Individuals and commercial environments have increasingly resorted to a variety of regulatory mechanisms to protect access to their personal or marketable possessions. Not everyone has a fully equipped car alarm or home security system; but a growing number of people would not own a highly marketable commodity without acquiring such a system. More significantly, Davis wrote about this trend even before Mayor Rudolph Giuliani of New York City declared war on the homeless and the deviant in what became a successful effort to sanitize the center of Manhattan in order to attract tourists.

According to Davis (1990: 224):

> The old liberal paradigm of social control, attempting to balance repression with reform, has long been superseded by a rhetoric of social warfare that calculates the interests of the urban poor and the middle classes as a zero-sum game. In cities like Los Angeles, on the bad edge of postmodernity, one observes an unprecedented tendency to merge urban design, architecture, and the police apparatus into a single, comprehensive security effort.

Long a characteristic of malls, this same merger of design and control elements, noted by Davis, has been successfully extended to the themed, commercial development projects within the city itself.

Davis discusses the way surveillance and other defensive measures are comprehensively engineered into the built environment of Los Angeles. They often take the form of architectural features, such as the heavy, wrought-iron gate in front of the Frank Gehry–designed public library, or the almost ubiquitous notices posted on affluent suburban residential properties warning of an "armed response" to intruders. His description of Los Angeles as an environment whose dominant theme is defense against strangers is convincing. The signs of a fortress mentality dominate the area as a grand motif.

I disagree, however, with Davis's assertion that these signs are symptoms of class warfare, and that fortress architecture is a phenomenon caused by middle-class paranoia about crime. Astoundingly, he ignores how poor people also protect themselves using defensive techniques, such as owning attack dogs, barring windows, and posting hostile warning signs. Fortress architecture is also characteristic of less-affluent, inner-city areas, where most stores have iron bars on the windows, bullet-proof counters, and surveillance cameras, and some even have armed guards.

The fear of crime is not a manifestation of middle-class paranoia, as Davis suggests; it is a realistic response of all residents to our increasingly violent cities—especially of the poor, who are most likely to be its victims. For example, in the inner city of Philadelphia, in December 1995, the owners of two different neighborhood food markets were gunned down by teenage intruders in separate incidents, leaving community residents without convenient access to food shopping. Then, too, it is not just the wealthy who deploy fortress architecture, as Davis would have us all believe. When the racially mixed, working-class neighborhood of Five Oaks, in Dayton, Ohio, was besieged by crime and the drug trade because of its proximity to the downtown, it hired defensive space architect Oscar Newman, who recommended the immediate construction of gates across most of the streets in the community. The result was a drastic decline in crime and an increase in property values, thereby allowing the neighborhood to regain stability (Collison, 1996). Those gates are the kinds of objects Davis exemplifies as aspects of fortress architecture, but they exist in and are used by a modest income, inner city community.

The problem with fortress architecture is the way it ruptures the urban fabric by isolating buildings from both the surrounding landscape and the street. In this connection, Davis zeroes in on what he dubs a "stealth house" (1990: 238)—a building that presents blank walls to the street, consciously avoiding both visual integration with adjacent buildings and open commerce with the contiguous area. Davis cites the Danziger Studio designed by Frank Gehry as one such case: "The street frontage of the Danziger was simply a massive gray wall, treated with a rough finish to ensure that it would collect dust from passing traffic and weather into a simulacrum of nearby porn studios and garages" (1990: 238).

Los Angeles, like other areas of the country, contains many residential communities that are surrounded by high fences. These are often termed "gate-guarded communities." Visitors must enter through a secured and guarded checkpoint, having first obtained clearance from the locals. Security walls, armed guard posts, and signs advertising gated security help create a theme of fortress living (see Langdon, 1994). Davis singles out the "armed response" signs in front of affluent homes as a particularly chilling feature of suburban life. They imply that in addition to the usual security devices such as burglar alarms and wired windows, a private police corps patrols the area. Apparently, when intruders or unwanted visitors trip the appropriate signals, armed guards are dispatched. For Davis this constitutes an "imbrication of the police function into the built environment" (1990: 250). By breaking down the distinction between publicly sponsored police departments and the lengths that individual citizens advertise they will go to in order to discourage visits from strangers, the private, standing armies further develop the theme of the fortress city or fortified residential space.

Elsewhere, in theme parks and casinos, in themed restaurants and airports, additional security measures also have been taken, but these operate principally through unobtrusive surveillance techniques that deploy hidden technological wizardry. We may be observed in the most minute detail when visiting a themed environment such as Disneyworld, but the visitor is made to feel comfortable by the landscape. At the very least, most themed environments encourage us to consume and "enjoy." This effect seems to be behind the success of the new Times Square renovation, which transformed that space from an urban "danger zone" to an extension of a Disney theme park. For ordinary cities in decline, by contrast, material forms dedicated to defense combine with environmental sign systems to create a belligerent and threatening milieu, a menacing world of estrangement that militates against the idea of a democratic community as the basis for city life.

## The Disappearance of Public Space

Recent critiques of the plague of theming have implicated it in the ongoing transformation and destruction of community ideals. For several decades, observers have lamented the decline of places that allow for free public interaction in our society (Sennett, 1977; Meyerowitz, 1985; Habermas, 1989; Chaney, 1993). Their analyses call attention to the decline of "public space"—community space in which the public can interact, where people can meet others at their leisure, and where free and open discussions can take place. When scholars discuss the concept of a public space, most often they have in mind, as the ideal type, the agora or open marketplace of the classical Greek cities. Behind the concept lies the idea that every society, no matter how commercial and business oriented, needs a free space for public interaction.

In an interesting study, William H. Whyte (1988) discovered that even in the hustle and bustle of the downtown in a large city (Manhattan), people meet others and talk, or schmooze, whenever opportunity permits. In Whyte's study, social bonding might include stopping to acknowledge a friend in the middle of a busy sidewalk or talking while sitting on low concrete walls outside office buildings, as well as the more common kinds of public interaction in commercial spaces including sidewalk cafes and al fresco restaurants, or in public parks. Because of the growth of homeless populations in the inner city and their redefinition as "nuisance" groups, some municipalities have taken to redesigning benches and low walls so that people can no longer sit or lie on them (Whyte, 1988; Davis, 1990). In such ways, public space is assaulted and diminished by city officials.

The most common complaint regarding the decline of public space concerns the social effects of high crime rates. Writers who disparage as hysteria the average person's concerns about crime—as does Davis (1990), who also likes to demonize the middle class as the cause of anticivic attitudes—ignore the overwhelming statistics on urban crime, especially compared to crime in other areas (Gottdiener, 1994b). American inner cities are, indeed, unsafe places to live, although within these spaces crime rates still vary according to the economic well-being of the neighborhood. Thus, the perception of unsafe cities, which is quite realistic, still masks the fact that affluent residents live in safe sections of cities, whereas poorer urban residents are often victims of crime.

People cope with the high rate of urban crime by adjusting their behavior accordingly. This change has had a negative effect on the use of public space. City parks, which were purposely dedicated to the concept of public communion, are now rightly perceived as unsafe places. Cases like that of the Central Park jogger (Gottdiener, 1994b: 215), and incidents of group violence directed against women, demonstrate the danger of using public spaces. If most residents view city streets as increasingly unsafe, then urban culture, which is dependent on the open interaction of people in public, will decline.

Many contemporary urban analysts confine their observations to the disappearance of public space and its effects (Sennett, 1977; Whyte, 1988;

Davis, 1990), and miss a more fundamental and important idea addressed by earlier writers on the subject—namely, the relationship between personal space and public space (see Habermas, 1989; Arendt, 1958; Marcuse, 1964; Lefebvre, 1971; O'Neill, 1972). The one cannot be isolated from the other.

As John O'Neill (1972: 20) suggests, all our desires are produced in the private realm of our own making. Within that domain, we exercise our personal as well as political/community imaginations. A nurturing private space allows for personal growth. It is complemented by a nurturing public space that enables the expression of a political consciousness. Public space, then, allows for self-realization in the community realm. Today, instead, as public space disappears, we have a greater emphasis on the limited self-realization of individuals through consuming. Working in tandem with this effect is the takeover of our city and suburban environments by themed spaces that are engineered to stimulate buying. Disneyfication of downtowns, environmental simulation of real places, surveillance and control of space, are all aspects of the growing reliance on theming that have a negative effect on the amount of free, public space available where citizens can realize broader and more important aspects of the self.

According to those writers who are concerned about the historical trend of civic decline, private space was assaulted by the twin forces of consumerism and the invasion of the mass media during the turn of the century, and was virtually eradicated. Marcuse, for example, asserts that individual opinion and the political consciousness were transformed by exposure to "public opinion"—that is, the aggregation of individual ideas by state-directed surveys into a "mass sentiment," through the "invasion of the private household by the togetherness of public opinion; [and the] opening of the bedroom to the media of mass communication" (1964: 19; see also Habermas, 1989). Through this process, individual ideas were no longer allowed to percolate in their own time from the household to the street level to political venues and to democratic mechanisms for the public expression of sentiments. Instead, democracy itself was undercut by the "top-down" aggregation of individual responses to surveys that were then marketed by the state and corporation alike as "public opinion." With this change came the objective decline of democratic processes in society. Small wonder that even during a presidential election only the minority of citizens exercise their right to vote. Public opinion polls, and media coverage of election results, heavily discourage individuals from leaving their homes or even initiating a political dialogue with their neighbors.

Consumerism further eroded both public and private space, thereby changing the way individuals interacted with the society. The interior spaces of homes began to be commodified in the 1920s, when households were systematically targeted by marketers of consumer goods (see Baudrillard, 1968; Gottdiener, 1995). Although household goods had been offered for sale on a mass basis since the previous century, the 1920s brought a more comprehensive marketing approach and a more consumer-oriented society. At this time, interior spaces were transformed by ensembles of furnishings designed for use in a particular room, driven by the marketing idea that each room's furnishings should express a unified theme (Baudrillard, 1968; Gottdiener, 1995). Thus, companies eschewed the marketing of individual objects for the selling of dining room sets, bathroom sets, bedroom sets, and the like, with each piece coordinated to fit the ensemble theme. The idea of thematic conformity within home interiors was further reinforced by fashion and architecture magazines for popular reading. The consummate reflection of this comprehensive approach to interior design came from the German Bauhaus movement, which greatly influenced the production and marketing of household commodities in this country as well as Europe.

The total commodification of interior space during the 1920s and '30s was one of the earliest manifestations of fully themed environments. Because this effect occurred within the home, it had a special role in transforming private space to a commodified interior that was less a reflection of personal self-expression and more a testament to current consumer fashion. Private space was eliminated, being replaced by the commodified logic of interior design. In the same way, the venues of public space—the marketplaces, parks, and city sidewalks—that had for thousands of years nurtured community and political communion, were threatened with competition from commodified public places such as cafes, restaurants, and bars. Nevertheless, the inner life of the individual, which was simultaneously personal and public, could still be nurtured, especially in the unevenly developed open spaces of society that were only marginally commodified prior to the 1950s.

After 1950, however, public space as a social resource began to disappear. Notwithstanding the claims of commentators such as Davis and Whyte, crime and civic ordinances were not factors in this trend. Instead, as earlier observers (Marcuse, 1964; Lefebvre, 1971; Habermas, 1989) noted, new forms of social organization, dependent on mass media and suburbanization, took their toll on public life through the twin forces of the powerful media with its public opinion polling and the transformation of material space. In suburban developments, for example, the common city center was eradicated in favor of privatized backyards. New residential areas no longer included public space. Suburbanization also introduced the hegemony of the automobile as the dominant form of transportation. The public space of mass transport also disappeared, except for its continued presence in the inner city and along rail commuter lines.

By the 1970s and '80s, little public space remained, as more and more places were redeveloped for consumption-oriented, themed environments. These new consumer spaces are not "public," because they are owned and controlled by commercial interests. As noted in this chapter, they allow for personal self-expression only within the constraint of consumer identity. The mall may be the new space of public communion, or the "new main street," as some have suggested; but it functions in that capacity only within the very restricted context of consumption. Some writers also refer to theme parks as the "new main streets of the nation." Such parks may be viewed as a kind of public space only if we forget that many people in our society are kept out by the price of admission. The crowds that we encounter within themed environments are selectively chosen and highly regulated by the structured, commodified experience of the theme park itself. Primed at home by mass media for self-realization through consumption, people enter the pseudo-public space of the themed environment without either the political or the social desires that their counterparts in earlier epochs may have had. They pursue self-fulfillment in these places in the only way allowed, through the realization of the consumer role. This is a far cry from the multidimensional everyday life of the past.

## The Other Side of the Picture:
## Citizen Protests Against the Spread of Theming

Despite the continued reliance on themes to sell commodities and environments, the transformation of everyday space by these projects is not always supported by local residents. Disneyfication and McDonaldization, in particular, are increasingly viewed as forces to be opposed. On the one hand, new projects have supporters in government because they most often lead to economic gains and real estate redevelopment. On the other hand, the simulated and crass commercial nature of themed environments often rubs locals the wrong way. This reaction is especially true of those who hold the values that many of the new projects seek to emulate, such as a strong

belief in the virtues of small-town living. The new urbanism, Disney simulations of "main street," the McDonald's corporate activities, all seem to
support preservation of community character. Over the years, however—
just as many people now protest the opening of a new Wal-Mart or megamall—residents of both cities and suburbs have viewed with increasing
alarm the activities of the giant, earth-moving and environment-simulat-
ing corporations. Through the increasingly frequent engagements between
the two sides, the negative effects of our society's reliance on themed attractions is becoming clearer and more publicly acknowledged.

## Anti-Disneyfication

One recent controversy involves the failed attempt by the Disney
Corporation to build a proposed $650 million history theme park called
"Disney's America" in a historic region of Virginia. Sited next to
Haymarket, a town of approximately 500, situated about 35 miles west of
Washington, D.C., the proposed project was expected to benefit from prox-
imity to two of the nation's historical environmental treasures—Manassas
National Battlefield Park, located 4 miles away, and the much revered
Shenandoah National Park, a storied wilderness lying about 30 miles fur-
ther west. Manassas, or Bull Run, as it is known by Northerners, was the
scene of two brutal battles in the Civil War that resulted in 25,000 soldiers
killed or wounded on both sides. The park itself is a 3,000-acre site that also
includes "13 historic towns, 16 Civil War battlefields and 17 historic districts" (Wiebner, 1994; see also Fordney, 1994). According to reporter
Michael Wiebner (1994):

> Things had been going according to plan. Company officials and lobbyists wooed
> and wowed Virginia politicians at all levels, from the board of county supervisors
> to its most enthusiastic supporter, Governor George Allen (R). Disney courted
> business leaders and local citizens with the same ardor, leading county Chambers
> of Commerce to form the Welcome Disney Committee and Virginians to support
> the park by a 2 to 1 ratio.

And yet, with a mounting environmental protest aimed at them, Disney
withdrew the project in November of 1994, just months after it had been
proposed. The corporation had not expected such deeply felt animosity
toward the theme-park simulation of the nation's historical heritage.
Highly motivated grassroots organizations, environmentalists, and local

community preservationists banded together to prevent what they believed was a genuine threat to their way of life. In Wiebner's words, "Disney was challenged in nearly every way imaginable: through free and paid media, protests, letter-writing campaigns, and legislative lobbying."

Joining the fight were an impressive number of national environmental and historical preservation groups, such as the National Trust, Citizen Action, the Sierra Club, and the Piedmont Environmental Council. With money and expertise behind them, they vigorously protested this example of the "Disneyfication of America." Almost overnight they made the project and their protest a topic of nationwide debate. Eventually, Michael Eisner, the CEO of Disney Corporation, pulled the plug on the project "because he concluded the park would cost too much, create negative publicity and absorb management's time and attention. . . . Constant negative publicity hurt the company's most prized corporate asset, its squeaky-clean corporate image" (Wiebner, 1994).

In this and other protests, the anti-Disney forces had found a strategy that worked. Afraid of negative publicity when the outcry got too sustained and when it acquired a national exposure, the corporation could not continue with its plans, despite the political groundwork it had done at the beginning to gain support for the project. Although companies like the Disney Corporation seem almost invincible, they are in fact vulnerable to the kind of organized protests that were witnessed in Virginia. Earlier, in the city of Anaheim, California, the home of the original Disneyland, a proposed $3 billion project called "Westcot," which would have been a west-coast analogue to Disneyworld's Epcot Center in Orlando, was also blocked by grassroots protest. In this case, the issue was less the threat to the environment and more the concern of taxpayers in Orange County when they learned that Disney was asking for one-third of the project's cost—that is, $1 billion—to be covered by a government subsidy. Yet, it was only when public protests achieved media exposure that the project was abandoned. Again, the presence of too much negative publicity proved effective against the giant global enterprise.

Anti-Disney protests also point to another important issue. With the increasing reliance on themed environments in our society, people are becoming progressively more concerned about the effects of simulation on our cultural heritage. The same fears are stirred up overseas when native cultures are threatened by the vacation- and tourist-oriented megaprojects of giant corporations. Although architects such as the new urbanists extol the virtues of small-town America, their projects—like Seaside and the

Disney-built town of Celebration, both in Florida—actually have more in common with other idealized and simulated environments, such as Main Street in Disneyland. These projects unleash forces in our society that drive up land prices, chew up undeveloped space, attract thousands of new residents to pristine locations, and sell a simulated, idealized vision of America to upper-middle-class people who can afford the cost. At the same time, the small towns that already exist languish for lack of young people, economic vitality, and government resources.

## Anti-McDonald's

Chapter 1 told of the actions of José Bové, the French farmer who trashed the local McDonald's when it opened in his small town and then started a national movement against the franchise. Reading news reports from that fall, one might get the idea that Bové's response was the isolated act of a madman rather than the start of a social movement. Yet nothing could be further from the truth. In the United States there are so many fast-food franchises, and McDonald's has so many successful competitors, that Bové-style protests are quite unusual. However, in Europe the concept of franchised fast food is relatively new, and the McDonald's Corporation is leading the way in its global expansion. You can find an outlet in just about any city around the world. In fact, during September I took a trip to the former Soviet Union to visit countries that had been impoverished after over a half century of communist rule. In the medieval town of Tallinn, in Estonia—a country that had been oppressed until opening its doors wide to Western capitalism after the fall—I discovered, right next to the 500-year-old gates of the medieval city, a brand-new McDonald's franchise. At first, the contrast seemed obscene to me; but then I realized that this site was probably the most obvious way the beleaguered Estonians could announce to the world that they were now part of Western capitalism. In France, however, the situation is quite different. Bové and his followers oppose the *malbouffe* (bad meal) offered by McDonald's on aesthetic grounds, as a direct assault on the French tradition of fine dining. He and his followers also have generally opposed the consumption of beef, due to the epidemic of mad cow disease. They object to multinationals driving out local, indigenous businesses, and they are in general against free trade and the World Trade Organization.

Bové is no isolated oddball, as one observer reports: "His admirers, known locally as *bovistes,* include the likes of Anita Roddick, the Body Shop founder, and Ralph Nader, the veteran American campaigner who joined Bové and the other militants of the citizen's movement in the protests that disrupted last December's Seattle summit of the WTO" (Bremner, 2000). Furthermore, there were protests against McDonald's in Europe even before Bové's. During the early 1990s, two Greenpeace activists in England, Helen Steel and David Morris, drafted a fact sheet about McDonald's franchise operations, entitled *What's Wrong with McDonald's*. They traveled around Britain, distributing this pamphlet in front of McDonald's fast-food outlets. Among other things, they accused McDonald's of marketing unhealthy, fatty food; of damaging the global environment through their worldwide operations; and of treating their workers poorly because of bad working conditions and low pay. Steel and Morris picked up many followers during the past decade, through their widespread canvassing in England. In response the corporation took the two activists to court, charging them with libel. Steel and Morris provided their own defense, whereas McDonald's had on staff a battery of legal counselors. The proceedings became "the longest running libel trial in England's history" (Ritzer, 2000: 214), and the company paid a high price for its lawsuit. Although it finally ended in January 1997 with a verdict against the defendants and for McDonald's, according to one account the judge also ruled that the corporation "exploits children, deceptively claims that its food is nutritious, and poses a risk to the health of its long term customers" (Ritzer, 2000: 214). Steel and Morris have appealed the judgment against them. McDonald's, meanwhile, was left with large legal bills and very bad publicity.

As we have seen also in the case of opposition to Disneyfication, local citizen protests may not be able to compete legally with giant corporations, but they can damage their operations through propagation of negative publicity. With global companies like Disney so concerned about their image, even weak citizen groups can mount effective campaigns against the expropriation of their local culture and the destruction of their native environment. McDonald's was within its rights to defend itself against people that picketed its franchises with leaflets criticizing its food quality and work arrangements. However, the corporation did not expect a judge to rule that its quality claims were deceptive and that regular consumers of their hamburgers and French fries are running a serious health risk. Such negative publicity has a damaging effect on the corporation, no matter how wealthy and powerful it is.

According to George Ritzer, the social movement started by Steel and Morris in England "has become the heart of a world wide movement in opposition to McDonald's." Their web site, www.mcspotlight.org, averages almost 2 million hits a month and "acts as a repository for information on actions taken against local McDonald's throughout the world" (Ritzer, 2000: 215). Other organizations and web sites also have mobilized worldwide against this corporation. On October 16, 1995, a World Anti-McDonald's Day was proclaimed by groups in various countries that coordinated protests around the globe. Mr. McCrappy and Mr. McLitter, characters devised to promote the protest message, showed up in front of many corporate outlets. In England, the *What's Wrong with McDonald's* leaflets were passed out in front of 300 of the 600 total franchise outlets owned by the company. Reportedly, several protests also occurred in the United States on that same day, including one outside the themed, Rock 'n' Roll McDonald's in Chicago. Protesters dressed up as well-known musicians exhorted passersby to oppose McDonald's. Every year since that time, protesters have held the anti-event and have organized demonstrations around the globe (see www.ainfos.ca).

## Summary of Main Points

1. Themed environments are popular among customers as well as business owners. People like to be entertained while they spend money. Every themed environment stands at the intersection of enjoyable personal experience and corporate profit making.
2. Different people view themes in different ways. The successful themed environments appeal to a broad audience and project several enjoyable aspects.
3. Themed attractions are also segmented to appeal to different consumer markets. This approach does not necessarily contradict the one in statement 2. Targeted market segments are always broadly based, too.
4. Every consumption act is a personal experience that calls forth an aspect of the self, the consuming self, which is a social construction. People must learn how to behave in spaces of consumption. Themes and symbols give people cues that stimulate shopping.
5. Whenever we enter a space of consumption, we are very much like tourists, orienting ourselves to a new environment. Our personality switches to the more specialized consumer role. Successful environments aid that transition through stimulation, by means of themes, fantasy, and symbols. Consumer environments appeal to

the consumer self that has been nurtured for years by mass advertising and media programming to spend money as a means of
being happy.

6. Themed environments are also segregated and specialized according to class, race, space, and gender.

7. Themed environments, like all consumer spaces in this country,
are increasingly subjected to constant surveillance. So extensive is
this "watcher" function of institutions that, in a sense, surveillance
can be considered a theme of all consumer spaces and even of
entire cities.

8. With a heavy reliance on economic concerns and the increasing
use of privately owned commercial spaces in the redevelopment of
our environment, progressively fewer locations are true *public*
spaces. Without adequate public space in our society and a social
life that freely transpires within them, several negative conse-
quences for personal and societal development follow that are of
great concern.

9. In the early 1990s, themed environments were increasingly popular among businesses. More recently, there are a growing number
of protests and examples of citizen resistance aimed at franchising,
theming, and their effects on local culture. Disneyfication and
McDonaldization are two targets of an active movement of protest
groups that are now organized worldwide. As a consequence,
theming is not always as popular a commercial option as it once
was.

# 7

# THEMES,
# SOCIETAL FANTASIES,
# AND DAILY LIFE

Friends of mine returned recently from a wedding in southern California. The bride and groom were in their forties and had previously been married. Both were successful businesspeople. Before knowing each other, they attended acting classes in the Los Angeles area, in pursuit of "personal growth." That is where they met. The wedding was a lavish affair, as expected of people at that career level. What marked the occasion was not its cost, however, but its explicit use of themes. This couple prepared a wedding celebration and ceremony deriving entirely from popular culture sources, bereft of any influence from religion or family background. Their affair was scripted, cast, produced, directed, costumed, and acted as a Hollywood movie. It had several acts, costume changes, and a small cast of characters.

The first act was a Western fantasy in which the couple, dressed in fancy Western garb, rode horses to a musical accompaniment. For the second act, scenery and costumes switched to medieval Venice, where the couple performed a scene from Shakespeare's *Taming of the Shrew*. The third act changed location back to the American southwest. At the end of the performance, the wedded pair disappeared, and the guests were invited to watch a professionally prepared video program entitled "The Making of the Wedding of . . ." that was very much like other pseudo-documentaries on the making of Hollywood films. Images from the ceremony were recycled one more time in this TV program format.

This wedding is remarkable for its ability to convey a highly personal family ceremony without the use of religious and ethnic symbols that have legitimized such occasions for thousands of years. A creative blending of popular cultural motifs along with an overarching theme of Hollywood cinema were sufficient. For many years people have been attending family celebrations that involve some contemporary themes along with those deriving from religious or ethnic culture. The modern motifs are veneered over the solid foundation of signs from the latter realms. The wedding or confirmation ceremony is often an articulation between the old and the new. However, the Hollywood wedding that took place in the summer of 1995 was qualitatively different. It represents a successful ceremony that has abandoned all cultural referents from traditional society.

Perhaps everyone has attended a themed family event of some type. These happenings are not unusual. What is remarkable, however, is the cultural shift to events that derive their symbols solely from contemporary culture. A few people in our society, at least, can strike out on their own with themed celebrations that make no reference to religious, ethnic, or family symbolism. Over the years, our society has accumulated an immense dross of signs from cultural expressions that people now recirculate and repackage for their own purposes. They choose from an overabundance of signifying repertoires. Commercial signs that are jettisoned after their initial use by films, rock stars, television, advertising campaigns, consumer promotions, catalogues, fashion magazines, and the like, find their way back as images used by other people, for all kinds of personal reasons. Mirroring this process is the media's own recirculation of the very same signs. Retro fashions, nostalgia, the endless retelling of basic plots by television and films with only slight variations, eclectic rock music, and in fact the entire postmodern mix-and-match culture borrow from the very same repertoire, as do individuals in fashioning a daily life.

As images, the original meanings of signs no longer matter. Stripped of their deeper significance, symbols become objects or "sign-vehicles" for individual and group self-expression, and media commodities that sell the new rounds of programming. Consequently, new uses and hybrid meanings constantly evolve in our society out of the flotsam and jetsam of popular culture symbols drifting our way from fashion, movies, television, and other media image factories.

## Cultural Criticism and Themed Environments

When popular, media-driven culture is so thick with symbols and themes that it can fully replace traditional culture, we might suspect that there is something very wrong with our society. Yet simply saying that we dislike popular culture or the hokey Hollywood decor of places like Disneyworld or Las Vegas is not a strong criticism, because so many *more* people actually like this kind of simulated culture. We must approach the negative transformation of our society by looking at deeper ways to grasp its shifts in that direction.

Traditional academic inquiry provides an approach to cultural analysis known as *critical theory*. Its earliest proponents belonged to "the Frankfurt School," because they were associated with the university at Frankfurt, Germany, before World War II. Because many members of the Frankfurt school were Jews and/or anti-Nazis, such as Max Horkheimer, Theodore Adorno, and Herbert Marcuse, they left Germany and established their critical theory tradition in the United States during the war years.

Critical theorists belonging to the Frankfurt School were particularly hostile to popular culture. They treated it, and rightly so, as a mass-produced product of newly emergent "media industries." That is, unlike high culture, such as classical music, produced selectively by artists in pursuit of lofty cultural ideals, popular culture was considered an industrial product of large corporations interested only in profit. For this reason, Frankfurt Schoolers considered popular culture a *debasement* of "culture," and therefore, of daily life, by capitalism, through its reduction of all cultural products to the status of commodity. They were especially appalled at the way white, capitalist media expropriated black American cultural traditions in order to sell records. The members of the Frankfurt School recognized only high art and folk art as true cultural forms because neither was based on commodification and profit making. As Doug Kellner (1995:16) observes: "Production for profit means that the executives of the culture industries attempt to produce artifacts that will be popular, that will sell, or, in the case of radio and television, that will attract a mass audience. In many cases, this means production of lowest common denominator artifacts that will not offend mass audiences and that will attract a maximum of customers."

As the previous chapters have argued, themed environments are controlled, commercial spaces designed to stimulate consumption for the *realization* of profits through mass marketing. In that sense, they are mere extensions of the social forms critically analyzed by the Frankfurt School. Themed environments display a surprisingly limited range of symbolic motifs because they need to appeal to the largest possible consumer markets. They have replaced the public space of daily life that was characteristic of early cities with a regulated place of consumer communion, access to which is restricted to the more privileged, affluent members of society. Today themed environments eclipse the role of the open urban fabric as the staging ground for social interaction. The duality of private-public space, which was once the constitutive basis for liberal democracy—as the Frankfurt School theorists believed—has been replaced by the implosion of consumption and public presence. This leads to the disappearance of the true space of social communion. All the efforts of new urbanists and other urban planners interested in the revival of community because of the neighborly, unalienated values that are associated with that mode of living, are doomed to fail because of their greater failure to acknowledge this critique of our daily life. A society that has already lost its habits of social communion cannot be revived merely by some new architectural forms.

Despite its power to delve into the very heart of matters, most critics today no longer subscribe to the Frankfurt School thesis regarding the debasement of high culture by popular culture. Now authorities take a more democratic view that appreciates the singularity of popular culture as an authentic form of symbolic expression. A more recent but equally critical perspective on popular culture was articulated in the 1970s, in the United Kingdom, as the Birmingham School of Cultural Studies. The Birmingham School rejected the Frankfurt argument regarding the strict division of popular and high culture, and also the debasement of the latter by the former. British cultural studies adopted a critical perspective much like that of the Frankfurt School, but combined insights from Frankfurt Schoolers with those of another European—Antonio Gramsci. Gramsci sought to understand why the working class did not rebel against the means of its own enslavement under the Fascist regime in Italy. This *Cultural Studies* tradition, and Gramsci before it, was more politically motivated than the Frankfurt School, because it sought to connect culture with social movements militating for change.

According to the Cultural Studies perspective, popular culture was a volatile domain within which the working class expressed its own desires, through support for certain commodities or group activities, and the capitalist class pursued the domination of society through the co-optation of culture's symbolic forms. Popular culture was considered a tool of ruling class domination because it assuaged or diverted class conflict into harmless forms of consumption. Consumer lifestyles, then, were considered essentially as forms of ideology that co-opted everyday beliefs to support the status quo. Television watching, for example, diverted the use of free time from after-hours worker assembly and political discussion to couch-potato leisure in front of the "boob tube." Class conflict was controlled by the production of a symbolic and meaningful world based on consumerism, that propagated ideological messages legitimating the domination of society by the capitalist system—or more basically, that diverted interests into socially useful consumption pursuits of personal self-realization.

The Cultural Studies tradition may sound as if it stressed static, functional arguments, especially through its emphasis on the role of ideology as a mechanism of legitimation, but this is a false impression. The British school followed Gramsci, who was a dialectical thinker. In particular, for every cultural expression that was functionally supportive of the status quo, Gramsci believed that the working class could respond with a countermeasure, or "counterhegemonic action." Boycotts of commodities or the debunking of legitimation symbols were two possible forms of resistance. British Cultural Studies, therefore, placed great weight on critical cultural theory precisely because it could supply the alternative readings that would expose the status quo ideology operating in popular culture. As described by Kellner (1995: 37), "A cultural analysis, then, will reveal both the way the dominant ideology is structured into the text and into the reading subject, and those textural features that enable negotiated, resisting, or oppositional readings to be made."

A good number of contemporary culture analysts subscribe to the dialectical premise of the Gramscian/British approach. While the Frankfurt School might condemn all television programming in the manner described above, adherents of the Cultural Studies tradition point to the ways in which average watchers can mobilize counterhegemonic readings and inaugurate forms of resistance to thoroughly commodified media institutions (see Fiske, 1987). Thus, even as themed environments are examples of commercially controlled spaces that restrict personal experience to domains dominated by consumption, they also can be viewed as places that allow for personal self-expression and self-realization through modes of resistance (see Langman, 1992; Shields, 1992; Davies, 1995).

I have little doubt, based on my field experiences with themed environments, that they offer opportunities for creative interaction in space. It is precisely for this reason that I reject the distinction between production and consumption, traceable to the early Frankfurt School, and allow for the Gramscian concept of counterhegemonic consumer behavior. As argued in Chapter 1, the act of consumption itself possesses the potential for productive creativity. Polysemic themed environments may control crowds, but they cannot orchestrate the *meaning* of the experience. Each individual user of themed, commercial space has the opportunity to pursue a form of self-fulfillment through the creative act of consumption. If these places can be viewed as modes of domination because of their singular emphasis on the realization of capital, they can also be considered spaces for the exercise of consumer resistance, especially when the ability to enjoy actually existing public spaces in the metropolitan region is severely curtailed for reasons listed in the previous chapter. As we have seen, even a critical perspective toward society can be generated by people's strongly felt need to defend local, traditional life from a homogenizing takeover by corporate themed and simulated environments. Anti-Disney, anti-McDonald's, and anti-consumerist organization in general are good exercises in regaining individual or group control of culture from the giant corporations that currently dominate consumption practice.

Despite these observations, however, many cultural studies scholars seem to go too far in their celebration of counterhegemonic tendencies (see, e.g., Fiske, 1987). One limitation is the dependency on "readings" as a way of describing the experience of culture. An important argument of this book is that culture today takes the form of *material* environments, not simply texts (see Gottdiener, 1995). Both the body and the mind are engaged by commercial spaces. As Doug Kellner (1995) astutely argues, an emphasis on readings alone reduces the experience of culture to the level of personal *interpretation* rather than the interrogation of action or practice. Resistant readings, as Kellner argues, may *not* be true forms of resistance at all. They often sound, when described by Cultural Studies writers, simply like different textual interpretations—different *opinions* about the significance of cultural forms. From the discussions above it should now be clear that polysemy characterizes the free play of meaning in themed environments, and that commercial spaces anticipate different and even counterhegemonic readings in that their design *allows* for a variety of personal interpretations.

The issue of resistance should really be framed according to physical behaviors as well as mental exercises. A counterhegemonic tendency must appear as a social practice (see Hall and Jefferson, 1976). An emphasis on the material forms that articulate with popular culture symbols, as in the present analysis of themed environments, avoids the Cartesianism of cultural criticism that limits itself to textual readings. Within these new spaces of communion, analysts should search for alternate and possibly resistant *behaviors,* in the manner of Goffman's studies of public interaction (1963, 1971). It is also important to remember that any *critical* approach to culture must account for the production process and the place of cultural products in the scheme of capitalist social organization, as the Frankfurt School showed, besides the personal experience of culture by individuals, whether they subscribe to or reject the manner of symbolic appeals to consume.

Now an emergent media/information network existing in hyperspace characterizes society and conditions people to desire commodities. Simultaneously the net links up with the material forms of the themed environment that are the physical spaces for the satisfaction of consumer desires. The virtual hyperspace of images and the material places of consumption are the dual components constituting our culture today. The current consumption-dominated, themed economy is tied to the production of desires through information flow and image circulation on the one hand, and the flow of money from consumers to businesses on the other. Popular culture has become a hybrid of ephemeral electronic networks of communication and place-specific, material enterprises for the production and realization of profit. If consumers also find represented in this combined ethernet/material mediascape some version of a personal vision, dream, or fantasy, they do so only through the commodification of all such imaging by the creators of the themed milieus.

## The Themes of Built Environments

Human interaction is always *meaningful.* Since the origins of society, people have related to their environment in symbolic ways, besides using it for functional reasons such as survival. I contend in this book that image making has moved a step beyond the infusion of meanings into the built environment. Everyday life has been set free from the wellsprings of religious, ethnic, and family signs by the plethora of popular culture symbols that now pervade our environment. Françoise Choay (1969) argued that the city under the spell of modernist architecture and planning had become "hyposignificant." By this she meant that unlike classical and traditional settlement spaces, contemporary cities no longer possessed an *overarching* theme that organized the symbolic content of the built environment (see Chapter 2). This was so despite the fact that it was always possible to find symbolic milieus in the thoroughly modern city, such as the highly stylized movie palaces and fantasy fairs or arcades. The modernist architecture dominating industrial cities prior to the 1960s discouraged the use of signs in the construction of buildings, even though when taken in the aggregate each building symbolized the ideology of modernism and progress. By the 1950s, design practices of this kind created an urban environment limited in its symbolic scope and restricted to the signs of affluence, capitalism, status both high and low, religion, and ethnicity. The industrial city extolled progress, technological advancement, the practice of building or construction, and the geometric austerity of efficient modernist design.

Nevertheless, the human quest for meaning and the need to endow our lived-in community space with a richly textured symbolic content could not be squelched by modernist architecture and urban planning. Themed environments now reassert their presence even in the most technologically advanced places. Among all the countries of the world, however, the United States stands alone as uniquely endowed with motifed places. Nowhere else is there such a variety of themed restaurants, amusement spaces, malls, airports, or fast-food franchises. Nowhere else are pleasure spaces and tourist destinations so heavily invested with symbols as are Las Vegas, Disneyworld, and professional sporting events. Although some lament the superficiality of symbols associated with such environments, many people draw upon them to express meaning in their daily life.

Looking back at the survey in the previous chapters, it seems remarkable that despite the wide availability of fantasies produced by the media, only a select number of themes have been materialized in space. The environment with the most examples is Las Vegas. Even there, however, casinos manifest a well-defined range of motifs. The influence of the media is important. Themed environments derive inspiration from Hollywood, rock music, and other media industries. The same codes structure the restaurant chains of the Hard Rock Café and Planet Hollywood. At times these codes articulate with others that are more socially grounded, such as the ubiquitous symbolic markers of high status or affluence. However, an important criticism of the culture of theming is the limited repertoire of its themes. This aspect constitutes a failure of imagination. It is a result of the corporate control of theming that seeks markets through appeals to the lowest common denominator. What follows is a discussion of the main ideologies that are used to structure the themed environment experience in our culture.

## Status

Bugsy Siegal's Flamingo Hotel, on the Las Vegas strip, was the first to mix signs of wealth with movie stars and Hollywood glitz. Most popular culture themes, in fact, combine media signs with those that derive from the code of social status or affluence in our society. Movies and popular novels are *rarely* about the poor and deal almost exclusively, instead, with the concerns of the upper class. Through the influence of media (e.g., in the daytime soap operas) and the phenomenon of celebrity, people are, in fact, implored to make the problems of the wealthy the most compelling issues requiring the audience's attention. Whether aping, celebrating, or satirizing high status, the symbols of wealth are most characteristic of our culture.

Status sign-vehicles were once central to the residential needs of the newly rich around the turn of the century. Their conspicuous consumption symbols defined the suburban mansion and, in turn, established the normative features for the construction of middle-class suburban homes that still dominate housing appearance today (Veblen, 1899; Gottdiener, 2000). Status also defines the fashion industry. Designer logos and expensive sneakers costing over $100 a pair belong to the extensive system of signs that define appearance in terms of status. This same system also regulates merchandise at the mall. Shops are aligned according to the relative status and prestige they enjoy, although this ranking varies with each social subgroup. In short, because consumption is the dominant activity in our society, signs of status, more than class, structure our symbolic universe and personal expectations.

## Tropical Paradise

A second popular motif, after status, is "tropical paradise." Real estate interests in Brazil first defined it as a themed environment when they reconstructed Copacabana Beach in Rio as a tourist mecca during the 1920s (Jaguaribe, 1991). Since then, the aura of "tropical paradise" remains powerful as an escapist fantasy. It can be found as the sign in appeals for tourists ranging from commercial places in Hawaii to the Caribbean to southeast Asia. Tropical paradise is the organizing sign of several Las Vegas casinos including the Tropicana, a name that evokes the Copacabana (also the name of a once-famous New York nightclub); the Rio Hotel and Casino; and the immense Mandalay Bay Casino-Resort, now at the southern end of the Strip; and it can also be found as the sign of commodities ranging from shampoo to candy and juice. Tropical paradise is also the premier ideology guiding tourist infrastructure development by third world countries. Of course, the paradise that is offered excludes local residents, who must contend with crushing conditions of life in underdeveloped countries. For this reason, the "tropical paradise" vacation motif is commonly transparent.

## The Wild West

The American "Wild West" is another code that organizes themed environments. Again popular in films and novels today, this thoroughly macho motif refuses to die. Its symbols are recycled periodically in various manifestations, including virtual reality arcade games in which participants engage in gunfights and barroom brawls. The Western motif is popular in airports and hotels in the southwest, as a simulation of place. Merchandising makes use of it in the sale of clothing, such as Ralph Lauren's "Chaps" brand, and men's and women's accessories, such as cologne; and in home furnishings. Las Vegas casinos, before strip development, were once totally expressive of this motif, mainly because it fit well the fantasy of gambling, sex, and alcohol served up in a free-wheeling town. Not too long ago, Hollywood revived this theme with the big-budget movie, *Wild Wild West*. Although the movie was a notorious flop, we have probably not seen the last of the Western and its male-gendered take on history.

## Classical Civilization

Classical themes seem to have limited uses in our society. Architecture influenced by Greece or Rome is reserved for powerful social institutions such as colleges, banks, and government buildings, such as the U.S. Supreme Court with its faux Greek facade. Although Las Vegas has casinos using classical motifs, such as Caesars Palace, such themes are not duplicated elsewhere. University campuses once constructed buildings almost exclusively in the classical style. Today, modern and postmodern design prevails. Despite its limited appeal, however, the classical code remains a sign of power. Consequently, it persists as an important symbolic referent in the design of state buildings.

## Nostalgia and Retro Fashions

One popular thematic source is nostalgia, especially the signs of American culture from the 1920s to the 1950s. A common retro style of restaurant is the newly constructed diner using a decor recalling the 1950s. The franchise chain Ruby Tuesday features an interior that is an implosion of signs from several decades. Some popular television shows also are inspired by an idealized sense of the past, which is recycled in various forms. Nostalgia permeates the personalized visions of both Walt Disney and Dolly Parton and, in turn, has left its mark on their theme parks. The past is recycled in great, simulated heaps by the theme park experience, as it is in Hollywood films, fashion, and advertising. Part of the allure of historical monuments relies on the idealized sign of nostalgia. Each of these elements—theme parks, monuments, historical sites, and folk museums—structure a simulated, idealized version of American history consumed eagerly by tourists. We rediscover our history not through books or college courses but from visits to themed environments that simulate the past. As shown by the concerned citizens of Virginia who blocked Disney's themed project *America,* some people prefer their history in an authentic form instead of looking at the past through the Hollywood lens of nostalgia or fantasy.

## The Desert Fantasy

A sixth theme, one used in a limited way today, is the desert fantasy motif. At one time, it was very popular among Las Vegas casinos with names like Aladdin, the Sands, the Dunes, the Desert Inn, and the Sahara, perhaps because of the desert setting and its exotic connotations in the pre–Gulf War days. Now both the Sands and the Dunes are gone, imploded to make way for new properties such as the Bellagio. Lately, this theme's sign-value has declined, especially as the entire southwestern tier of the United States has become thoroughly urbanized. Also events like the Gulf War and the continuing tensions and terrorism in the Middle East deflate the cache of "Arabian" symbols. However, this motif of eastern "otherness" can occasionally be found in new Hollywood movies, such as *The Mummy,* and in tourist projects in other areas of the world (outside the Middle East). Several hotels in Hawaii, for example, have developed an Arabian, or more specifically, a Moroccan theme. When in tropical paradise, a tropical theme is redundant, just as the Arabian motif would also be redundant in Arabia. Commercial enterprises vying for tourist dollars in places that have already been plundered for their sign-value are forced to think up new codes in order to remain competitive. In the above example, one idealized, exotic locale borrows signs from another across the globe. Exoticism remains an important consumer fantasy even if its manifestations have changed from the Parisian arcades of the nineteenth century to the Las Vegas of the 1950s to the present eclectic mix of simulated "otherness."

## The Urban Motif

In our discussions of the important commercial places, such as malls and theme parks, I observed that the themed environment sought to recycle the ambiance of the pedestrian city. This urban motif is replicated in many forms, and recently became the basis for several successful new Las Vegas casinos such as the Venetian, the Bellagio, Caesars Forum Shops, and New York–New York. The idealized street setting that creates a condition of safety for pedestrian crowds is one consistently popular motif. There are personal and commercial reasons for this success. On a commercial level, a built environment capturing urban ambiance is used to sell commodities through a re-creation of the marketplace. This form has been in existence for thousands of years. People may go to a market for one thing, but sellers have always known that through proximity they can maximize their chances of attracting impulse buyers. What once worked in the Greek agora or the Istanbul bazaar thousands of years ago, also works now in malls and airports and in all the other environments that combine with the mall form, such as casino-malls, multiplex cinema-malls, and the like.

There are also personal reasons for the popularity of the urban ambiance theme. People crave a public experience, because true public space is disappearing, as is the public realm of social interaction (see Chapter 6). There is a certain attraction to people-watching and a certain eroticism in being watched. Communion with the crowd, even a crowd of strangers, means participation in the larger collectivity of society. Because most Americans live in suburbia, not the central city, and have limited opportunity to experience the anonymous crowd of public space, malls, theme parks, and large themed casinos fulfill this need. People enjoy these environments as entertaining spaces. Since the urban/pedestrian theme is replicated in so many different contexts, from Universal Studio's CityWalk to theme parks and casinos, we can conclude that people probably derive considerable satisfaction from the crowd milieu. In contrast to suburbia and its car-oriented culture, the pedestrian ambiance of secure, themed, city-like spaces satisfies desires of which we may be only dimly aware. Crimes in the city and the uncertainty of encounters that are unwanted in urban society prevent most people from enjoying the large metropolis in the same way; but the craving for the communion of public space and the anonymous crowd remains strong.

The urban ambiance created by malls, airport retailing spaces, theme parks, and new city simulations such as CityWalk works because they are controlled spaces. Mall police, security forces, video surveillance, and in the case of amusement places, the high cost of tickets, filter and control the crowd. Owners and operators of themed environments devote a substantial expenditure to such measures. Every Las Vegas casino, for example, contains banks of 360-degree, high-speed cameras in the ceiling. Both plainclothes and uniformed security patrol the corridors of malls, and so on. For the most part these spaces are safe, in contrast to the large city, where anything can happen. I do not mean to imply, however, that no crimes are committed within themed, commercial environments. Recently, for example, a gang-related murder took place at Disneyland, in Anaheim, California. Muggings and robberies can occur anywhere, including malls. However, not only is the level of crime comparatively low in the highly surveilled commercial spaces, but more importantly the public *perceives* them as safe.

For these and other reasons discussed above, the themed environment is enjoyable. People are amused not only by the attractions of these places; they also derive satisfaction from being within the built space itself. This phenomenon makes a unified cultural critique of theming quite difficult to achieve. Las Vegas, for instance, once attracted visitors because of its legalized gambling and tolerance for loose morals. Now tourists flock to the area because they find the entire milieu created by the newly constructed casinos entertaining. Vegas has become one big theme park, with different attractions on every corner of the Strip. The city itself has become an amusement space through its varied sites.

Another core element in the attraction of these themed environments is their structure, which resembles that of a state fair. Rural residents for years have enjoyed the crowds at the state fair, a kind of urban milieu. But, unlike the city and very much like Disneyland, state fairs feature one attraction after another, interspersed with places to eat. Theme parks now replicate the urban ambiance *and* the state fair ambiance, by mixing pedestrian crowds and food. So do giant megamalls, with their abundant food courts, and Las Vegas casinos, with their shopping spaces and their offerings of food and drink at bargain prices.

## Fortress Architecture and Surveillance

Ironically, an eighth theme is the obverse of the controlled and secured urban environment—namely the fortress sign systems of the "uncontrolled," actually existing city discussed in the previous chapter. This sign system consists of defensive architecture and belligerent warnings. Some of its components are so subtle and unobtrusive that they do not contribute to the visible theme of defensiveness. Surveillance needs and intruder countermeasures, in particular, articulate with the most advanced technological devices. In other contexts, defensive signs can be so common that they constitute an overarching theme for a particular space.

Security seems a ubiquitous need of all communities in the contemporary metropolis. In cities of the past, this desire might have been met on a formal level by municipal policing of streets or the construction of a tall defensive wall, or informally through armed security, or later, youth gangs and even the Mafia. Today many residents of cities have lost faith in the ability of the police to keep them safe, especially within their own neighborhoods. Clearly the relatively high levels of crime in today's urban areas have contributed to this perception. A second factor in the case of Los Angeles and other, newer sunbelt cities is relatively low population density. Street policing works best in compact, dense places like Manhattan, but is less effective, even when patrol cars are used, in the sprawling, heterogeneous metropolitan regions of the southwest.

Consequently, architects and local residents have responded with their own security measures, especially in the newer, sprawling areas of the nation. Fortress-like buildings, gate-guarded communities, visible signs advertising "neighborhood watch," or "armed response" posted in the front of houses (as well as graphic signs, such as the picture of some vicious dog, that may be purchased in any pet store for hanging on home gates), work together to create a new thematic texture for the urban landscape. Symbols of defensiveness and belligerent counterattack against strangers or intruders have eclipsed the previously inviting neighborhood decor of open streets and accessible buildings characteristic of the pre-1960s era. Now the sign system of the fortress city provides the theme, making the city seem a meaner, less neighborly place.

## Modernism and Progress

A consistently important theme that pervades many environments is the belief in progress and the superiority of technological improvement over time. Early modernism of the nineteenth century championed these related themes, as did the modernist architects of the International School, such as Le Corbusier. The exact purpose of a building constructed within a city in the modernist style was to announce the advent of modernism. Keeping up-to-date is often signified even today by the building of structures with an avant garde look. This symbolic function even extends to the new, *post-modern* examples of architecture. Because so many city centers have been taken over by the modernist, international style and its classic flat-roofed skyscrapers, the construction of a new, postmodern building, with its deviant shape and often pointed roof, signifies—veritably shouts—that the host city is "with it" and "up-to-date."

The theme of progress has been celebrated for hundreds of years in public events such as world's fairs and in commodity advertisements on television. Presently, this motif remains a potent form of packaging for new commodities. People may have their suspicions about the attractiveness of modernist architecture, but they retain their soft spot for merchandise that advertises itself as the "latest" or "newest," and they seem enthralled by the most recent marvels of technology. Successful mall interior spaces, for example, make use of the high-tech, glitzy style of chrome, neon, and glass that first appeared in the multistory-type mall known as the galleria. The latter is possibly the most popular form of mall. It combines the natural lighting and plentiful small shops of nineteenth-century arcades with the most modern department-store merchandising. In areas with severe winters, such as Minneapolis, or stifling summers, such as Atlanta, climate-controlled, fully enclosed malls are attractive and entertaining places to visit. Both the high-tech decor and the commodities of the stores underscore the emphasis on newness or technologically advanced commercialism.

## Representing the Unrepresentable

Along with the many themes discussed above, we have also considered an emergent system of sign vehicles that attempt to represent the unrepresentable. Conceptualizers of such themed spaces refer to some highly emotional historical event without making recourse to simplistic signs or clichés. In this category the most successful form is Maya Lin's "blank wall with names," which has been replicated across the globe. Museum spaces, where themes have always been used to organize individual shows, have recently been enhanced by socially conscious exhibits that depict monumental events in human history. The Jewish Extension of the Berlin Museum is one example. It pays homage to the cultural accomplishments of Berlin's Jews and simultaneously wraps visitors in a space that memorializes the Jews' demise at the hands of the Nazis, thereby functioning as a museum exhibit of culture *and* a personal experience. In time people will overuse the "blank wall with names," creating the need for another inspirational means to represent heart-rending human events without the clichés of obvious symbolization. Themed environments of this kind may intertextualize through exhibits with other cultural forms, such as novels, films, or computer-assisted visuals/texts that are already successful at expressing deep emotions. A planned museum in Washington recalling the slavery experience, if built, would undoubtedly make use of the multimedia objects that our nation has already produced over the years on this subject.

## Societal Domination by Consumption

In the main, we do not possess a culture with an expanding repertoire of themed environments, but a recycling of the arcade, the state fair, the world exposition, and the ambiance of the cosmopolitan, pedestrian city. The themes of modernism—progress, technological wizardry, and the "new"— are intertwined with themes of status, nostalgia, and fantasies derived from the most hackneyed examples of Hollywood cinema—ancient civilizations, tropical paradise, the Wild West, and, to a lesser extent, "Arabia," "Rio," or "Hawaii"—that is, some fantasized geographical scene of exoticism, straight out of the Saturday matinee. The realization that the indulgence in fantasy environments consists of a limited repertoire that in many ways apes Hollywood cinema is, perhaps, the biggest disappointment of this study. New, projected themes seem to be settling down into variations on the pedestrian street scene—perhaps because it lends itself so well to complementing the mall form and commercialism. Airports, casinos, restaurants, theme parks, and malls combine entertainment with shopping and eating. Simultaneously, we recognize the irony of these simulations. While the society and its development have functioned to destroy both the central city and the small town, nostalgic yearning for the ambiance of urban, pedestrian culture has continued to grow and to define new themed environments. Similarly, as the rain forests are systematically destroyed across the globe, the signs of this space resurface as animatronic simulations (e.g., the Rainforest Café). Slowly, we are replacing real places that we still need with their artificial counterparts.

There may also be another logic at work that limits the variety of fantasy elements used by themed milieus. Nearly all the types discussed above— malls, restaurants, airports, theme parks, casinos, and spectacular places of nature—are constructed and owned by commercial enterprises. The motifs chosen for environments designed and mass-marketed for profit are very much like the programs sanctioned by commercial sponsors and owners of television networks. Profit seeking dictates that they conform to the common denominator of tastes. This is so even with the important role of segmentation, which splits markets into several alternate lifestyle choices. Throughout the immense diversity of American popular culture, there remains little variety. The margins of "good taste," of acceptable aesthetic or artistic expression, of color schemes and recreational activities, are jealously kept from straying out of the mainstream. The "tropical paradise" theme, for example, borrows from the sultriness of Rio but stops short of the eroticism of Rio's beaches and nightlife. Inside the "Rio" casino in Las Vegas is a very ordinary gambling hall.

Commercialism and the profit motive carefully control the mall. We find a great variety of goods at stacked-and-packed, multistory galleries, but they are sold in stores franchised from some chain. Despite an appearance of diversity, all of the stores are vaguely familiar. Every large mall across the country has almost the exact same kinds of outlets. I can buy Hickory Farms sausage, Footlocker sneakers, Mrs. Field's cookies, and the like at malls in upstate New York, the midwest, Colorado, Kansas, the deep south, and California.

Themed restaurants such as Planet Hollywood and the Hard Rock Café, and themed parks such as Dollywood, use motifs and images that are already proven commercial products from the competitive worlds of moviemaking and popular music. Familiar shopping experiences at the mall also make a visit to Disneyland seem familiar. As a core activity of the consumer society, advertising paves the way for the popular acceptance of commercial images. Through habits of TV watching, popular magazine reading, and fashion, consumers are conditioned to mall environments and theme parks. On August 1, 1995, the Disney Corporation merged with Capital Cities/ABC, creating the largest movie/theme park/TV empire in the world. This corporate move, which cost $19 billion, exemplifies one of the many methods used by information, media, communications, and entertainment corporations to consolidate their profit making. According to a newspaper account regarding Disney's future *and ours* (Barber, 1995: A–15):

> Its goods are as much images as products, creating a common world taste that is identifiably American. Music, video, films, theater, books and theme parks are the outposts of this civilization in which malls are the public squares, gated suburbs are the neighborless neighborhoods and computer screens the virtual communities.... The distinctions between information and entertainment, software and hardware, product and distribution are fading fast anyway.

If we seek truly varied, entertaining fantasies from our themed environments, we may have to look for relief from sources other than the giant corporations that control our increasingly integrated media-information culture. However, these same corporations and the owners of Las Vegas casinos seem to consistently be one or several steps ahead of consumers in innovating entertaining variations on similar, salable environmental themes.

## The Social Context of Themed Environments

As we have seen, therefore, environments not only convey themes that are enjoyable; they also play an important role in the economy. In Chapter 3 we discussed how, in a highly competitive consumer-oriented society, owners of businesses must face the challenge of *realizing* profit from production. Increasingly, they accomplish their desires through the medium of thematic consumption. People purchase images along with goods. Typically, the former is more important than the latter in the individual's decision to buy. During the nineteenth century, the realization of capital was effected by better selling arrangements. This effort culminated in the success of the large department store first unveiled in Paris and later copied by the rest of the industrialized West. The department store worked because it facilitated shopping, as does the Internet today. Supplementing this structural change were limited attempts at the thematic presentation of commodities through window displays and dramatic staging within the interior.

Selling techniques were superseded by marketing as the consumer society evolved. Mass advertising became a major component of profit making, as it still is today. Advertising appeals developed the earliest themes of the consumer society, such as the desire for status, and the attraction of mechanical marvels. Progressivism and prestige-envy were complemented by advertising copy that created the persona of the consumer through direct enticements stimulating the desire for objects. This marketing mix of fantasy themes and appeals to the consuming—or desiring—self remains most important today for the realization of profit making. Marketing considerations are more important than other components of the production process, and now most products are conceived, designed, and produced with consumer markets in mind. The population of our society is split into segments characterized by lifestyle. Products are designed and sold expressly for the active consumer segments among these population clusters. Marketing practices reduce lifestyles to various themes or textual codes that can be mechanically replicated in advertising. Commodities, images, signs, themes, and constructed consumer environments all meld together to lubricate the rapid sale of products.

Lifestyles are organized by symbols and depend on signs for their social differentiation from each other; but they also have a material correlate, because they use objects as sign vehicles. Despite its overall focus on movies and media images, the Disney Corporation, for example, makes millions off tie-in merchandising, as do other mass entertainment businesses, including professional sports. Beneath the image-driven society, we retain a world of ordinary objects produced for sale. Most consumption involves the marketing of these material correlates to the symbolically organized lifestyle clusters. Themed environments physically encapsulate this vast domain of commodities.

Themes work in a second way to aid the economy. As we have seen, business interests use motifs as sign vehicles to sell their particular location in competition with other places. A specific spot can promote itself through the construction of a themed environment that attracts visitors. Vacation areas are typical examples of this phenomenon. In the 1920s, Rio entrepreneurs transformed its fringe area beaches into the first "tropical paradise" tourist area, with great success. The same theme has been replicated since then by other third world places desiring a tourist industry. Fantasy images and imagined delights play an increasingly determining role in the desire for overseas vacations.

Presently, city boosters combine several attractions to compete as a location with other places. These may include a successful sports team, a shopping mecca, an entertainment zone, a renovated historical quarter, richly themed restaurants, and in the case of Las Vegas, themed casino gambling. All of these elements are marketed as signs of location through the extraction of their symbolic value. Advertisers promoting a specific place use images of happy shoppers, spectacular forms of entertainment, couples in romantic or active settings, facades of themed milieus, and exciting vistas of waterfronts, downtown skyscrapers, or other grand city settings. As tourism has increased in importance to local economies, the marketing of place has become more competitive. The city has become the sign vehicle for the profit-making activities of capital tied to the tourist, shopper, and spectator markets.

Previously I discussed the melding world of themed environments, mass media, and giant entertainment corporations, in connection with the commercial control of consumer fantasies. These aspects comprise an ephemeral, image-driven environment existing in a hyperspace of TV programming, communications networks, computer internets, film images, and virtual fantasy simulations. In tandem with this world is a second one of material relations, involving the manufacture of common objects, from cars to sportswear. Objects that are correlates of or sign vehicles for the images of consumption are manufactured mainly by cheap labor in third world settings. Sports teams and their players make millions from T-shirts and logo-imprinted hats, but these image-objects are manufactured in Latin American or Southeast Asian sweatshops at minimal corporate cost. Beyond the worlds of entertainment, fundamental principles of making money, such as the control of labor and the selling of commodities, still decide the success or failure of image-exploiting enterprises. Consequently, the themed environments that we experience as consumers/tourists rest on top of relations of exploitation within a world of manufacturing that includes a political economy of global reach. In short, as Henri Lefebvre (1976: 21) once remarked, "Capitalism has found itself able to attenuate (if not resolve) its internal contradictions for a century, and consequently, in the hundred years since the writing of *Capital*, it has succeeded in achieving 'growth.' We cannot calculate at what price, but we do know the means: by occupying space, by producing a space."

Our environment is dominated by the space of consumption/consumer communion, which has replaced the public/private duality that was the cornerstone of the early modernist city and the cradle of local democracy. Increasingly, commercial environments that combine shopping, eating, entertainment, and a pedestrian city culture while utilizing some obviously simulated theme from the limited repertoire of mass market appeals have increasingly invaded suburbia, central city redevelopment, and tourist spots around the globe. These artificial, themed environments are limited substitutes for the rich public spaces that are nurtured in a healthy society with open cities and a strong public sphere of action. These environments also cannot replace the *real* rain forests, tropical paradises, and important local cultures, although they may well contribute to their destruction.

## Summary of Main Points

1. Our culture is increasingly dominated by sources of meaning that do not derive from traditional societies, such as religion and ethnicity, but that come from the mass media and consumer themes.
2. The field of *cultural criticism* can be used to analyze the current changes in our society with great effect.
3. One approach, that of the *Frankfurt School*, emphasizes how popular culture debases and threatens folk culture, local sentiments,

and the world of high culture. This argument fuels objections to the way simulations in today's mass media and themed environments debase and even replace real places and experiences.

4. The approach of the *Birmingham School* does not distinguish between high and low culture. Rather, it focuses on the negative effects of commodification. Those who adopt this approach believe that people can resist as well as be manipulated by our powerful consumer culture. Whether we resist or not depends on how we define the consumer act in our own minds and also through group processes of resistance.

5. Although our society is increasingly themed, the symbolic inspiration seems to be coming from the mass media and the most hackneyed aspects of Hollywood cinema. Despite the freedom to fantasize and simulate, themes that are used seem to be limited to a disappointing range of ideas.

6. Popular themes include: status, tropical paradise, the Wild West, classical civilizations, nostalgia and retro fashions, the desert fantasy, the simulation of urban pedestrian culture, fortress architecture, the theme of progress, and representations of the unrepresentable.

7. The negative effects of theming derive from the way our society is increasingly dominated by consumption. Free public space disappears. Our complex selves are reduced to the consumer-obsessed self. Commercialism and profit making dominate our daily built environment.

8. The powerful aid that themed environments provide to our present economy makes them useful now and for the future. They help solve the *realization problem* of capital in an economy dominated by the need to sell commodities that are produced in global locations.

9. Simulated and commodified themed environments are no substitute for genuine local culture and open cities with free public spaces for social action, nor for much-needed natural environments, such as rain forests, and other renewable resources.

# BIBLIOGRAPHY

Aglietta, M. 1979. *A Theory of Capitalist Regulation.* London: New Left Books.

*Amusement Business.* 1991. Sept. 2.

_____. 1992. May 11.

Applebome, P. 1995. "Franchise Fever in the Ivory Tower." *New York Times Educational Life Supplement.* April 2. Section 4A, p. 16.

Arendt, H. 1958. *The Human Condition.* Chicago: University of Chicago Press.

Aronowitz, S. 1974. *Food, Shelter and the American Dream.* New York: Seabury Press.

Banham, R. 1971. *Los Angeles.* New York: Viking Penguin.

Barber, B. 1995. "From Disney World to Disney's World." *New York Times.* August 1, p. A-15.

Barbour, D. 2000. "Dining with the Stars: Light Menus at the Next Generation of Themed Restaurants." *Lighting Dimensions.* September.

Barnes, E. 1996. "Can't Get There From Here." *Time Magazine.* February 19, p. 33.

Barthes, R. 1967. *Elements of Semiology.* New York: Hill and Wang.

_____. 1970–1971. "Semiology and the Urban." *L'Architecture d'aujourd'hui,* December-January, 153: 11–13.

_____. 1972. *Mythologies.* New York: Hill and Wang.

_____. 1983. *The Fashion System.* New York: Hill and Wang.

Baudrillard, J. 1968. *Système des objets.* Paris: Denoël-Gauthier.

_____. 1973. *The Mirror of Production.* St. Louis, MO: Telos.

_____. 1983. *Simulations.* New York: Semiotext(e).

_____. 1993. *Symbolic Exchange and Death.* Newbury Park, CA: SAGE.

Benjamin, W. 1969. *Reflections.* New York: Schocken.

Bluestone, B., and B. Harrison. 1982. *The Deindustrialization of America.* New York: Basic Books.

Bramlett, M., and M. Sloan. 2000. "The Commodification of Sport." Pp. 177–203 in M. Gottdiener, ed., *New Forms of Consumption.* Lanham, MD: Rowman and Littlefield.

Braudel, F. 1973. *Capitalism and Material Life: 1400–1800.* New York: Harper and Row.

Bremner, C. 2000. "The New Asterix." *Times of London.* October 25, p. 3.

Broadbent, G. 1994. "The Semiotics of the Void." Unpublished.

Bruegmann, R. 1989. "Art and Life Under the Runways: United's O'Hare Tunnel." *Twenty/One.* Fall, pp. 6–17.

Carney, G., ed. 1995. *Fast Food, Stock Cars and Rock-n-Roll.* Lanham, MD: Rowman and Littlefield.

Carson, T. 1992. "To Disneyland." *LA Weekly.* March 27-April 2, pp. 16–28.

Cartensen, L. 1995. "The Burger Kingdom." Pp. 119–128 in G. Carney, ed., *Fast Food, Stock Cars and Rock-n-Roll*. Lanham, MD: Rowman and Littlefield.

Castells, M. *The Rise of the Network Society*. Oxford, UK: Blackwell.

Chaney, D. 1993. *Fictions of Collective Life*. New York: Routledge.

Choay, F. 1986. "Urbanism in Question." Pp. 241–258 in M. Gottdiener and A. Lagopoulos, eds., *The City and the Sign*. New York: Columbia University Press.

CNN FN. 1999a. "Stars Eatery Gets Bail-Out." August 17. Available on line at www.cgi.cnnfn.com/output/pfv (cited October 12, 2000).

_____. 1999b. "Café This, Café That: Themed Restaurants Are Struggling." August 20. Available on line at www.cnn.com/food/ (cited October 12, 2000).

Cohen, S., and L. Taylor. 1992. *Escape Attempts: The Theory and Practice of Resistance in Everyday Life*. New York: Routledge.

Collison, K. 1996. "Urban Planner Gives Advice on Creating Safer Neighborhoods." *Buffalo News*. March 23, p. C-1.

Davies, I. 1995. *Cultural Studies and Beyond*. New York: Routledge.

Davis, M. 1990. *City of Quartz*. London: Verso.

_____. 2000. *Prisoners of the American Dream*. London: Verso.

Davis, S. 1992. "Streets Too Dead for Dreamin'." *Nation*. August 31-September 7, pp. 220–221.

de Certeau, M. 1984. *The Practice of Everyday Life*. Berkeley: University of California Press.

de Saussure, F. 1966. *Course in General Linguistics*. New York: McGraw-Hill.

Debord, Guy. 1970. *Society of the Spectacle*. Detroit, MI: Black and Red.

Delaney, S. R. 1999. *Times Square Red, Times Square Blue*. New York: New York University Press.

Dollywood, Inc. 1995. *Guide Map*. Pigeon Forge, TN.

Eco, U. 1976. *A Theory of Semiotics*. Bloomington: Indiana University Press.

Edwards, J. 1998. "That's Eatertainment." *Las Vegas Review-Journal*. Feb. 16. Available on line at www.lvrj.com (cited October 12, 2000).

Eliade, M. 1963. *Myth and Reality*. New York: Harper and Row.

Ewen, S. 1976. *Captains of Consciousness*. New York: McGraw-Hill.

Feireiss, K., ed. 1992. *Extension to the Berlin Museum with Jewish Department*. Berlin: Ernst und Sohn.

Fiske, J. 1987. *Television Culture*. London: Methuen.

Fjellman, S. 1992. *Vinyl Leaves: Walt Disney World and America*. Boulder, CO: Westview.

Fordney, C. 1994. "Embattled Ground." *National Parks*, 68, 11-12: 26–32.

Frantz, D., and C. Collins. 1999. *Celebration, U.S.A.: Living in Disney's Brave New Town*. New York: Henry Holt.

Frisby, D. 1985. *Fragments of Modernity*. Oxford: Polity Press.

Galbraith, J. K. 1978. *The New Industrial State*. Boston: Houghton Mifflin.

Garfinkel, H. 1967. *Studies in Ethnomethodology*. Englewood Cliffs, NJ: Prentice Hall.

Gergen, K. 1991. *The Saturated Self*. New York: Basic Books.

Geyer, F., ed. 1996. *Alienation, Ethnicity and Postmodernism*. Westport, CT: Greenwood.

Goffman, E. 1959. *The Presentation of Self in Everyday Life*. New York: Anchor-Doubleday.

_____. 1963. *Behavior in Public Places*. New York: Free Press.

_____. 1971. *Relations in Public*. New York: Basic Books.

_____. 1974. *Frame Analysis.* Boston: Northeastern University Press.

Goldman, R. 1994. *Reading Ads Socially.* New York: Routledge.

Goldman, R., and R. Papson. 1996. *Sign Wars.* New York: Guilford.

Gottdiener, M. 1986. "Recapturing the Center: A Semiotic Analysis of Shopping Malls." Pp. 288–302 in M. Gottdiener and A. Lagopoulos, eds., *The City and the Sign.* New York: Columbia University Press.

_____. 1994a. *The Social Production of Urban Space.* Second Edition. Austin: University of Texas Press.

_____. 1994b. *The New Urban Sociology.* New York: McGraw-Hill.

_____. 1995. *Postmodern Semiotics.* Oxford: Blackwell.

_____, ed. 2000. *New Forms of Consumption: Consumers, Culture and Commodification.* Lanham, MD: Rowman and Littlefield.

_____. 2001. *Life in the Air: Surviving the New Culture of Air Travel.* Lanham, MD: Rowman and Littlefield.

Gottdiener, M., C. Collins, and D. Dickens. 1999. *Las Vegas: The Social Production of an All-American City.* Oxford: Blackwell.

Greimas, A. 1966. *Semantique structurale.* Paris: Larousse.

_____. 1976. *Semiotique et sciences sociales.* Paris: Seuil.

Griaule, M. 1966. *Afrique noir.* Paris: Musée Guimet.

Habermas, J. 1989. *The Structural Transformation of the Public Sphere.* Cambridge: Massachusetts Institute of Technology (MIT) Press.

Hall, S., and T. Jefferson, eds. 1976. *Resistance Through Rituals.* London: Hutchison.

Hannigan, J. 1998. *The Fantasy City.* New York: Routledge.

Hart, W. 1985. *The Airline Passenger Terminal.* New York: John Wiley and Sons.

Harvey, D. 1988. *The Postmodern Condition.* Oxford: Blackwell.

Heller, S. 1994. "Dissecting Disney." *Chronicle of Higher Education.* February 16, pp. A–1, A–9.

Heritage, J. 1984. *Garfinkel and Ethnomethodology.* Cambridge: Polity Press.

Hervey, S. 1982. *Semiotic Perspectives.* London: Allen and Unwin.

Hodson, C. 1999. "Café This, Café That: Themed Restaurants Are Struggling." August 20. Available at www.cnn.com (cited Oct. 12, 2000).

Hoston, J. 1989. *The Modernist City.* Chicago: University of Chicago Press.

Jaguaribe, B. 1991. "The Modernist Epitaph: Brasilia and the Crisis of Contemporary Brazil." Unpublished.

Jakle, J. 1995. "Roadside Restaurants and Place-Product-Packaging." Pp. 97–118 in G. Carney, ed., *Fast Food, Stock Cars and Rock-n-Roll.* Lanham, MD: Rowman and Littlefield.

Jameson, F. 1984. "Postmodernism or the Cultural Logic of Late Capitalism." *New Left Review.* 146: 53–92.

Johnson, G. 1995. "It's a Mall World at Airports Nowadays." *Buffalo News.* Jan. 1, p. F-2.

Jung, C. G. 1964. *Man and His Symbols.* New York: Dell.

Kellner, D. 1995. *Media Culture.* New York: Routledge.

Knaff, D. 1991. "Shopping Centers Have Become World, Culture of Their Own." *Galleria Supplement. Press-Enterprise* [Riverside, CA]. October 16, p. 4.

Konig, R. 1973. *A la Mode: On the Social Psychology of Fashion.* New York: Seabury.

Lagopoulos, A. 1986. "Semiotic Urban Models and Modes of Production." Pp. 176–201 in M. Gottdiener and A. Lagopoulos, eds., *The City and the Sign.* New York: Columbia University Press.

Langdon, P. 1994. *A Better Place to Live.* Amherst: University of Massachusetts Press.

Langman, L. 1992. "Neon Cages: Shopping for Subjectivity." Pp. 40–82 in R. Shields, ed., *Lifestyle Shopping.* New York: Routledge.

Lanza, J. 1993. *Elevator Music.* New York: Picador.

Leach, W. 1993. *Land of Desire: Merchants, Power and the Rise of a New American Culture.* New York: Pantheon.

Lefebvre, H. 1971. *Everyday Life in the Modern World.* New York: Harper and Row.

_____. 1974. *La Production de l'espace.* Paris: Anthropos.

_____. 1976. *The Survival of Capitalism.* London: Allison and Busby.

Livingston, E. 1987. *Making Sense of Ethnomethodology.* London: Routledge.

Lucas, L. 1991. "The Galleria." *Galleria Supplement. The Press-Enterprise.* Oct. 16, p. 4.

Luckmann, T. 1967. *The Invisible Religion.* New York: Macmillan.

MacCannell, D. 1976. *The Tourist.* New York: Schocken Books.

Mall of America. 1992. *Guide.* Minneapolis, MN.

Marcuse, H. 1964. *One Dimensional Man.* Boston: Beacon.

Marling, K. 1999. "Books of the *Times*: Nice Front Porches, Along with the 'Porch Police.'" *New York Times.* September 6. Arts/Culture Section, p. 1.

Marx, K. (1967 [1868]) *Capital.* New York: New World.

Mayer, T. 1994. *Analytical Marxism.* Newbury Park, CA: SAGE.

McCalla, J. 1999. "Hypertheme Restaurants: Hyped Out?" *Philadelphia Business Journal.* Available at www.bizjournals.com (cited Oct. 12, 2000).

Meyerowitz, J. 1985. *No Sense of Place.* Oxford: Oxford University Press.

Miller, M. 1981. *The Bon Marché: Bourgeois Culture and the Department Store.* Princeton: Princeton University Press.

Miller, R. 1990. "Selling *Mrs. Consumer:* Advertising and the Creation of Suburban Socio-Spatial Relations." Unpublished manuscript.

Mullings, B. 2000. "Fantasy Tours: Exploring the Global Consumption of Caribbean Sex Tourisms." Pp. 227–250 in M. Gottdiener, ed., *New Forms of Consumption: Consumers, Culture and Commodification.* Lanham, MD: Rowman and Littlefield.

*New York Times.* 1996. "Mohegans Open Connecticut's Second Casino." October 13. Metro Section, p. 44.

Oh, M., and J. Arditi. 2000. "Shopping and Postmodernism: Consumption, Production, Identity and the Internet." Pp. 71–92 in M. Gottdiener, ed., *New Forms of Consumption.* Lanham, MD: Rowman and Littlefield.

O'Neill, J. 1972. "Public and Private Space." Pp. 20–40 in *Sociology as a Skin Trade.* New York: Harper and Row.

*Pages of Time.* 1951. N.a. Millersville, TN: Kardlets.

Peirce, C. S. 1931. *Collected Papers.* Eds. P. Weiss and C. Hartshorne. Cambridge: Harvard University Press.

Piore, M., and C. Sabel. 1984. *The Second Industrial Divide.* New York: Basic Books.

Pollan, M. 1997. "Town Building Is No Mickey Mouse Operation." *New York Times.* May 16, Section A, pp. 28–29.

Postman, N. 1985. *Amusing Ourselves to Death.* New York: Penguin.

Purdy, M. 1995. "Theme Park Atmosphere Is Part of Proposal for Yankee Stadium." *New York Times.* Wednesday, January 25, p. B–1.

Real, M. 1977. *Mass Mediated Culture.* Englewood Cliffs, NJ: Prentice Hall.

Redfield, R. 1947. "The Folk Society." *American Journal of Sociology.* 3 (January): 293–308.

Ritzer, G. 1993. *The McDonaldization of America.* Newbury Park, CA: Pine Forge.
———. 2000. New Century Edition. Newbury Park, CA: Pine Forge.
Ritzer, G., and S. Ovadia. 2000. "The Process of McDonaldization Is Not Uniform." Pp. 33–50 in M. Gottdiener, ed., *New Forms of Consumption: Consumers, Culture and Commodification.* Lanham, MD: Rowman and Littlefield.
Roberts, B. 1993. "Household Coping Strategies and Urban Poverty." Pp. 135–168 in M. Gottdiener and C. G. Pickvance, eds., *Urban Life in Transition.* Newbury Park, CA: SAGE.
Ross, A. 2000. *The Celebration Chronicles.* New York: Ballantine Books.
Rybczynski, W. 1986. *Home: A Short History of an Idea.* New York: Viking Penguin.
Schama, S. 1995. *Landscape and Memory.* New York: Knopf.
Schickel, R. 1968. *The Disney Version.* New York: Simon and Schuster.
Schneider, M. 2000. "Welcome to NBA City." Available on line at www.abcnews.go.com (cited October 12, 2000).
Seiler, C. 2000. "The Commodification of Rebellion: Rock Culture and Consumer Capitalism." Pp. 203–276 in M. Gottdiener, ed. *New Forms of Consumption.* Lanham, MD: Rowman and Littlefield.
Sennett, R. 1977. *The Fall of Public Man.* New York: Alfred Knopf.
Shields, R., ed. 1992. *Lifestyle Shopping.* New York: Routledge.
Simmel, G. 1957. "On Fashion." *American Journal of Sociology.* 62: 541–558.
Smoodin, E. 1994. *Disney Discourse: Producing the Magic Kingdom.* New York: Routledge.
Sorkin, M. 1992. *Variations on a Theme Park.* New York: Hill and Wang.
Stone, G. 1962. "Appearance and the Self." Pp. 86–118 in A. Rose, ed., *Human Behavior and Social Processes.* Boston: Houghton Mifflin.
Thomas, B. 1977. *The Walt Disney Biography.* New York: Simon and Schuster.
*Travel Weekly.* 1986. July 17. Vol. 45, p. 14.
Veblen, T. 1899. *The Theory of the Leisure Class.* New York: Macmillan.
Venturi, R., D. S. Brown, and S. Izenour. 1972. *Learning from Las Vegas.* Cambridge: MIT Press.
Warren, S. 1994. "Disneyfication of the Metropolis." *Journal of Urban Affairs.* 16: 89–107.
Warson, A. 1998. "Entertaining Canada." *Building: The Magazine for Canada's Development.* August/September. Available on line at www.narer.com/building (cited October 12, 2000).
Weber, M. 1968 [1921]. *Economy and Society.* Totowa, NJ: Bedminster.
Weiss, M. 1988. *The Clustering of America.* New York: Harper and Row.
Whyte, W. H. 1988. *City: Rediscovering the Center.* New York: Doubleday.
Wiebner, M. 1994. "The Battle of Bull Run." *Campaigns and Elections.* Dec.-Jan. Vol. 16, no. 1: 44–46.
Williams, R. 1973. *The Country and the City.* New York: Oxford University Press.
Williams, R. 1982. *Dream Worlds: Mass Consumption in Late 19th Century France.* Berkeley: University of California Press.
Williamson, J. 1978. *Decoding Advertisements.* London: Marion Boyars.
Wright, T. 1989. "Marketing Culture, Simulation and the Aesthetization of Work and War." *Social Text.* Spring.

# INDEX

197